THE PROJECT MANAGER'S MBA

THE PROJECT MANAGER'S MBA

How to Translate Project Decisions into Business Success

Dennis J. Cohen

Robert J. Graham

JOSSEY-BASS
A Wiley Company
San Francisco

The quote on page 57 from Louis J. Gerstner is from *Investor's Business Daily,* August 11, 1999, in Section, Leaders & Success; p. A8 by Curt Schleier. Used by permission of Investor's Business Daily. Copyright 1999 Investor's Business Daily, Inc.; all rights reserved.

The quote on page 85 from Barbara Tuchman is from *The March of Folly* by Barbara W. Tuchman and is used by permission of Alfred A. Knopf, a Division of Random House, Inc.

The quote on page 153 from C. Michael Armstrong is from Peter Elstrom, "Get Busy, Mr. Armstrong," *Business Week,* November 3, 1997, and is reprinted by permission of Business Week.

 Manufactured in the United States of America on Lyons Falls Turin Book. This paper is acid-free and 100 percent totally chlorine-free.

Library of Congress Cataloging-in-Publication Data

Cohen, Dennis J.
    The project manager's MBA : how to translate project decisions into
business success / Dennis J. Cohen and Robert J. Graham.—1st ed.
      p. cm.—(The Jossey-Bass business & management series)
    Includes bibliographical references and index.
    ISBN 0-7879-5256-7 (alk. paper)
    1. Industrial project management.   I. Graham, Robert J.   II. Title.   III. Series.
HD69.P75 C63 2001
  658.5—dc21

                                                     00-010062

FIRST EDITION
HB Printing 10 9 8 7 6 5 4 3 2

THE JOSSEY-BASS BUSINESS & MANAGEMENT SERIES

To our partners, Ann and Jean

CONTENTS

PREFACE

This book is for project managers, project team members, and managers of project managers who want to increase the contributions of their projects to their organization's desired results. Every day business management decisions are driven more and more by the need to meet shareholder expectations: "the simplest, most visible, most merciless measure of corporate success in the 1990s has become this one: Did you make your earnings last quarter?" ("Learn to Play the Earnings Game," 1997, p. 77). There is every reason to believe that this need will continue into the 2000s. In order for a company to meet its projected earnings in a given quarter it must have a history of projects during previous quarters that are now producing the capability to meet those projected earnings. When project managers manage their projects without having the company's future earnings in mind, meeting earnings targets is less likely to happen. Project management is not just a technical process. It has become a very important business process. For project managers, their managers, and their team members, successful project management requires the broad business-based view described in this book. Given the acceleration of change in every organization's environment, similar pressures are being felt by not-for-profit and governmental organizations as well. The lessons in this book apply to project managers in these sectors as well.

The concepts and suggestions we offer in this book were chosen in the light of our consulting experience and our work in training project managers in leadership and organizational skills. In our development and consulting work and in delivering our project management course (based on Robert Graham's *Project Management as If People Mattered,* 1989) over the past ten years, we have met with thousands of project managers. During these years it has become obvious to us that there is a wide gap between the world of the project manager and the world of the upper manager. Upper management craves predictability (to make the company's quarterly earnings) whereas risk and contingency characterize the world of the project manager. Given the resulting lack of mutual understanding, upper managers have been likely to pressure project managers to not follow best practices in project management. This has led to project failures. In our leadership courses we work with project managers to help them gain confidence in best practices and to learn to persuade upper managers to support those practices. Robert Graham and Randy Englund's *Creating an Environment for Successful Projects* (1997) is a recent effort to approach the issue from another direction and educate upper managers on project management best practices.

This book that you are about to read takes another step toward helping project managers better understand and act on the upper-management perspective that is driven by the need to generate economic value. Project managers and team members who learn the principles discussed here will be able to engage in a more meaningful dialogue with the upper managers in their environment. When one is speaking *truth to power,* a familiar activity for most project managers, it helps immensely to use the language of those in power to reveal those awful truths that they do not want to hear (as Randy Englund reminded Dennis Cohen in a recent conversation). Project managers might think of the contents of this book as a vaccine that they can use to inoculate their organizations against a delusion that often takes over upper-management thinking—the delusion that the company can have its cake and eat it too.

Our belief is that the standard way of interconnecting the business perspective of upper management with the technical and tactical perspective of the project team and project manager is outmoded. In quieter more placid environments, management could set a strategy and then program it into a static set of project constraints. Today things move so fast, this method prevents rather than produces the desired results. Project managers must be able to make decisions on the fly as the environment is changing. This means that project managers must have the latitude to think more like CEOs and the information to act more like entrepreneurs, taking responsibility for a project as a total enterprise. Project managers' responsibility no longer ends at the end of the project development stage; instead it continues throughout the implementation, or the outcome, of the project—what we call the project outcome lifecycle (POL)—the selling of the new product, the delivering of the new service, the use of the new facility and so forth. (This also implies that upper managers need to think more like project managers and master the technical knowledge that drives projects today, but that is the topic of another book.)

Audience

The Project Manager's MBA will benefit three distinct audiences. The first consists of project managers who do not have the background and training in business to feel confident in managing projects as if each were a new enterprise. The second consists of managers who manage project managers or who create the environment for project success. Project managers will need their managers' help and support to follow the new approach we describe. The third consists of technical professionals and any other individual contributors who work on project teams.

Project managers. The profession of project management grew out of the construction industry. Project managers are often trained in techniques that recall the stable days of construction or the early days of defense contracts. Projects could be managed successfully based on a budget, a plan, and a set of specifications that stayed fairly stable during the life of the project. These same techniques have come to be applied in business, first for new product development and then for software development; however, the conditions in which they are applied are now changing. Project managers now find themselves operating in highly turbulent environments and with company expectations that they will manage their projects to contribute to "the bottom line." This book offers project managers a set of tools and concepts that will lead them to better appreciate the perspective of upper management. This book will help to answer the questions of what economic value means for the company and what managers have to do to get it. Most important, it will suggest ways that project managers can manage their projects to increase the probability that the outcome of each project will make a significant contribution to economic value. The principles we present apply to all kinds of projects in business, not-for-profit, and governmental organizations: new product or service development projects for the market, internal projects to improve infrastructure or process, and client engagement projects. Stated in the most direct terms, this book will help project managers to always think of a project as an investment of company funds and the outcome of the project as a vehicle for producing an adequate return on that investment to satisfy the expectation of shareholders and lenders.

Managers of project managers. For managers of project managers and of line managers who touch projects in some way *The Project Manager's MBA* will help to support a more business-oriented approach to project management. We assume that these managers already understand many of the concepts that we introduce in this book to help project managers better understand their world. What managers of project managers will gain is a new perspective from applying these concepts specifically to projects. In addition they will learn ways to support project managers in improving the contribution of projects to economic value. This may require a change in the organization's project management system, but this change should result in better returns for the company over the long run. This change will also require a change in management and leadership behavior so that upper management emphasizes global controls rather than local controls. Managers will need to ask themselves, What would we rather have, control or results?

Project team members. This book will also give team members a better understanding of how their project work contributes to their company's success. It is a principle of sociotechnical design that the parts of a sociotechnical system work better when the people involved understand the purpose of the system as a whole. This applies to companies because they are sociotechnical systems, having a social system (the people) and a technical system (the work). So, if it is the purpose of a company to produce a return for its shareholders, the people who work in that company ought to understand how their work contributes to that purpose. They can then engage in an improvement process to better contribute to that purpose over time. Because maximizing economic value most often drives upper management, the ability to contribute to the goal should enhance the career of project team members. It will also prepare them to take the reins if they ever decide to become project managers.

Overview of the Contents

Chapter One introduces the business systems approach to project management. In it we explain how thinking about projects in terms of a framework based on such business concepts as increasing shareholder value and Economic Value Added can contribute to better decision making throughout the project lifecycle and ultimately result in more successful projects. Increasing economic value is becoming the criterion for success in the future of project management, and this chapter also presents an influence model showing the interaction of project factors that influence a project's contribution to economic value. We also introduce a business systems diagram that guides the structure of our discussion throughout the chapters, and an on-line calculator that reflects the functions on that diagram and that readers can use to gain a better understanding of examples in the book and to apply the concepts we discuss to their own projects.

Chapter Two discusses basic accounting and finance for companies and projects. It covers the basic terms and concepts that all project managers need to know to understand how projects contribute (or fail to contribute) to company success. Some readers will be able to skim or skip this chapter, but we wanted to include it so anyone could pick up this book and benefit from it without having to consult an additional source.

Chapter Three is all about strategy and the significance of the changing environments in which businesses must function. Business environments are no longer as placid and stable as in the past. They have become more turbulent. Change is happening more often, at a faster pace, and in less predictable ways, requiring organizations to undertake more projects in less time with greater risk. Because of this, management behavior and focus must change rapidly too, and this change needs strategic direction. Setting strategy, once often an academic exercise has become a necessity, an active process of setting a direction for the company, formulating priorities, guiding managerial action, and evaluating results so that the business can stay aligned with the changing environment. Under conditions of turbulence it becomes especially important for project managers to understand and internalize strategy, because the decisions that implement strategy must be made where the action is, that is, at the project level.

Chapter Four examines the effect of project management practices on the creation of economic value. The way a project is managed determines when it will be done and thus when the project outcome will take place. The date that the project outcome is ready has an enormous effect on that outcome's cash flow, profitability, and subsequent increase in economic value.

Chapter Five examines the revenue side of cash flow. This revenue is generated by the project outcome, and it is influenced by the decisions that project managers make during the project. The major themes of the chapter are crafting the project outcome for market performance and timing that outcome for maximum cash flow. We present a process for developing a project outcome that solves problems for and will meet the needs of the intended users of that outcome, and that delivers that outcome when intended users are ready for it.

Chapter Six focuses on costs and the factors that influence how much it costs for the project outcome to produce the revenue it earns. A project income statement does not tell a lot about a project as a business enterprise unless it covers both the life of the project and the life of the project outcome, becoming an enterprise income statement. A project income statement that covers only the life of the project shows only expenses and no revenues. Conversely, if project managers look only at the project outcome, they may miss some of the expense incurred during the project itself. In this chapter we present a break-even chart that combines project costs, post-project costs, and project outcome revenue to show when the project outcome will begin to earn a profit and how much profit can be expected over the project outcome lifecycle.

Chapter Seven explains why finance matters for project managers. It shows how projects develop assets that produce a return to the company and its shareholders. Unless a business demonstrates an ability to produce an adequate return on investments made in the company, it will not get the cash it needs to invest in projects. No cash to invest means no projects and probably no business. This chapter covers a number of financial concepts, including the amount of time required to reach breakeven, the capital charge, WACC (weighted average cost of capital), and economic profit, also known as Economic Value Added.

Chapter Eight illustrates how an understanding of the business system can help managers in making project management decisions. This chapter goes further into the use of the on-line business systems calculator introduced in Chapter One and used to illustrate examples throughout the book. Here we demonstrate how various project management decisions can be evaluated, using sensitivity analysis and the calculator to determine their effect on economic value.

Chapter Nine summarizes what all these concepts and perspectives mean for the project manager and project management. We offer some ways for you to think differently about how to manage your project so that you can better apply insights gained from this book.

Acknowledgments

We are grateful to all the people who helped us to complete this project. Ann Cohen provided editorial as well as emotional support. Jean Graham, as always, was a cheerleader for our two-person project team. Ben Cohen supported this work with his patient understanding. Aaron Hillegass contributed to the business calculator. Valerie Smith of the Strategic Management Group helped us with the preliminary graphics for the business systems diagrams. The Strategic Management Group provided support and permission to use parts of its CD-ROM interactive learning program *Why Finance Matters*. A special thanks goes to Bridget Doyle, Dawn Francis, Christie Hutton, Ann Wilson, Marianne Morris, Valerie Smith, and Phil Charon. Their great teamwork was an inspiration. Finally, we thank all the project managers who have shared their trials and tribulations with us over the years. We have learned the most from you. One of our mentors, Russell Ackoff, was right. In a student-teacher relationship, it is always the teacher that learns the most. For the help of these friends, family, and everyone else who assisted us, we are grateful. Only we are responsible, of course, for the ideas expressed in this book.

September 2000

Dennis J. Cohen
Philadelphia, Pennsylvania

Robert J. Graham
Mendocino, California

THE AUTHORS

DENNIS J. COHEN is a partner, senior vice president, and managing director of the Project Management Practice at Strategic Management Group (SMG). He works with clients to enhance business results in the areas of leadership, team building, organizational change, strategy implementation, and project management.

Cohen coauthored a chapter on the politics of project implementation in the book *Project Management as if People Mattered* by Robert J. Graham. He has delivered a number of papers at the Project Management Institute's yearly symposium and at Project World. In addition, he has worked with a large number of organizations, including GTE, MCI, PWC, Schlumberger, AT&T, Schering-Plough, Merck, Glaxo, The World Bank, Pfizer, Chevron, Unisys, William M. Mercer, U.S. Postal Service, General Accounting Office of Congress, Pacific Bell, American Express, Walt Disney, Applied Materials, Matsushita, Vanguard, and Sony.

Before coming to SMG, Cohen was a research associate at the Wharton School's Management and Behavioral Science Center and a senior fellow with the Wharton Center for Applied Research. He has been an adjunct assistant professor of management for the Wharton School, teaching courses in management and entrepreneurship. Cohen has also led seminars in the Wharton Effective Executive Education program, Wharton's Executive Development Program, and the MBA leadership curriculum.

Cohen holds B.A. and M.A. degrees from the University of California, Berkeley, an MBA from the Wharton School of the University of Pennsylvania, and M.A. and Ph.D. degrees from the University of Wisconsin.

Dennis Cohen can be reached at dennis.cohen@smginc.com.

ROBERT J. GRAHAM is currently an independent management consultant in the areas of project management and organizational change and is a senior consultant with the Strategic Management Group. Previously he was a senior staff member of the Management and Behavioral Sciences Center at the Wharton School, University of Pennsylvania.

Graham has also held visiting professor positions at both the University of Bath, in England, and the University of the German Armed Forces in Munich, Germany. He continues as adjunct professor at both the University of Pennsylvania and as a part of the Project Management Unit at Henley Management College in Henley, England.

Graham's first book is *Project Management as if People Mattered,* his second book, coauthored with Randy Englund from Hewlett-Packard, is called *Creating an Environment for Successful Projects.*

Graham has a B.S. degree in systems analysis from Miami University, as well as an MBA and Ph.D. degree in operations research from the University of Cincinnati. He was also a postdoctoral fellow at the Wharton School. In addition, he has an M.S. degree in cultural anthropology from the University of Pennsylvania.

Robert Graham can be reached at robert.graham@smginc.com.

THE PROJECT MANAGER'S MBA

FIGURE 1.1. BUSINESS SYSTEMS DIAGRAM.

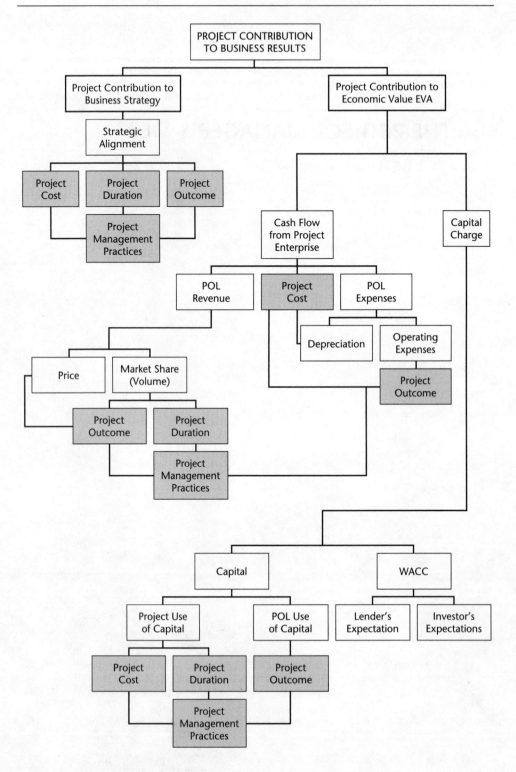

CHAPTER ONE

AN ENTREPRENEURIAL APPROACH TO MANAGING PROJECTS

The old order changeth,
Yielding place to new.

ALFRED LORD TENNYSON, "THE PASSING OF ARTHUR," 1869

"Make it fast. Make it good. Make it cheap." So goes the project management folklore about what senior management always asks for. "Pick two," is the traditional project manager reply. Almost always, "make it cheap" is one of the two project goals upper management chooses. However, only when upper managers and project managers understand the wider business implications of their decisions do they realize that "make it cheap" may not contribute to successful business results as often as they think. This is because the cost of the project, or the cost of producing the product, is only one factor in determining the economic success of the project. In this book we develop a framework for thinking about projects based on business concepts such as increasing economic value, or Economic Value Added (EVA); this framework can contribute to better decision making throughout the project lifecycle and ultimately result in more successful projects. In addition we show that the old success criteria of meeting outcome, cost, and schedule constraints are no longer adequate and that increasing economic value will become an important, if not the most important, criterion for success in the future of project management.

The use of economic value as a decision criterion indicates a change in the way project success is determined. In the past, project managers were assessed primarily on project performance up to the point of project completion. This resulted in evaluations based on outcomes that met the project specifications, a fixed budget, and a given deadline. The ensuing economic success of the product produced was normally someone else's concern. However, in the future project managers must think more broadly about what a *successful outcome* really means. To for-profit businesses it means a level of customer satisfaction high enough to produce sales that result in enough cash flow to cover project and operating expenses, make a profit, and pay back the cost of the capital used to produce the product. At this point the project begins to produce the economic value known as shareholder value.

Shareholder value is a term that has become familiar in the world of business. Those who work for publicly owned corporations are likely to have some idea of its increasing influence on upper-management behavior in those companies. Those who work for not-for-profit or governmental organizations may have to do a little translation to relate the idea of shareholder value to their projects. We suggest mentally substituting the term *stakeholder, taxpayer,* or *voter value* for the terms shareholder value and economic value (which we use interchangeably throughout). At first glance, shareholder value, or economic value, seems to be a purely financial term. Besides its financial element, however, it contains a dynamic balancing of competing values. In order for a business to maximize shareholder value, it must balance customer satisfaction and competitive market forces with internal cost and outcome considerations. Shareholders of a for-profit company want a return on their investment. Stakeholders of a not-for-profit organization want its desired outcomes achieved within the economic constraints necessary to ensure the survival of the organization so that it can continue to do good in the world. Stakeholder value may not involve a profit, but it must necessarily involve an outcome that somehow recoups any actual or implied cost of the capital used by the project. In addition, many not-for-profit organizations are finding themselves in competition with for-profit businesses and thus subject to similar competitive and economic forces (Ryan, 1999). Taxpayers, for example, want the highest quality outcome from a governmental project for the lowest relative cost. This outcome must also include considerations of cost of capital, which is lower for governments than for businesses but still not inconsequential. We believe that the dynamic new approach to projects we are describing here will serve you well whether your project is in a business, a not-for-profit organization, or a governmental agency.

In any of these organizations, the criteria for economic value are now or soon will be *your* responsibility, because management will measure your performance by them. This, then, is the future of project management. As a project manager, you must recognize it as your future as well.

Welcome to the world of business systems. The only way that you will attain success given the new project management paradigm will be as a business systems thinker. In more direct terms this means of thinking of your project as if it were a business and you were the chief executive officer, the CEO. This chapter outlines the change in thinking managers must undertake to work within the new project management paradigm. In any sociotechnical system the people in the system work better when they understand how they fit into the system as a whole. This understanding is developed when people share the perspective of the CEO, the person who is responsible for the whole business and whose results are measured by an increase in value for the stakeholders of the organization. The board of directors represents the stakeholders, and the CEO works for the board. He or she must manage the whole company from the top. Therefore, the entrepreneurial approach to project management requires the project manager to manage the project as if it were an independent business venture. But like the CEO, the project manager must also manage with the larger organizational system in mind, even though the project manager will be influencing the system from the project standpoint rather than from the top. He or she will need to understand how the elements of the project affect the business as a whole and how elements of the business influence the project. By thinking in business terms project managers will better understand the interaction between the project and the overall organization. In addition, they will be better able to explain the business implications of upper-management decisions about a project. That is, they will be able to speak to upper managers in a language that those managers understand. Managing this interaction between the project and the larger organization is fast defining the role of the project manager. The new project managers will act like entrepreneurs as they treat their projects as businesses and think like CEOs as they view each project as part of the wider organization.

Moving from Project Focus to Organizational Focus

What does it mean to think like an entrepreneur and act like a CEO? First and foremost, it means understanding how any organization creates value for its major stakeholders—shareholders, customers, and the business team. It also means taking responsibility for delivering that value. For shareholders the business creates value when it provides a rate of return on investment that meets their expectations for the level of risk they are taking. The fuel that powers this return is the cash flow provided by customers who pay for products or services because they meet or exceed the customers' expectations relative to competitors' products or services. A company's ability to provide this cash flow and thus shareholder value by using resources efficiently depends on business team members who have been recruited intelligently and managed well.

Project managers are an important part of the business team. They manage projects that for the most part are vehicles for investing resources to produce assets that will provide the foundation for future cash flow. Developing a new product and building a new factory are examples of projects that will produce cash flows in the future. A process improvement project or marketing project may have a shorter time horizon and may not produce additional cash flow during that time period, but it too is an investment for the future. Thus, managing a project is managing the application of capital to provide a required return so the business can satisfy its customers, shareholders, and ultimately the business team. In the end, project success is based on the ability to choose the right project and then execute it successfully.

To meet and exceed customer expectations, the business team needs to follow an overall organizational strategy. Strategy is an agreed-on guide to action that should lead the business to success in the marketplace by satisfying customer needs better than the competition does. However, no matter how well thought out a strategy is, it is useless if implemented poorly or not implemented at all. In fact, a strategy that is implemented poorly or not implemented at all is really not a strategy; it is simply a plan, an intention to do something that remains undone. A true strategy is a plan that has been executed so that the consequences of carrying out the strategic intention can be observed. In most companies a strategy is implemented through projects. The portfolio of projects planned, in progress, and completed represents the process of strategy implementation. Best practice companies such as Hewlett-Packard, Chevron, IBM, 3M, NCR, Boeing, IBM, and Motorola do a good job of managing the project portfolio and linking it to the organization's overall strategy (Graham, Englund, and Cohen, 2000).

From the project manager's viewpoint then, the success of a particular project depends on how well that project helps to implement the overall strategy. For example, some projects, such as developing new products, may be expected to return high levels of profit whereas other projects, such as entering a new geographical market, may be lucky to break even. However, they could both be considered successful if they met a strategic objective. So, even though a given project may not produce a return that justifies the capital invested, it may nevertheless add value because it helps the organization achieve an overall strategy that increases value. This is the first step in the business systems approach to project management—understanding that the new measures of project success involve the project's contribution to overall organizational strategy. Linking projects to strategy is one of the best ways to increase shareholder value (Cohen and Kuehn, 1997; Englund and Graham, 1999).

The portfolio of projects in process in any company is an important manifestation of that company's strategy. A typical organization has many types of projects that are necessary to help it achieve its strategy. Some projects involve new research and define new products, whereas others concentrate on refining business practices. Some projects respond to competitor actions, whereas others respond to government regulations. We do not cover in detail all the different types of projects that make up the business enterprise. Instead, we focus on the three broad project categories that we have found in most organizations:

1. *New product, service, or facility development projects.* These projects produce something new in the organization. It could be a new product or service for the external market or a new production facility for new or existing products. Because their outcomes normally generate new income for the organization or a change in income that can be easily measured, these projects are the most amenable to the business systems approach. Adding a new feature to an existing product is also a kind of new product development project.

2. *Internal projects.* These projects involve infrastructure development and improvement that is internal to the organization. Internal projects include reorganizations, reengineering and other change initiatives, and new process and software development projects that aim to make internal operations more efficient. The results of these projects do not normally generate new income; instead they produce cost savings, operating efficiencies, or a slowing of an erosion of current product sales. In most cases the financial results of such projects are not easily measurable, and thus the projects have not been thought amenable to a business systems approach. However, it seems clear that almost all internal projects ultimately have a financial effect on the organization, and this effect can be estimated as a part of the business plan for such projects. Given such estimates, internal projects become amenable to a business systems approach.

3. *Client engagement projects.* These projects are conducted for an external client or customer. They are the type of projects for which project management techniques were first developed. They are also the type of project traditionally evaluated in terms of the outcome, budget, and schedule constraints mentioned previously. These measures have been used because such projects are carried out under a contract that specifies them and because it has traditionally been of little concern to the project manager what the customer does with the project outcome once the project is completed. However, customers now expect *total solutions* for their problems and thus expect contracting organizations to work with them to help them market or otherwise employ the project outcomes. In such a market-driven business systems approach, the project manager will be much more aware of the customer's situation and thus much more likely to create successful solutions. This should lead to more successful projects. So even for this type of project the old days of measuring success strictly by outcome, cost, and schedule are gone. Those measures are being supplemented by measures of increased economic value for both the project organization and the client organization.

The move from project focus to organizational focus points the way toward the future of project management. Outcome, cost, and duration will still be important factors for measuring project progress. However, these factors will be augmented by business factors that will be used to measure project success. The new project manager will have to understand the interactions between these project and business factors.

Understanding Project and Business System Interactions

The business systems diagram shown in Figure 1.1 illustrates the relevant interactions between a project and a business enterprise, from the project manager's point of view. At the top of the system is its ultimate goal, the project's contribution to business results. The boxes below that final goal represent the business factors that go into producing the economic value, and the lines connecting the boxes represent interactions among those factors. The boxes shaded in Figure 1.1 represent the outcome, cost, and schedule constraints that previously defined successful project management. The unshaded boxes represent the new factors that must be considered in the entrepreneurial approach to project management. Thus the diagram illustrates that the business systems approach is built on the old triple constraints of project management but goes beyond the use of these constraints to consider factors for developing business results.

The left-hand section of the business systems diagram is concerned with *strategic alignment*. Because achieving the organizational strategy is part of the goal of any project, all other project goals must be aligned with that strategy. Strategy formulation is a major task for the company entrepreneur and the CEO, but it is the task of middle managers and project managers to carry this strategy out and eventually turn it from talk to action to results. Strategic alignment is affected by the project outcome, project duration, and project cost. Issues important to achieving strategic alignment are covered in Chapter Three.

The right-hand section of the business systems diagram is concerned with a project's contribution to economic value. This contribution consists of the *cash flow from the project* outcome minus the *charge for the capital* used to create that outcome. Near the bottom of the right-hand side the project factors of outcome, cost, and duration reappear. As is well known, the way a project is managed and led will have a direct effect on project outcome, duration, and costs. The business systems diagram, however, also emphasizes that the results of project management processes will ultimately influence economic value. Our emphasis will be on showing how best practices in project management support the major goal of creating positive business results. This information will help project managers to influence upper management to adopt these best practices by indicating their effect on business results. These project management processes are covered in Chapter Four.

Now, in the middle of the diagram, examine the components of the cash flow from the project enterprise, or outcome, looking first at the *revenue* side of cash flow. The basis for revenue is the design and delivery of products, services, or processes that help customers solve problems and meet or exceed their expectations, at a price customers are willing to pay. This is the *project outcome*. The time over which the outcome has a useful life is the *project outcome lifecycle* (POL). The project outcome features influence market share. When they are better aligned with customer needs and expectations than competitive offerings are, these features will increase the probability that customers will buy the output or that internal customers will be able to use the output to enhance external customer satisfaction. Project duration also influences market share, in that market entry timing is often critical to sales performance. Product price is also influenced by the project outcome. Market share and price determine sales revenue. Sales revenue (minus expenses) is the primary driver of cash flow, and this ultimately influences the project's contribution to economic value. So far, this seems pretty elementary, but it is just the beginning. The older methods of project management often did not even go this far. The customer was often left out of the equation, and market considerations of any kind were often considered to be someone else's problem. But this is not the case today, so these important marketing topics are covered in Chapter Five.

The remainder of the cash flow section of the diagram represents the need to balance the features in the design with *project cost* and *POL expenses* considerations. Every set of features has cost implications for the project cost, post-project costs, and the cost of the final product or service. These costs ultimately influence the total cash flow and the rate of cash flow. The rate of cash flow influences the *time to breakeven,* or time to profit—that time when the net income from the project outcome has finally paid back the costs of the project. The time to breakeven is an important element in the project's contribution to economic value. We explain this in more detail in Chapter Six.

The final section on the right-hand side of the business systems diagram centers around the financial aspects of project outcome, cost, and duration. As mentioned, project outcome features and project duration influence the time to breakeven. This time is important because it is the amount of time that the project is a user of capital. As long as it has not reached breakeven, it is a net user of capital and thus incurs a charge for the use of that capital. This *capital charge* is based on the amount of capital used, the length of time it is used, and the company's *weighted average cost of capital* (WACC). The WACC reflects the cost to the company of raising capital through taking on debt and selling equity. Project managers have little influence over WACC in the short term, yet over the long term a consistent stream of outstanding projects will reduce the WACC by increasing overall cash flow and raising the price of the company's stock (Strategic Management Group, 1997).

As we discussed earlier, CEOs and entrepreneurs think a lot about increasing shareholder value. Thus the economic value of a project becomes critical to the success of the business. If the project produces a positive economic value, then it is contributing to shareholder value. If it produces a negative economic value, it is subtracting from the value to shareholders of the company as a whole. Briefly, shareholder value, or economic value, may be understood as the equivalent of the *net present value* (NPV) of the project given a required rate of return (often called a *hurdle rate*) equal to the weighted average cost of capital of the company. NPV is a financial measurement of the present value of future cash flows given an assumed rate of return (Strategic Management Group, 1997). These topics will be introduced in Chapter Two and covered in detail in Chapter Seven.

The length of time to breakeven is an important focus of pressure from upper managers. They want the project done fast. As long as it is unfinished the company cannot begin to realize the cash flow that will offset the cost of development and the cost to borrow the capital. However, there are trade-offs to be considered as well. Factors such as project costs and customer satisfaction also ultimately affect cash flow and time to breakeven. There is also sometimes a trade-off between project cost and project deadline that involves buying more resources (and raising the project cost) to reduce the time it takes to get the project done. The business systems diagram illustrates that most decisions made during the life of a project are the result of trade-offs. Understanding the effect of these various trade-offs on the project's contribution to economic value will become the main decision tool for project managers in the future. These topics in quantitative decision making are covered in Chapter Eight.

Defining the Evolving Role of the Project Manager

Taking the business systems approach requires knowledge of accounting, strategy, organization and motivation, marketing, cost control, finance, and quantitative decision making. These are the subject areas typically covered when taking an MBA degree. This book covers those areas from the project manager's perspective; that is why we have called it *The Project Manager's MBA*. For most project managers, understanding these subject areas in order to think like an entrepreneur and act like a CEO means acquiring new skills and behavior.

As we have been discussing, today project managers have to think of the project as a business enterprise and to manage the project as a business venture. Thus project managers have to consider not only the success of the project itself but also the success of the project outcome that is the result of the project endeavor. As Jaafari (2000) comments, when the project management focus is shifted from the creation of a final product to the creation of a business to service project objectives, "it becomes clear that the traditional project delivery approaches will have to give way to a new system in which project lifecycle objectives will be the basis for decision making throughout the project's life" (p. 44). This *new system* is the basis for the entrepreneurial approach to project management, which essentially expands two dimensions of the project management process. The first dimension is time. Considering the project outcome and its lifecycle (POL) expands time beyond the traditional horizon of project completion. The second dimension is the project boundary. Stakeholders from all kinds of organizational areas become more important as partners, not just stakeholders, in the enterprise. Market forces beyond the customer and end-user also become important. Most important, these additional forces now include the competition.

In the past, many of the business objectives important for project success were imbedded in the outcome, cost, and schedule constraints that were given to the project manager. For example, upper management might have chosen the project outcome on the basis of organizational strategy, but this was often not discussed with the project manager. The assumption seemed to be that "if the project team builds it to specification, strategy will be achieved." This made it easier to transfer the project from upper managers to project managers and to measure project success, but it made it more difficult for the project manager to make the right decisions during project execution. The new role of the project manager requires an intimate knowledge of the strategy the project is supporting. The new role of the project manager also requires knowledge of marketing, post-project costs, and finance. Figure 1.2 summarizes the evolving role of the project manager.

Turning the Triple Constraints into Possibilities

Today, project managers have to think of projects as having two parts. First, there is the project itself, which creates an outcome. And then there is the outcome lifecycle, in which the outcome is used or sold. Both parts contain elements of risk. The first part contains technical risk, which is concerned with the probability that the project team can actually produce the desired result. The second part contains marketing risk, which is concerned with the probability that the company can sell the result. In the past the project manager was concerned mainly with the technical risk and so concentrated on creating the outcome. This resulted in the narrow orientation project managers were often given and the focus on the triple constraints of outcome, cost, and duration. Those commissioning the project saw this approach as giving them control. They were concerned with the marketing risk and adding value to the company. They apparently felt that if a business could get specific things done at a fixed cost and time, the value would be there and the market would respond. This orientation of working within constraints led to many bad practices by both project managers and upper managers. In particular many new possibilities that arose during the execution of a project were often ignored because they were not in the budget nor in the specifications nor in the schedule.

The business systems approach is concerned with discovering possibilities for adding value to the organization, not with finding solutions within given constraints. This approach requires a business as well as a technical orientation. The business orientation concentrates on the entire life of both the project and the project outcome, from birth to death, from "lust to dust." Now the project manager thinks not of constraints but of the possibilities throughout the entire life of the project and its outcome, both outcome creation and use. Such thinking is essential today because change in the marketplace is accelerating and occurring in increasingly random patterns. Such change increases market risk and the ne-

FIGURE 1.2. NEW PROJECT MANAGEMENT PARADIGM.

Factor	From	To
Organizational strategy	Not my concern.	Number 1 determinant of project success.
Project management processes	Scheduling processes are important. Behavioral factors are "frills."	Behavioral factors are linked to project success and economic value and are essential.
Marketing	Something done by people in the Marketing Department.	Something that must be understood during the project for project success (market-driven project management).
Costs	Only project costs are important.	Costs are important during both the project and the life of its outcome.
Finance	Something of no consequence to the project.	Something important in determining project contribution to economic value.

cessity of having project managers make important decisions at the project level. Any imposed constraints become obsolete in weeks, and there is no time to constantly check in with upper management before acting to keep up with changing conditions. Remember that D-day underwent more planning than any military endeavor before that time. Yet on the beaches of Normandy it was the few junior officers who survived the initial hours and who reacted to the situation who carried the day.

The table in Figure 1.3 compares the old triple constraints to the new processes and results, discussed in the following paragraphs.

Crafting for market performance. This process was the old outcome constraint. It stresses understanding the customer and the competition so that the project outcome performs well in the market and adds value to the organization. The new emphasis is on understanding the dynamics of competition. The outcome constraint was about collecting technical specifications. Crafting is about developing a viable commercial solution for the marketplace directly by creating a new product or service or indirectly by supporting the commercial enterprise of the business or by creating an outcome for a specific client that the client will then use in the marketplace.

Timing for maximum cash flow. This process is much more than just meeting a schedule and deadline. Timing for maximum cash flow rests on the realization that decisions made during the project that affect the timing of project completion will also affect the potential cash flow from the project outcome and thus affect economic value. Timing can affect both the price and the sales volume of the project outcome. The timing process helps project managers time product completion for maximum cash flow.

Investing for competitive advantage. Projects are not just a cost to the organization. They represent an investment. In the past the budget was the control on investment in the project. However this control can negatively affect project results. It might prevent an increase in spending, say for better product features, that would

FIGURE 1.3. FROM OLD CONSTRAINTS TO NEW PROCESSES.

Old Constraint	New Process	Result
Outcome	Crafting for market performance	Market performance
Duration (fixed deadline, schedule)	Timing	Maximum cash flow
Cost (budget)	Investing	Competitive advantage

pay off in increased competitive advantage. Thus the project manager should not be constrained by a budget but armed with knowledge of competitors and ways to develop competitive advantage. When a competitive advantage is reached, cost is transformed to one component of the total investment. Rather than concentrate on budget, the entrepreneurial project manager will calculate the incremental investment and its expected return in order to determine whether a project cost increase will or will not produce a greater return.

Viewing the Business System as a Balanced Approach

As shown in the business systems diagram, business skills for project leaders require learning more than accounting and finance. This is because a business is more than finance. A business is a system of interrelated factors of people, strategy, management, products, competitors, suppliers, and owners. True, the language of business is finance (and that is why we devote Chapter Two to a discussion of financial terms, covering the basics of the balance sheet, income statement, and cash flow). However, in considering the overall system we take the *balanced scorecard* approach of Kaplan and Norton (1996). In this view, organizations prosper by achieving strategy, and they achieve strategy through balancing four factors or perspectives: the learning and growth perspective, the customer perspective, the internal process perspective, and the financial perspective. We believe projects succeed the same way, as illustrated in Figure 1.4. In that figure the wheel on the right balances the four factors and turns smoothly. However, too much emphasis on one area, say financial, can lead to the lack of balance shown on the left wheel. In addition, lack of emphasis on any area, say process, can also lead to suboptimal performance.

In the past, project management has suffered from the dual problem of too much emphasis on operations and not enough emphasis on finance, which has led to a wobbly wheel of performance. In the future, project management should emphasize all areas equally in a balanced, business systems approach. Thus this book is about business skills for project leaders, not only finance skills for project leaders.

Achieve strategy. The primary goal of any business is to increase shareholder value. It does this by achieving its strategy. Projects are the primary means for achieving organizational strategy. Therefore all projects should be aligned with the organizational strategy so they can in fact contribute to it. Because the project manager's job is to help the organization achieve a particular strategy, it is important that project managers know the basics of the business strategy.

Learning and growth perspective. The learning and growth perspective concerns the human side of the organization. A business enterprise must develop employee

FIGURE 1.4. IMPORTANCE OF A BALANCED STRATEGY.

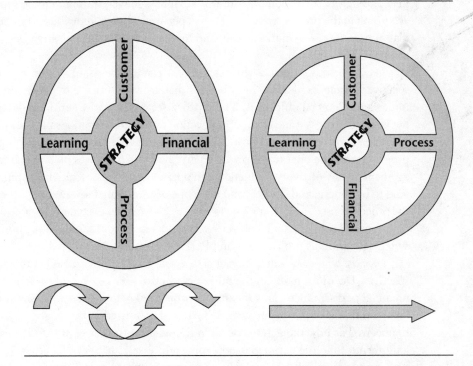

capabilities in order to drive organizational learning and growth. This perspective emphasizes current, sustained investment in people and the systems and organizational processes that support them. This is an important perspective for project managers because the way the people involved in a project are managed today will affect the success of the project outcome in the future. That is, decisions regarding project team structure, communication, motivation, and management will have an effect on how well the project outcome contributes to shareholder value. On the business systems diagram these are the *project management practices* that lead to project outcome, cost, and duration.

Customer perspective. The customer perspective identifies the market in which the organization has chosen to compete. This perspective addresses the customers, competitors, market segment, and market strategy. The customers are the sources that will deliver the revenue component of the company's financial objectives. If businesses are to achieve long-run superior financial performance, they must create and deliver products and services that are valued by customers. Thus, if a project outcome is to meet financial objectives, the project manager must translate the mission and strategy statements into specific market- and customer-based objectives. To do this the project manager must know the market and identify the *value propositions,* the product features that will be delivered to targeted segments according to the project strategy. This perspective is shown in the business systems diagram as the price, market share, and project outcome and duration that contribute to POL revenue.

Internal process perspective. In taking an internal process, or operations, perspective, managers identify the processes that are most critical to achieving customer and financial objectives. These processes are typically considered part of the internal process value chain of innovation processes, operations processes, and post-sale service processes. The innovation process is the process of managing the project itself. The operations processes are the basic processes of business management. Many of these production and operations processes and measurements tend to be generic and thus beyond the scope of this book. However, regardless of the processes used, project managers need to know the expected effect of cost decisions on reaching financial objectives. This perspective is shown in the business systems diagram as project costs and POL expenses.

Financial perspective. The financial perspective links together the other three perspectives. Decisions made in the other perspective areas eventually culminate in financial performance. This means the project manager must understand how long-run financial performance is defined and measured in the larger organization as well as how the actions taken in the other perspectives affect the desired long-term economic performance (a topic addressed further in Chapter Seven). This perspective is shown in the business systems diagram as the capital charge, the project and project outcome use of capital, and WACC.

Changing the System of Control

Having project managers make decisions in terms of the principles of the business system will require radical change in the measurement and control systems of most organizations. Companies sometimes say they want project managers to understand the business and manage to optimize shareholder value, that is, to act like CEOs of their projects. To this we say, "Really?" for we do not believe most organizations are ready for the change in control that must occur before the entrepreneurial project manager can emerge. For project managers to act like CEOs they must be treated like CEOs. They must be assessed not simply by a detailed emphasis on project outcome, duration, and cost but by broader measures based on how well a project increases economic value. Mitchell (1979) argues that such detailed, or *local,* controls restrict behavior and often become ends in themselves. Many of the controls put on project managers are local, go or no-go controls. Focusing on these controls may get a project done as specified but may not get the desired results of increasing economic value. Upper management may have close control but may not get the results it wanted. Mitchell argues for more global controls based on organizational goals, controls that focus on the results desired. Business-oriented controls focused on market performance, timing, and investing for return offer this more global approach; they are much more likely to get results but much less controlling. Thus the organizational question becomes, Do you want control, or do you want results? All too often we have found that organizations reward control more than results, and it is these organizations that we ask, Do you really want your project managers to act like entrepreneurs? For those organizations that can truly reward results and live with minimal control, a new world of project management awaits.

For example, examine the effects of controlling on outcome, duration, and costs. Begin with outcome. Controlling on outcome usually results in an emphasis on outcome specification. However, as the project proceeds, the need to change the specifications may arise in order to meet customer expectations or competitor actions. Von Moltke's dictum that "no plan survives contact with the enemy" (Mitchell, 1979, p. 22) has its counterpart in project management: few specifications survive contact with the market. However, when change procedures are too onerous or specification controls too tight, needed changes may not be done. As a result, the product may meet outcome controls but fail in the market. So controlling on outcome may not yield desired business results.

Now consider the problems with controlling on duration or schedule. A desired change may also be ruled out because it would alter the schedule. But deadlines and schedules should be set according to market conditions and changed according to those same conditions. With tight schedule control the deadline often becomes an end in itself and product changes are ignored if they cannot fit the schedule as it was first planned. One often hears managers saying, "If we make that change, we will miss the deadline."

A final problem is control on the budget. Many possibilities are missed because they are "not in the budget." For example, it is frustrating to project managers to be told to act like entrepreneurs but to be constrained from visiting potential customers because there is no money in the budget for travel. Under more global controls focused on increasing shareholder value, project managers would be free to travel to potential customers in order to understand the market better, without fear of budget recriminations. They could then change product features if they thought this change had the potential to increase profit. They might also change the schedule to respond to competitor actions. All these changes would be based on and evaluated in terms of the ability of the project manager to increase shareholder value and not just to keep within outcome, schedule, and cost constraints.

An additional problem is the imposition of overall company controls on the project process. The farmer who eats his seed corn will have a poorer crop in the future. Upper managers often eat their seed corn by imposing organization-wide limits on expenses, travel, and so forth. Such limitations may keep the project outcome from being introduced at the best time or with the best set of features, severely reducing product revenues and subsequent shareholder value. So the responsibility for success belongs to the organization as well as the project manager. Although the project manager must produce an outcome that increases shareholder value, the organization must provide an environment that allows that outcome to happen. This means the organization must provide the necessary funding and also shield the project manager from organizational restrictions that prevent people from achieving company goals. It is only in this way that the project manager can think like an entrepreneur and act like a CEO.

The result of the new orientation for project managers means that the ways they measure success must also change

From meeting fixed specifications to satisfying customers and contributing to strategic intent

From coming in on a fixed budget to managing cash flow so as to increase shareholder value

From meeting a fixed deadline to selecting the best time to market and time to breakeven

From having an internal focus on the project to having an external focus on the customer, market, competition, and entire project lifecycle

From just getting the project done to helping to implement organizational strategy

Project managers will have to understand what these new measures mean and how to manage their projects to attain favorable results. These results are not static. They are interactive. Projects are influenced by turbulence in the organizational environment, especially by global market forces. In short, projects have the properties of a business system. Project managers can influence this system only if they recognize these properties and act accordingly.

Using the Business Systems Calculator

One of the best ways to understand the interactions of the business variables and the effect of various decisions on potential economic value is to examine numerical examples and do *what if* analyses. For example, favoring the financial perspective by not traveling to potential customers for the project outcome may harm the customer perspective because the product may never reach its full sales potential. However, the extra sales generated by incorporating more features desired by customers may not be worth the cost when viewed from an economic value perspective. That is, the extra sales revenue may not be enough to cover the costs of the travel and of incorporating the features, including the cost of the capital used. In making a decision on such issues, it is useful to numerically calculate the economic results of the different decisions that might be made.

Understanding the interaction between factors in the business system is one thing, and calculating the potential results of decisions is quite another. To help project managers understand the potential consequences of decisions from a business systems standpoint, we have provided a on-line business systems calculator. Access it at www.projectmanagersmba.com. Examples of the functions that can be performed with the calculator are shown and explained throughout the book.

The calculator is based on the factors and interactions shown in the business systems diagram. The calculator uses data and assumptions developed for the business case for a specific project and allows the project manager to do what if analyses for various project decisions and to see the effect of potential decisions on economic value. Because the calculator uses data developed by organizational managers and presents results in terms that are important to those managers, it increases the chances that the project manager's decisions will be understood and accepted by those managers. That is, using the results of the calculator (or the results of making similar calculations yourself), you can encourage organizational managers to abandon their old go–no-go controls on projects and to adopt the more global control of increasing shareholder value.

In this book we divide the calculator input and output categories into four major parts, and each part is explained in one of the subsequent chapters. The first part is concerned with the project investment (Chapter Four), and the second part is concerned with project outcome revenues (Chapter Five). The third part addresses the project and post-project costs for producing or operating the project outcome (Chapter Six). The final part works with the costs of financing the work of the project and the operation of the project outcome as well as with the final calculations for determining any increase in shareholder value (Chapter Seven).

The main output of the calculator is a graphical representation of project costs, cash flow from the project outcome, and financing charges over the assumed life of the project outcome as well as the potential increase or decrease in shareholder value. Additional outputs from the calculator, such as monthly income statements, are also explained in the following chapters.

For example, Figure 1.5 shows the monthly financial progress of a project and the project outcome lifecycle. Beginning above the x-axis, which represents months, are familiar numbers for most project managers, namely cumulative project costs and sales revenue. Project costs climb during the project duration then level off.

FIGURE 1.5. INTERACTION OF PROJECT MANAGEMENT FACTORS.

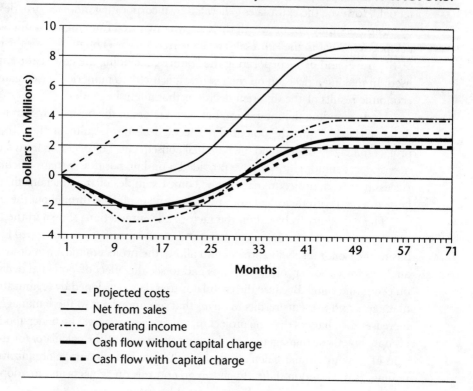

- – – – Projected costs
- —— Net from sales
- ·—·— Operating income
- —— Cash flow without capital charge
- ■ ■ ■ Cash flow with capital charge

Sales revenue begins after the project costs become level, as the project outcome lifecycle begins. Some of the numbers shown beginning below the *x*-axis may not be as familiar to all project managers (they are explained further in Chapter Two). Cumulative operating income, basically sales revenue minus operating expenses, at first decreases as the organization loses money during the project, then it turns up as sales revenues begin to climb during the POL. Cash flow is not as negative as operating income (loss) during the project due to the effect of the tax credit for negative income. In the same vein, cash flow is less than operating income after the losses stop, as some of the operating income goes to pay the now positive tax charge. (The tax man giveth during losses but taketh away during profits. Fair enough.) The final line shows the cash flow with an additional capital charge. This charge, the WAAC, is levied to pay for the financing needed during the losses.

In short, the calculator asks the project manager to supply various assumptions about his or her project, and the project manager can compare the outputs for different sets of assumptions as an aid to understanding the potential effects of project decisions on economic value. As mentioned, a variety of these assumptions are discussed in Chapter Eight to help the project manager understand the relative importance and the interactions of the various components of the business system.

Preparing the Business Case and the Business Plan

Projects often require some form of business case analysis as part of the selection process, and project managers may become involved in developing the business case. At the very least they should have a copy of the case as completed by some other manager. The material in this book will help you to contribute to a better business case or simply to understand a case better if it is handed to you. It will also do much more than that, however. It will help you to take the business case and use it to develop a business plan. All too often we have seen that the business case developed to justify a project never becomes part of the project plan, is never used as a basis for decision making during project execution, and is never used for evaluation during the project close out and the operation of the project outcome. However, entrepreneurs run their businesses from a business plan. And project managers should do the same thing.

Most companies that use business case analysis have their own processes and methods. However, the Appendix to this book offers a generic outline for constructing a business case. The case becomes a business plan with the addition of more detail. This requires additional analysis and testing of all the assumptions in the case as well as learning more about the market. Once completed, the business plan becomes a powerful guide for making project decisions that enhance shareholder value and for conducting an evaluation at the end of the project outcome lifecycle.

The following are the key questions that you will need to answer in order to write a competent business plan. You will find methods for answering these questions in this book and methods for doing the analysis with the aid of the business systems calculator. Using the calculator as an aid to decision making will extend the business case analysis into the reality of daily project management and help ensure that the project is being run according to the business plan. The calculator will help you use the business plan as a living guide to action.

How will this project contribute to and support the strategy of the company? (Chapter Three)

What are the major market forces that will influence the expected revenue during the POL? (Chapter Five)

What return on investment must the project have in order to contribute to positive cash flow and shareholder value? (Chapter Seven)

How will the project and its outcome produce this return?

To determine the answers for these questions, you will construct a financial model of the project and its outcome. The contents of the model will vary depending on the type of project. For a new product development project the model will include the total project cost and all the financial elements of the project outcome lifecycle including sales volume and price, operating costs, and overhead expenses. For an internal project the model will include the total project cost as well, but the financial elements of the POL will be different. They will include operating costs, maintenance costs, and the net savings the company realizes from the operations of the project outcome. The model for a client engagement project will include the cost of the project and the financial elements of a very short POL, including cash payments received from the client, any continuing clients payments, and any continuing costs for warranty or maintenance.

You will also need to list all the assumptions that go into the information that you use to build the model. What are the schedule and the costs that go into the project budget? What is the relationship between the times of the project completion and the POL start-up and cash flow? What is the sales volume and price of the new product (if the project is a development project)? What is the relationship between the quality of the project outcome and the assumptions made about price and sales volume during the POL? What are the operating costs and overhead expenses? How did you estimate all this information?

You will need to test your assumptions by referencing market research, operations analysis and experience, strategic alignment, and any other relevant information. As the project and POL unfold you will need to retest these assumptions at major milestones in order to control the project and influence the POL process.

The questions we suggest here and the basic business plan outline we offer in the Appendix are very basic. Once you begin applying the ideas in this book, you will begin to expand on these materials to develop a plan outline of your own (if your company does not already have one). In addition many publications on how to write a business plan are available. They are aimed primarily at budding entrepreneurs (see Tiffany and Peterson, 1997, for one good example). Even more relevant for project managers are guides from the literature on internal corporate venture development (see Pinchot and Pellman, 1999; Block and MacMillan, 1995).

Examples

To end this chapter and subsequent chapters, we look at two examples of project decision making. Using these examples we show first how these decisions are approached using the old triple constraint model of project management and then how they are approached using the business systems approach.

Newprod Project

The first example is a new product development project, the Newprod project. Assume this project was selected in order to develop a product that will open a new market for your company, and you are the project manager. The company wants this product to be the product leader in this market. The project is currently scheduled to take twelve months and cost $3,000,000. Competitive analysis shows that several other companies are working on similar products and they all could be ready in about twelve months. Thus the market for this product will begin in twelve months whether Newprod is ready or not. Market analysis indicates that the demand will peak to twenty thousand units about twenty-four months after the market for this product begins. Demand will decline from the peak and cease about twenty months after the peak. If Newprod is ready in twelve months when the market begins, it could capture a 30 percent market share. If not, it will gain only a 20 percent share. The price will begin at $300 per unit when the market begins and is expected to decline at 5 percent per year. Projected production costs are $240 per unit and are expected to decline 8 percent per year once Newprod goes into production. Cost of overhead, often called *selling, general, and administrative* expense, is 5 percent of revenue, and WACC is 12 percent. (These are also the assumptions used to generate Figure 1.5.)

Now assume that midway through the project a team member comes to you with an idea for an additional feature for Newprod. Of course any new feature represents *project scope creep*. Most project managers have learned to control scope creep by using the old triple constraints. The following lists compare the kinds of questions project managers ask when using the triple constraint approach to the kinds of questions they ask when using the business systems approach.

Triple Constraint Approach Questions

Outcome. Does this new feature conform to the specifications? Is it needed to achieve performance criteria? Can we get management approval for this change in time to include it in this version of the product?

Cost. How much will this new feature cost? Is there enough money in the budget? If not, can we get a budget increase? Can we get the increase in time to include the feature in this version of the product?

Duration. How much time will this add to the schedule? Is this acceptable to upper management? If not, can we get an extension?

Normally, if the feature does not satisfy the three criteria or if extensions are not granted, then it is rejected. This approach pits project manager against upper manager and often leads to rejection of good ideas.

Business Systems Approach Questions

Strategy. Does the new feature fit with the strategic alignment of the project?

Project processes. Do the team members feel they can add this feature with the current people on the team? If not, can it be done by outside people? How much will adding this feature delay project completion?

Market. Are there customers who want this feature? How much will any project delay decrease the potential market share for this product? How much more will customers be willing to pay for this product with the new feature? Will competitors have this feature? How much will having this feature increase the potential market for this product? For example, will it attract new customers not previously considered? What assumptions can we test regarding competitor and feature effects on market share? (See Figure 1.6 for an example.)

Costs. How much will adding this feature add to the cost of the project? How much will it add to the cost of the project outcome?

Finance. How much will the feature add to the capital charge?

Economic value. What will be the expected effect on economic value?

FIGURE 1.6. ASSESSING A NEW FEATURE'S EFFECT ON THE POTENTIAL MARKET.

	We have the feature	We don't have the feature
They have the feature	+ 5%	−15%
They don't have the feature	+ 20%	0%

Obviously, the set of questions for the business approach is quite different from the set a project manager would ask to satisfy the triple constraints. Although the business systems approach is still concerned with outcome, cost, and schedule, it considers them by looking at effects on market demand, revenue, and economic value rather than seeing them simply as constraints. Also notice the lack of concern with upper-management approval in these questions. The business systems approach seeks market approval, not management approval.

In subsequent chapters we examine ways to answer each of these questions. In addition, we show how to use the calculator to get some numerical answers to these questions.

Newsys Project

Newsys, our second example, is an internal project to select and install a new telephone system. Our ongoing description of the Newsys project will point out the typical differences between this internal project and the Newprod project and should apply to most internal projects that have the development of a new system or process as their outcome.

You are the project manager chosen to select, install, and start up a new telephone system that will move beyond the company's current analog system to a digital system that can expand as the company grows. Management has decreed that this system should provide consistent, high-quality telecommunications. The current system does not have sufficient line capacity to handle the company's rapid growth. Because of its memory constraints, the system drops calls, arbitrarily locks callers out of voice mail, and automatically purges voice-mail boxes. It does not distinguish between inside and outside lines and does not have a caller ID function. All of this makes for an unprofessional company image and difficult communications. The project is currently scheduled to last seven months and the cost has been projected to be $50,000 a month, for a total project cost of $350,000.

This project is fairly straightforward given triple constraint thinking. You have a budget of $350,000 to select, install, and start up a new phone system. The outcome needs to conform to the desires of upper management as just stated and be ready in seven months. We will demonstrate in the following chapters that the principles of this book can be applied to this kind of project as well as new product or service development projects and client engagement projects. Indeed, once we illustrate how to do a basic economic analysis of this internal project using marginal differences in cash flows, this example will closely parallel the Newprod example.

CHAPTER TWO

ACCOUNTING AND FINANCE BASICS FOR THE PROJECT MANAGEMENT ENTREPRENEUR

Never ask of money spent
Where the spender thinks it went.
Nobody was ever meant
To remember or invent
What he did with every cent.

ROBERT FROST, "THE HARDSHIP OF ACCOUNTING," 1936

This chapter is designed for the project manager who needs to learn or review some essential principles in business accounting and finance. To determine whether you should continue with this chapter, ask yourself the following questions: Do I know the difference between cash and accrual in the various kinds of reports that businesses use? (This involves such concepts as the principle of matching, the difference between an expense and a use of cash, and the difference between revenue and a source of cash.) Have I ever heard the phrase, "debits on the left, credits on the right," or laughed at a joke using this phrase as a punch line? Can I keep a straight face when told that a company was making a profit but still had to declare bankruptcy? Can I define an income statement, balance sheet, and cash flow statement and explain what each one is used for and how to use each one? Do I never get queasy if asked to read one of these reports for any reason? Finally, do I know specifically how my project fits into these three reports? If you can answer yes to all these questions, you may want to skip to the next chapter. If

This chapter draws heavily on the Strategic Management Group's *Why Finance Matters* (an interactive CD-ROM), sections 3 through 5. ©1997 by Strategic Management Group. Used by permission.

you can answer yes to all but the last question, you will benefit from skimming the chapter and reading the sections that relate the financial concepts specifically to projects. If you answered no to every question and perhaps also had difficulty understanding the questions themselves, we suggest that you read this chapter and also look at a basic learning resource on finance and accounting. (Our favorite is the interactive CD-ROM program developed by the Strategic Management Group, 1997.)

This chapter is about basic accounting and finance for companies and projects. It includes what we consider to be the basic terms and concepts that all project managers need to know to take on the new role that today's business requires of them. As we described in Chapter One, the traditional project manager had to be able to deal with static constraints of project schedule or duration, cost or budget, and outcome. Now the project management entrepreneur has to deal with a more dynamic business system. This requires a broader understanding of the whole business and the way each project fits into the dynamics of the business system. When project managers accept a budget and simply manage to that budget, the economic and financial decisions underlying the budget remain fixed as long as the budget is fixed. Once they understand the economic and financial dynamics of a business enterprise, managers will also be prepared to fine-tune the project budget and the project as a whole in the light of current problems and opportunities. They will be able to manage for broader economic and financial gain for the project and project outcome lifecycle, thereby contributing increased shareholder value to the company. The terms and basic concepts in this chapter are a foundation on which to build this competency.

We begin with the topic of money, the fuel on which all businesses run. An examination of the cash cycle of the firm traces how businesses get cash, spend it, and make more of it. We then explain how the three basic financial reports that businesses use—income statement, balance sheet, and cash flow statement—are windows for viewing the cash cycle over a given period of time. The cash cycle is continuous. These statements allow businesses to take a snapshot of the cycle at regular intervals to assess what is going on and whether the company is producing an economic surplus over time. Only by producing this surplus can a business flourish over the long run and meet the expectations of its investors. The income statement shows whether the business is making a profit, has the potential to produce cash, during a given period. The balance sheet shows what the business owns at a given point in time and the cash that has been invested in the business to buy or produce what the business owns. The cash flow statement explains the sources and uses of cash over a given period.

Different organizations, organizational functions, and groups use these basic financial statements for different but related purposes. Publicly owned companies use external versions of them in their published annual reports and 10K reports to conform to Securities Exchange Commission (SEC) regulations. Shareholders and potential investors use external versions of them to understand the financial health of a company and to compare the performance of companies in order to make investment decisions. Managers use detailed internal versions of them to understand a company's financial health and also to look for opportunities to improve the financial performance of their area of responsibility and of the company as a whole. This chapter discusses these statements as important managerial tools for the project manager.

Cash Cycle of the Firm and the Project

Each company or project has a cash cycle. The cash cycle involves acquiring cash, using that cash to grow and to operate, and returning any cash necessary to the creditors and owners (see Figure 2.1). Once a business starts up, this is a continuous process, and it becomes difficult to isolate each phase at any given period of time because all the phases are happening continuously. For the start-up business or a project, it is easier to isolate and understand each phase of the cycle. The start-up business must attract funds from financial institutions and investors to have the capital needed to start the business (the *financing phase*). It then invests the funds in labor and equipment required to develop the business (the *investing phase*). During the *operating phase,* the company continues to use these funds to operate the business, adding funds generated by the operations. Finally, to keep going, it must pay the interest on any loans and provide a return on investment required by investors (the *returning phase,* using return as in the phrase "return on investment").

FIGURE 2.1. CASH CYCLE OF THE FIRM.

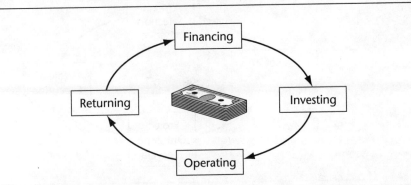

Source: Strategic Management Group. Used by permission.

Projects are really just like start-up businesses. The essential difference is that whereas a project usually has a beginning, middle, and end, a business does not have an end as long as it is successful. In the beginning, just like a business, the project must attract funds. It gets these funds from upper management, which decides how to invest the company's money and therefore which projects to select. Project selection and approval is equivalent to the business's financing phase. The project manager invests that money in developing a product, service, process, or some other outcome that will eventually generate more cash. The project itself, then, is most often the equivalent of the investing phase. In most cases the official end of the project happens well before the project outcome produces any cash. Operations of the project outcome over the project outcome lifecycle (POL), constitute the operating phase. In this phase upper management will be able to assess whether the company has made a sufficient return on its investment. It needs this return in order to pay back company creditors and shareholders. The end of the cash cycle for the project comes at the end of the useful life of the outcome that it produced (Figure 2.2).

A major problem for the project manager is that projects are often conceptually and managerially isolated from the cash cycle as a whole. The project outcome is usually pooled with all the other operating assets. Under these circumstances it becomes difficult to isolate the cash cycle for an individual project. However, the cash cycle for the company as a whole depends on the cash cycles for the ongoing projects in the project portfolio. If these projects are not

FIGURE 2.2. CASH CYCLE OF THE PROJECT.

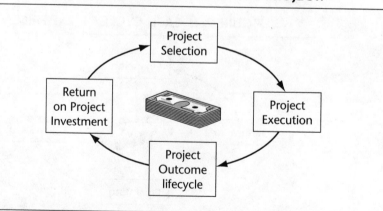

successful in generating sufficient cash, the company cannot succeed. This issue will come into sharper focus as we discuss each phase of the cash cycle in more detail.

The Story of DDI

To illustrate the cash cycle and, later, the format and use of financial reports, we use the example of a fictitious small start-up company. As we suggested earlier, project managers should think of their projects as total enterprises rather considering them from the conventional project point of view, and the total enterprises they are most like are start-up companies.

Digital Development Inc. (DDI) was started in a backyard cottage somewhere in California during the early 1970s. A professor of computer science, Barry First, had an idea for developing an operating system for the small microcomputers that hobbyists were beginning to buy and use. Reading hobby magazines, he noticed that people were writing letters to the editor complaining that once they acquired the new computer kits and built them, they were having a difficult time making the computers work because they did not know how to program an operating system. Barry knew that he could develop such a software system, but he needed cash to buy computers and other equipment to develop the system and then make copies of the software that he could sell to hobbyists. Barry had some cash himself, but it was not enough. So he asked a friend of his to contribute some cash. He also went to his local bank for a small loan, which was approved after Barry agreed to a second mortgage on his house.

Barry used part of the cash to buy computers and the other equipment needed to develop and copy the program. He also found a great deal on a small office condo. It was being auctioned in a sheriff's sale, and he bought it as a space for setting up the business. He also used part of the cash to pay the wages of an assistant programmer who would help him develop the system. Once the product was ready, the assistant also helped produce copies, take orders, and ship the finished product. DDI took orders through the mail from individual hobbyists. It also sold copies to a computer kit maker, the Computer Company, which included a system with each kit to attract new customers. Most individuals paid by check, but the Computer Company paid for its systems only after it received payment from its customers. During production, Barry made payments to the bank on the loan and paid taxes on DDI profits. From the beginning the business was successful and began to grow nicely. After two years Barry paid back the principal on the bank loan and paid a share of the profits to his friend who had invested in the company. Then he reinvested the remaining cash in the business. Looking at this process as it evolved during DDI's first year, gives a good illustration of the cash cycle of any project or business.

Financing Phase

What does it take to start a business or a project? Cash. Where does that cash come from? It usually comes from the pocket of the entrepreneurs who start the business, but this cash is usually not enough. The good news is that there are other sources of funds for sound business propositions. The bad news is that this money comes at a price. Individuals or financial institutions may become lenders, providing some of the money in the form of a loan. They will require that they be paid interest on the loan while the money is being used by the business. They will also require that the principal be returned after a given period of time. Individuals and other financial institutions, such as investment banks, may also provide some of the money in return for a share in the profits of the business. They then become shareholders along with the original entrepreneurs. Shareholders have a right to a share of the profits in proportion to the amount they have contributed to the business. When projects are started up within an existing business, they increase the business's need for cash. This extra cash must come from the same basic sources. The business can borrow money from banks, or it can issue and sell bonds. It can get more money from existing or new shareholders by issuing new stock and selling it, or it can use surplus cash being held within business.

To return to the DDI example, Barry calculated that he needed $6,000 to start the business. He had $3,000 of his own cash that he could contribute. He was able to get $1,000 from his friend in return for a share in any profits. The friend's share would be in proportion to the amount he invested in the business. In this case, he invested $1,000 of the total $4,000 invested, or 25 percent. This $4,000 is called *equity*. Equity represents the amount contributed by the shareholders in the business. Barry then borrowed the remaining $2,000 from his local bank. This debt amount is called a *liability*. Because the bank did not become an owner of the business, Barry simply had to promise to pay back the amount of the loan after a specified period of time and to make interest payments during this period. Because DDI was a new business and quite risky in the eyes of the bank, Barry had to put up his house as additional security to guarantee that the loan would be repaid. This loan and the interest on it had to be repaid whether or not the business became a success. The friend who became a shareholder, or owner, however, would get a return only if the business made a profit. However, the shareholder expected a return on his investment that was higher than the lender's interest rate. This expectation was based on the fact that the shareholder's investment was at a higher risk. If anything went wrong with the business, the law gave the lender first call on available funds to get back its money (not to mention its right to foreclose on Barry's house). Owners were last in line.

Investing Phase

During the investing phase the money acquired during the financial phase is spent on labor, materials, and equipment to develop new assets. An *asset* is anything of value that can later be converted into cash. In most cases these assets will be used in a sales and production process to produce more assets—such as products and services—to be sold in the marketplace. In this way the assets are ultimately converted into cash. The investing phase of the cash cycle corresponds to the project execution phase. For ongoing companies the investing phase applies to the projects that have been initiated but are not yet completed.

In the investing phase at DDI, Barry hired an assistant to help finish and debug the operating system. He then registered the system for copyright protection. The operating system consequently became an asset called intellectual property. Barry bought a machine that could copy his program in a form he could send out to hobbyists who wanted to buy it. He also bought two computers to further develop and test the system, and other equipment needed to package and ship the product. These machines were also assets. His programmer had to refine the program and the copying machine so that the final product was error free and usable by the buyer. Meanwhile Barry placed advertising in hobby magazines and traveled to a hobbyists' convention to demonstrate his system. At this point in time project development was finished and the product was ready for production and sale. Of course, Barry and his assistant were already working on version two of the program, a new project.

Operating Phase

During the operating phase the company uses the assets it acquired or developed in the previous phase to make products and services, which it then sells in the marketplace or uses to support the manufacturing or selling process. For the project, this is the project outcome lifecycle. It represents the conversion of the project outcome into cash. For the company as a whole this phase corresponds to ongoing operations, which is the process of converting existing assets into cash. Projects are never ends in themselves. Financially they are always a means to an end, cash. Projects need to be planned and executed with this end in mind or they will not be as effective as they could be in contributing to this stage in the cash cycle.

At DDI, Barry's assistant bought materials needed to make copies with the new machine and materials to package the copies. He then produced copies of

Barry's operating system and put them into packages and stored them in a storage room ready to be shipped. At this stage DDI was very low on cash. Most of the cash it had acquired in the financing phase had been spent on equipment and wages to develop the product and produce the product, but there was no cash coming into the business yet. This is the pattern in most projects as well. They produce assets that will eventually be converted into cash, but during project execution and the first part of the project outcome lifecycle, or operating phase, this conversion into cash has not begun because the selling part of the operating phase has not yet begun. Because Barry had gone to computer shows and advertised in hobby magazines, people started ordering individual systems fairly soon. They sent checks with their orders, and once the checks cleared the bank, the cash started coming in. After making sales calls on some of the computer kit manufacturers, Barry convinced one company to include a copy of his operating system with the kit to make it more attractive to hobbyists. This increased the volume of systems out the door, but the company had promised to pay for each system only after its customers paid it. This took about sixty days from the time DDI shipped the program copies to the computer maker.

Returning Phase

During the returning phase of the cash cycle, investors are paid and available cash is reinvested in the company. Lenders expect interest payments on their loans, and eventually they want these loans repaid. The owners, the shareholders, want a return on their investment. Shareholders can realize a return in four ways. The company can make a dividend payment, the company can buy back the stock from shareholders, or the shareholders can sell their stock to other people. These first three ways return cash to the shareholder. The fourth way shareholders can receive a return is for the company to reinvest the surplus cash in the company, with the intention of eventually creating more cash. If this reinvestment is successful, it will increase the value of the company and thus increase the value of shareholders' stock.

Cash generated in the operating phase must be enough to allow these returns to happen, or the company will eventually fail. A project should be subject to an ongoing evaluation of the project outcome's return on project investment during the project outcome lifecycle. A company will be looking at periodic loan payments to lenders, dividend payments to shareholders, its fluctuating stock price, and the reinvestment of cash in new projects. All of these returns are made possible by the cash flow produced during the operating phase.

During its first year of operations, DDI earned enough cash to pay the interest on its bank loan. It reinvested the rest of the cash in the business as working capital, to fund the growth of the business.

Projects and Cash Management

A business must manage its overall cash flow. If DDI had not been able to produce enough cash to pay its financial obligations and continue to invest in the business, it would eventually have failed. As head of the company, Barry had to think broadly about managing cash for the company as a whole. He also had to take into account the flow of cash during each phase in terms of sources of cash and uses of cash. *Sources of cash* add to the overall balance of cash in the business, whereas *uses of cash* deplete that balance. Barry needed to think of strategies for maximizing the sources of cash and minimizing the uses of cash and for balancing the short-term needs of the business with the long-term strategic and business goals. The cash invested in the business was DDI's total *capital*. It included cash invested for the long term in buildings, equipment, machinery, and intellectual property, that is, *long-term capital*. It also included cash needed to run the day-to-day operations of the business, that is, *working capital*. Managing working capital successfully requires managing the time lags accompanying various operational processes, such as paying for materials and collecting money owed to the company by its customers. It is important to minimize the time lag for sources of cash and maximize the lag for uses of cash in order to keep the highest cash balance possible in the business. This high balance means cash is available for use as long-term capital for investing in new equipment or new product development.

The three types of projects—development, internal, and client engagement—all represent a use of cash. At DDI, its development project (getting the operating system ready for production and shipping) took a while. During this time the business was not able to generate any cash through operations because there were no operations yet. The sources of cash to finance the project were the shareholders and the bank. The outcome of the project, the product for sale, however, was the central source of cash for the business during the first year. If the project had not produced a system that met the needs of the people who were potential customers at a price they were willing to pay, there would have been little or no cash from operations and no additional sources of cash to repay lenders and shareholders. And so it goes for new product development projects. They are significant users of cash, but ultimately they create the essential sources of cash.

This is also true of internal projects to build facilities or install systems. They are initial heavy uses of cash, but for the business as a whole they must contribute to increasing the sources of cash. Other types of internal projects also classify as uses of cash, but they are often efforts to fine-tune the operations to increase sources of cash or decrease uses of cash or both. Examples are projects to make the manufacturing process more efficient, initiate Total Quality Management, or create an error-free billing process or a more efficient and effective sales process.

Client engagement projects are also uses of cash, but they are also most like companies. They usually have the shortest time gap between uses of cash and sources of cash. As initiating, planning, and executing the project uses cash, periodic client payments at agreed milestones become sources of cash. Nevertheless, as in companies, there is often a significant lag in the cash cycle of a client engagement project. Applying the principles of working capital management will help to control these lags in this type of project.

In all three types of projects, project managers need to incorporate two dimensions in their management decisions. The first dimension is the cash management during the project itself. The tendency here is to spend less and to hurry project completion because the project is a heavy user of cash and cannot produce cash until it is complete. The second dimension is the cash management during the project outcome lifecycle, when the project outcome is expected to produce cash. It is important to think about both dimensions when making project decisions and to think about how these dimensions influence one another. In very basic terms good project management is managing uses of cash in a way that maximizes the sources of cash for the company over the total period of the project and the project outcome lifecycle. Organizational culture, measurement and reporting systems, and other company incentives do not often encourage a project manager to develop this long-term horizon. Yet we believe the only way to manage projects as if shareholders mattered is for project managers to adopt this point of view, manage their projects from this perspective, and be measured and rewarded on this basis.

Financial Reports

During DDI's first year, Barry ran the company out of his checkbook. By the end of that year he knew he was going to have to produce financial reports so that he could better understand what was happening in the business financially and thus make better decisions. He was also starting to think about applying for another bank loan to expand the business. He knew that the bank would need financial reports to make a decision on whether to approve the loan. He also wanted to supply accurate information to his other shareholder. Of course he needed to file his tax returns as well. These circumstances defined his need for the three kinds of each basic report that all businesses need to produce. External reports are for investors and lenders so that they can determine the financial state of the company and compare it to other companies that they might invest in. Internal reports allow managers to view and understand the phases of the cash cycle and act to improve it. Finally all companies must file reports that give local and national governments the information to enforce regulations and collect taxes.

Barry hired an accountant to help him set up a financial reporting system for DDI. The accountant explained that Barry needed to set up three basic statements: a balance sheet, an income statement, and a cash flow statement. The balance sheet shows all of the assets that the company owns, its financial obligations to lenders and creditors, and any other claims on those assets for a given period of time. The income statement shows whether the company is producing a profit. A profit is a surplus of revenues over expenses for a given time period. The cash flow statement summarizes the flow of cash in the business during a given period in order to show exactly where the cash that the company used during the period came from and where the cash that the company produced during the same period went. All these reports would help Barry and his partner better understand the financial state of their business and whether it was creating value for them as shareholders. After all, there were other investments that they could make with the cash that they now had invested in DDI. These reports would help them to compare their investment in DDI with any alternative they might have.

The rest of this chapter will explain the basics of the three financial statements, detailing what they report and how project managers can use them.

The Balance Sheet

It is especially important for project managers to understand the nature of a balance sheet because a balance sheet is all about assets. Most projects are endeavors to produce assets for the company that will later be converted into cash. The balance sheet shows what the business owns (its assets) and tracks how much cash has been invested in the business to develop, buy, or produce these assets. It also tracks where that cash came from at a selected point in time. However, it is also important to realize that because of the reporting rules for financial accounting, not all the asset information may show up on the balance sheet. Concrete project outcomes such as a new factory or the purchase and installation of new equipment are recorded as long-term assets on the balance sheet. The costs associated with new product development projects or process reengineering projects are more likely to show up on the income statement as an expense (as explained in the next section). This is because most of the costs associated with these types of projects are the salaries of the project team members, and salaries are considered current expenses.

The balance sheet has two sides. The left-hand side of the balance sheet reports the company's investment or assets, what it owns. These assets are divided into two kinds. *Current assets* are items that will be normally converted into cash in a year or less. Examples of current assets are raw materials used to make a product and inventories of uncompleted products or of completed but unsold products. *Long-term assets* are items that will be converted into cash over a period of time longer than a year. The right-hand side reports the financing of the company, where the cash came from to support the investments reported on the left-hand side of the report. This side of the balance sheet consists of liabilities, obligations that have to be paid back, and shareholders' equity, the cash that belongs to the owners that is invested in the assets. Liabilities are classified in the same way as assets. *Current liabilities* must be paid back within a year, and *long-term liabilities* can paid back over a period longer than a year. Shareholders' equity also has two parts. The first is stock, valued at the amount that shareholders originally paid when they purchased shares of stock from the company. This amount does not include any adjustment for what shareholders may have paid when they bought shares of the stock on the open market. The second part of shareholders' equity is retained earnings. Retained earnings are the surplus cash created by the business, cash that is kept in the business rather than paid out to shareholders as dividends. This statement is called a balance sheet because the total amounts on the left side and the right side are always equal, that is, in balance. This is the accounting formula that always applies to the balance sheet: Assets (the left-hand side) = Liabilities and Shareholders' Equity (the right-hand side).

To illustrate in more detail how the balance sheet works and relates to projects and project management, we will track the first year of DDI through the company's balance sheet. We begin with the balance sheet as it would appear at the end of the financing phase of the cash cycle (Figure 2.3). Remember that Barry was able to put together $6,000 in cash to start the business. Before he started investing that cash by buying things and paying wages, it existed as cash in the bank ready to spend. So at this point in time, it is reported as cash on the asset, or *investment*, side of the balance sheet. Cash is always the most current of current assets. DDI's total assets in the financing phase are $6,000. The liabilities and equity, or *financing*, side of the balance sheet accounts for the source of the cash. Two thousand dollars was a loan from the bank that does not have to be repaid for two years and is thus listed under long-term liabilities. The rest of the money came from Barry ($3,000) and his friend ($1,000). They are shareholders in the business, and their money is reported as common stock under equity. Both sides of the balance sheet have the same total because they are reporting two sides of the same thing, the cash invested in the business: what it was spent on (investment) and where it came from (financing). This follows the equation: Assets ($6,000) = Liabilities ($2,000) + Shareholders' Equity ($4,000).

As DDI moves from the financing phase of the cash cycle to the investing phase, the balance sheet changes (Figure 2.4). The investment side reflects how Barry took the cash and invested it in assets that can generate more cash during the operating phase. The company purchased its small office condominium for

FIGURE 2.3. DDI BALANCE SHEET: FINANCING PHASE.

Investment		Financing	
Assets		**Liabilities**	
Current assets		Current liabilities	
Cash	$6,000		
		Long-term liabilities	
		Bank debt	$2,000
Long-term assets		**Equity**	
		Common stock	4,000
Total	**$6,000**	**Total**	**$6,000**

FIGURE 2.4. DDI BALANCE SHEET: INVESTING PHASE.

Investment		Financing	
Assets		**Liabilities**	
Current assets		Current liabilities	
Cash	$800		
Work in progress	1,200	Long-term liabilities	
		Bank debt	$2,000
Long-term assets		**Equity**	
Property, plant, & equipment	2,000	Common stock	4,000
Operating system code	2,000		
Total	**$6,000**	**Total**	**$6,000**

$1,000. In addition it spent $1,000 on the copying machine and two computers. Thus $2,000 was subtracted from cash and moved to *property, plant, and equipment* to account for these transactions. Because there was no change in the sources of the cash, the financing side of the balance sheet remained unchanged. Barry worked part time on completing the operating system code, supervising his assistant. It took them four months of intense work to finish the code and test it. At the end of this phase it was ready to be copied and sold. The coding project cost $2,000, including the assistant's wages. During development these costs were recorded as a current asset called *work in progress*. Once the project was completed it was moved to the long-term asset section and labeled *operating system code*. It was recorded this way because it was an important asset that DDI paid cash to develop. DDI was going to use that asset to generate more cash. It was considered long-term because Barry and his accountant had determined that the software had an expected useful life of longer than one year. (We have simplified this situation for the example. The accounting rules for capitalizing software are much more complicated in reality.) In addition, during these four months the assistant spent the rest of his time helping to set up the office and beginning to advertise the operating system. His wage for this other work, $300 per month ($1,200 total), was paid out as cash. For the time being it was recorded as work in progress.

A look at just the first month of the next phase in the cash cycle, the operating phase, will illustrate the kinds of information that go on the balance sheet during this phase. During the first week of this month, DDI bought enough materials to make one hundred copies of the operating system. The materials cost $200, which was charged on the company credit card. This amount became an account payable. An *account payable* is the recording of an obligation to pay cash sometime in the near future. The labor of making each copy cost $8. Because Barry paid his assistant every week and the assistant made one hundred copies over the month, this expense depleted cash at the end of the month by $800. If the assistant had not been paid so often, DDI would have had to add a category called *wages payable* on the liability side of the balance sheet to record wages earned by workers but not yet paid by the company. By the end of the month seventy-five of the one hundred units had been sold and shipped. The first fifty units were sold directly to individuals for $25 per unit. Individuals paid by check, and all these checks, miraculously, cleared the bank by the end of the month. The other twenty-five units were sold to the Computer Company for $20 per unit. The Computer Company promised to pay in sixty days. DDI also spent $600 on shipping the product and general administrative expenses. So at the end of the month DDI had twenty-five units in inventory at $10 per unit ($8 for labor plus $2 for materials), or $250. It had paid out $800 in wages and another $600 in expenses and owed $200 on its credit card for materials, but it had also collected $1,250 in cash from individual sales. And it had another $500 in sales to the Computer Company for which there was no cash payment yet, but the promise to pay was reported as an account receivable. An *account receivable* is the recording of a promise to pay in the near term. The organization that makes this promise has the promise recorded on its balance sheet as an account payable.

Because the balance sheet in Figure 2.5 is a snapshot of DDI at the end of the first month of the operating phase (the fifth month of its existence), it does not show all the steps in recording events that took place during the month. At the time Barry's assistant bought the materials to make one hundred systems and charged the amount on the credit card, two entries were made on the balance sheet. The account payable for $200 on the right-hand side of the balance sheet was balanced at that moment with an item called *raw materials inventory* on the left-hand side. This

FIGURE 2.5. DDI BALANCE SHEET: OPERATING PHASE, FIRST MONTH.

Investment		Financing	
Assets		**Liabilities**	
Current assets		Current liabilities	
Cash	$650	Accounts payable	$200
Accounts receivable	500	Long-term liabilities	
Work in progress	1,200	Bank debt	2,000
Inventory	250		
Long-term assets		**Equity**	
Property, plant, & equipment	2,000	Common stock	4,000
Operating system code	2,000	Retained earnings	400
Total	**$6,600**	**Total**	**$6,600**

showed that the materials had not yet been converted into a finished product. The assistant then began to make copies of the operating system. When a copy was started but not yet complete, it was recorded as *work in progress inventory.* Once that copy was finished—ready to be sold but not yet sold—it was recorded as *finished goods inventory.* To keep the balance sheet less complicated, we have combined all three of these types of inventory under the single line item *inventory.* We are also going to leave the work in progress account on the balance sheet until we finalize the balance sheet for the first year of operations (in Figure 2.11).

At the end of this first month of operations, the most notable factor is that the balance sheet still balances but now it balances at a higher number. DDI started with $6,000. Now it has $6,600. Where did the new investment come from? It came from both lenders and owners. It incorporates the additional $200 in short-term debt that DDI borrowed through the company credit card. More important, however, it incorporates the amount on the line labeled *retained earnings.* This line reflects the cash from selling the operating system, cash that the owners have a right to but have left in the business to be used to create additional value (cash). Barry and his partner were very happy about the prospects of the company. They wanted to declare a small dividend of $200 to be distributed in proportion to share ownership. Barry would get $150. His friend would get $50. On the balance sheet, this would have been recorded as minus $200 from cash and minus $200 from retained earnings (Figure 2.6). Notice that when the owners chose to take some of their money, they reduced the value of the business as it is recorded on the balance sheet. This is what happens when a corporation pays out a dividend to its shareholders. It pays cash out and reduces the cash available internally to invest in more assets

FIGURE 2.6. DDI BALANCE SHEET: RETURNING PHASE, WITH OWNERS' DIVIDEND.

Investment		Financing	
Assets		**Liabilities**	
Current assets		Current liabilities	
Cash	$450	Accounts payable	$200
Accounts receivable	500	Long-term liabilities	
Work in progress	1,200	Bank debt	2,000
Inventory	250		
Long-term assets		**Equity**	
Property, plant, & equipment	2,000	Common stock	4,000
Operating system code	2,000	Retained earnings	200
Total	**$6,400**	**Total**	**$6,400**

to develop and grow the business. However, Barry and his partner never followed through on this. They realized that it was much too early to declare a dividend at this point and decided to wait until the end of the year to see what the state of their business was then.

These balance sheet examples set the foundation for understanding how projects fit into the wider business system picture. The project that started DDI created an asset. This asset was a piece of intellectual property that consisted of software code that could be copied and sold as a product. This operating system code was reported on the balance sheet as a long-term asset along with the plant and equipment on the investment side of the balance sheet. The long-term liabilities and the shareholders' equity on the financing side of the balance sheet financed these long-term assets. During operations these assets produced a product that eventually was converted into cash and this added value to shareholder equity in the form of increased retained earnings. This extra cash was available either to be reinvested in the business to create more value for the owners or to be paid out as a dividend. Of course the dividend payout would deplete cash and deplete retained earnings. These are ways that the company satisfies shareholders' expectations for a return on their investment.

The Income Statement

An income statement is based on the accounting principles of matching and accrual. The *principal of matching* requires accountants to try to match revenues with the expenses associated with those revenues during a given reporting period. The *principle of accrual* requires accountants to count the inflows and outflows of all assets, not just cash. These principles are part of a system developed by accountants so that managers and investors can determine whether, during a given period of time, a business is producing revenue greater than the expenses necessary to produce that revenue. Subtracting *all* expenses is important because often cash is paid out during one period, say a month, for a piece of equipment that produces a product that is sold during the next month. The cash from the sale of that product may not get to the company's bank account until the month after that. This could make it difficult to determine whether profit exists. Without this knowledge, managers cannot make timely adjustments for problems or opportunities. The income statement's basic function is to track the revenue of a company minus its expenses and to do so in a way that resolves the problem just described.

The revenue of a company minus its expenses equals its net income. If net income is positive, the company has made a profit. If it is negative, the company has suffered a loss. This is why the income statement is sometimes called a *profit and loss statement,* or P&L statement. It is important to remember that profit and loss does not refer to an actual surplus or shortage of cash but rather to the ability to produce cash over the long term or the propensity to lose cash over the long term.

Project managers have not traditionally paid much attention to income statements because these statements represent what happens after the project is over. Income statements are important for project managers in today's businesses, however, because they match the expense of the project with the revenue or cost savings produced during the project outcome lifecycle. From the organization's point of view, it is during the project outcome lifecycle that the project proves (or fails to prove) itself as a worthy investment. It is successful if its outcome can produce enough cash to justify the investment made to create it unless there are other strategic considerations. The income statement reports whether or not this is happening over a given period of time. By better understanding the dynamics of the income statement, a project manager should be able to manage the project to optimize profitability. This is a first step to the ultimate objective of optimizing cash flow and economic profit to increase shareholder value.

In its most basic form, then, the income statement tells managers and investors whether or not they are making money during a specified period of time. It matches the revenue associated with the sales of a product or service made during the time period with the expenses associated with producing the products or services sold. This means that expenses are not necessarily recorded when they are paid out. Rather they are recorded when the product or service that was created by the expense is actually sold. We will explain this in more detail as we explore the income statement. What is important to understand at this point is that the reason for accounting for expenses in this way is directly related to the principles of matching and accrual. The object is always to match revenue with the expenses incurred to produce the revenue so the company has the best measurement of whether or not it has a surplus of revenue over expenses during a given time period.

So far we have followed the operations of DDI through the company's fifth month. For the rest of the year, DDI had its ups and downs, but the average monthly sales were very similar to the sales during the first month of sales (the first month of the operating phase). Total revenue for the year was $14,000 from the sale of six hundred operating systems. Four hundred operating systems were sold to individuals over the eight months of active sales. For each of these systems DDI had been paid $25. It also sold twenty-five units per month to the Computer Company. For each of these it had been paid or had received a promise to be paid $20. Barry and his friend added up all of the expenses for the year. Expenses, as the accountant had explained, were all of the costs associated with producing and selling the systems. This included costs for salaries, materials, shipping, advertising, financing, tax costs, and so on. The expenses for the year were $12,585. When they were subtracted from the revenue, DDI had a positive net income, or profit, of $1,415 (Figure 2.7). This made Barry and his friend very happy. They knew that most start-up businesses did not make a profit in the first year. However, as they began to work with their accountant to produce a more detailed income statement, they learned that their profit was not as large as they had first thought.

Barry showed the rough income statement he had put together to the accountant and asked her how he could improve it so that it showed more about how the business was operating. The accountant began her work with Barry and his friend by helping them to determine when they would recognize a sale, so that their revenue numbers would be based on consistent data. There were two rules that DDI had to follow. First, it could not recognize the sale until the buyer actually owned the product. Second, it had to have a reasonable expectation that the buyer would actually pay it for the product. Barry decided that DDI would recognize a sale when it shipped the product to the buyer. This meant that twenty-five units that had been ordered but not shipped during the last month of the year

FIGURE 2.7. DDI FIRST PRELIMINARY INCOME STATEMENT: YEAR 1.

	Amount	Percentage of Revenue
Revenue	$14,000	100%
Expenses	12,585	90
Net income	$1,415	10%

could not be counted as revenue for the first year. It also meant that even though most of the sales for the last month of the year were still recorded on the balance sheet as accounts receivable (because the checks had not yet arrived or not yet cleared the bank), they were recorded on the income statement as revenue. Barry could have chosen another time to recognize a sale and record revenue. For example, some companies recognize a sale when they receive an order, when the product is actually received by the customer, or when the customer begins to use the product. The most important factor is not which method a company chooses but that it uses the same method every year so that revenue is comparable from year to year. Given the method of recognizing sales that Barry chose, the revenue for the year remained at $14,000 on DDI's new, more detailed income statement.

Next they began to take a closer look at the expenses. First, the accountant asked Barry to identify all of the expenses directly associated with company operations. These expenses came to $12,000 and were recorded as *operating expenses* on the income statement. The accountant subtracted this amount from the revenue and recorded the difference as *operating income*. This represented the profit generated from the operating activities of the company. She then combined the taxes and the cost of financing capital as *financing and tax expense* and subtracted the resulting $585 from the operating income. The resulting number was net income (Figure 2.8).

The accountant then began to ask questions about the operating expense numbers. She explained that if Barry and his friend wanted to better understand their business, they would have to break these expenses down into more categories. As they went through the records they began to see that the operating expenses fell into two main categories: expenses directly connected to the production of the product they were selling and expenses connected to selling and shipping the product and just keeping the business as a whole running. The first category included all the cash Barry had spent in making copies of the system for

FIGURE 2.8. DDI SECOND PRELIMINARY INCOME STATEMENT: YEAR 1.

	Amount	Percentage of Revenue
Revenue	$14,000	100%
Operating expense	12,000	86
Operating income	2,000	14
Financing & tax expense	585	4
Net income	$1,415	10%

sale and shipment. It included wages for the assistant's labor in copying the systems and packaging them. It also included the cost of materials for copying the system and the packaging materials. As we noted earlier, however, not all the cash that Barry spent during this first year on making all the systems was recorded in the income statement. The accounting definition of expense is the depletion of the value of an asset. From the company's point of view, any product not yet sold has not been depleted of value. So the cash associated with that product's manufacture is not recorded on the income statement. The value of these assets remains recorded as inventory (specifically, finished goods inventory) on the balance sheet. DDI will realize value from its unsold systems during the reporting period when they are sold. So the expenses directly associated with making the six hundred units that DDI actually sold during the first year, at $10 per unit, were $6,000. These expenses are called *cost of goods sold*. The name accurately describes the labor costs and manufacturing expenses associated only with the products that are actually sold and produce revenue. So cost of goods sold is "any expense associated with the making of a product or the delivery of a service" (Strategic Management Group, 1997, p. 6).

The accountant then subtracted the cost of goods sold from the revenue and derived an important measurement for DDI, *gross margin*. The gross margin for this first year of operations for the company was $8,000 (Figure 2.9). This measurement is important because it compares the revenue received for the manufacture of a product or the delivery of a service directly with the salary, materials, manufacturing costs, and other costs associated with its creation. When a project manager is making decisions during a project, this is one important category to keep in mind. Decisions made during the project can influence gross margin during the project outcome lifecycle. For instance, a decision on how a product will be assembled can have a profound affect on the cost to manufacture that product. This decision might result in a lower cost of goods sold and a higher gross

FIGURE 2.9. DDI THIRD PRELIMINARY INCOME STATEMENT: YEAR 1.

	Amount	Percentage of Revenue
Revenue	$14,000	100%
Cost of goods sold	6,000	42.9
Gross margin	8,000	57.1
Selling, general, & administrative	6,000	42.9
Operating income	2,000	14.3
Financing & tax expense	585	4.2
Net income	$1,415	10%

margin, or a higher cost of goods sold and a lower gross margin. A higher gross margin means there is more revenue left over to pay other expenses and eventually to flow to the bottom line as profit.

DDI still had operating expenses not accounted for in the category cost of goods sold. These were the expenses that it had incurred over the year to advertise in the hobby magazines, go to the computer shows, ship the product, answer the phones to respond to questions about the product, keep up the office space, and to do anything else not directly associated with the manufacture of the product. These additional expenses were labeled *selling, general, and administrative* (SG&A) and came to $6,000 for the year. This amount included the $1,200 that DDI had recorded during its first five months as work in progress. Part of the reason SG&A was so great in relation to cost of goods sold and revenue was that many of these expenses had to be paid before the product was ready for market (back when they were recorded as work in progress). During the second year of operations, these expenses would be spread over twelve months of sales and therefore should be less as a percentage of revenue. In general, SG&A expenses may include the following:

- Salaries for anyone not directly associated with manufacturing a product or delivering a service
- Rent for any space not directly connected with the product manufacture
- Sales commissions
- Utilities
- Shipping, handling, and delivery
- Research and development
- Marketing expense
- Advertising
- Customer service
- General office expenses

SG&A may also be called *indirect expenses, selling expenses,* or *period expenses.* Project managers are often first introduced to SG&A as an indirect expense or overhead expense charged to the project as part of the project budget. It is important to remember that these expenses continue as part of the project outcome lifecycle. And as you look over the expenses just listed, you will see that although the project manager has no influence over some of them, he or she can influence others through decisions made during the project that affect the product outcome lifecycle.

Barry was quite proud that he had achieved a 10 percent return on sales after tax and financing charges during his first year of operations, but his accountant had to burst his bubble. "We have one other expense left to account for," she explained. Barry then remembered that depreciation represented a loss of value of a company's long-term assets. Each year some assets are in effect used up as part of the process of producing revenue. On a more complete balance sheet than those shown so far, an expense called *depreciation* represents this using up of assets. It is also charged as an expense on the income statement because it has been employed to help produce revenue for that time period. To keep things simple Barry's accountant simply created an additional line item called depreciation. (A more accurate recording of the depreciation expense would have been to charge depreciation of equipment and the system code, which were directly associated with production, as part of cost of goods sold. The depreciation of the office condominium and any other equipment would have been charged as part of SG&A.) The accountant chose straight-line depreciation with no salvage value over fifteen years for the condominium and over five years for the equipment and the operating system software code. Using the standard formula for straight-line depreciation, (Value of the Asset − Salvage Value) \ Years of Useful Life, the accountant calculated the depreciation expense for the three long-term assets of the company. This resulted in a depreciation charge of $50 for the condominium (($1,000 − $0) \ 20 Years), $200 for equipment (($1,000 − $0) \ 10 Years), and $400 for the system code (($2,000 − 0$) \ 5 Years). The total depreciation charge was $650. This was subtracted from gross margin even though this was cash that had already been paid out. It was important to do this in order to complete the principle of matching all expenses associated with the revenue for a given time period. Without accounting for depreciation, net income would be overstated. Both investors and management might look at DDI with more enthusiasm and optimism than they should.

Finally, to complete the income statement the accountant suggested that Barry and his friend separate the interest expenses over which they had some control from taxes over which they had little control. This created an additional income category called *income before taxes*, which was all the revenue left over after subtracting all of the expenses except taxes. Net income was then derived by subtracting taxes from income before taxes (Figure 2.10).

The net income at the bottom line of the income statement represented the profit, or the earnings of the shareholders. Once Barry saw that it was only 5.5 percent of revenue he realized that the best decision was to keep it in the business to reinvest for growth. There would be no dividend this year.

The balance sheet at the end of the year (Figure 2.11) reflected the additional value of the retained earnings, but it also showed the depreciation of the assets. The property, plant, and equipment (PP&E) and the operating system code (OSC) are stated at original value less accumulated depreciation resulting in the line items *net book value of PP&E* and *net book value of OSC*. In addition it showed a reduction

FIGURE 2.10. DDI COMPLETED INCOME STATEMENT: YEAR 1.

	Amount	Percentage of Revenue
Revenue	$14,000	100%
Cost of goods sold	6,000	42.9
Gross margin	8,000	57.1
Selling, general, & administrative	6,000	42.8
Depreciation	650	4.6
Operating income	1,350	9.7
Interest expense	200	1.4
Income before taxes	1,150	8.3
Taxes	385	2.8
Net income	$765	5.5%

FIGURE 2.11. DDI COMPLETED BALANCE SHEET: YEAR 1.

Investment		Financing	
Assets		**Liabilities**	
Current assets		Current liabilities	
Cash	$615	Accounts payable	$200
Accounts receivable	1,000	Long-term liabilities	
Inventory	2,000	Bank debt	2,000
Long-term assets		**Equity**	
Property, plant, & equipment	2,000	Common stock	4,000
Less accumulated depreciation	250	Retained earnings	765
Net book value PP&E	1,750		
Operating system code	2,000		
Less accumulated depreciation	400		
Net book value OSC	1,600		
Total	**$6,965**	**Total**	**$6,965**

in cash to pay tax and interest expense but also an increase in accounts receivable to reflect the money owed to DDI by the Computer Company for sixty days worth of sales. The completed balance sheet also showed $2,000 worth of inventory. This came from the fact that Barry's assistant had continued to make one hundred systems every month even though DDI sold only seventy-five of these. So DDI had built up an inventory of twenty-five units each month for eight months that at yearend equaled two hundred units at a cost of $10 per unit, or $2,000. Barry and his friend hope these will be converted into cash during the second year of operations. Either sales will begin to increase, or DDI will have to cut production.

The Cash Flow Statement

The final statement that Barry needed to manage his new business was the cash flow statement. The external version of a cash flow statement employs *generally accepted accounting principles* (GAAP). This statement helps outside investors evaluate how well management of any given public company is managing the cash needed to run the company. It tells them where the cash needed to run the business has come from and how that cash has been used. It builds on the income statement and balance sheet, but it is different from them because it combines the operating activities and the financing activities of the company and it make adjustments to convert accrual accounting into cash accounting. Internally, management uses a slightly different version of the cash flow statement to focus more closely on what is called *free cash flow*. Free cash flow is the net cash generated by the operations of the business after subtracting cash used for investment activities. If free cash flow is positive, the business does not have to seek new financing. If free cash flow is negative and the business does not have enough cash from previous years to finance its ongoing operations, it may have to attract new investment or take on more debt. If free cash flow is negative for a long time, the company will not be able to get additional financing and may eventually go bankrupt. Thus free cash flow is an important measure of the ability of the company to provide positive returns to its shareholders.

The accountant began with a comparative balance sheet for DDI (Figure 2.12). By looking at the change in cash from one year to the next she could see the net change in cash for the company. Then, by creating a cash flow statement, she could explain why the cash balance changed. For DDI this was quite simple because the company was in its first year of operations. Every account for the previous year was therefore zero. To construct the comparative balance sheet, the accountant listed the assets and the liabilities and equities in a single column so that she could list the figures for more than one year.

DDI's income statement for the year (Figure 2.10) showed a net income of $765, but that does not tell Barry and his friend everything they need to know about the cash in the company. The difference in cash on the balance sheet from Year 0 to Year 1 is $615, a different number from that for net income. The cash flow statement documents the changes in cash during the year. It groups cash flows in a manner that reflects the cash cycle described earlier. There are cash flows from operating activities, cash flows from investing activities, and cash flows from financing activities. The cash balances from these three activities are added together to get a total change in cash for the company for the period. This amount is then added to the cash balance from the beginning of the period to determine the cash balance for the end of the period. This process records where and to what degree

FIGURE 2.12. DDI COMPARATIVE BALANCE SHEET: YEARS 1 AND 0.

	Year 1	Year 0
Assets		
Current assets		
Cash	$615	$0
Accounts receivable	1,000	0
Inventory	2,000	0
Long-term assets		
Property, plant, & equipment	2,000	0
Less accumulated depreciation	250	0
Net book value PP&E	1,750	0
Operating system code	2,000	0
Less accumulated depreciation	400	0
Net book value OSC	1,600	0
Total assets	$6,965	$0
Liabilities		
Current liabilities		
Accounts payable	200	0
Long-term liabilities		
Bank debt	2,000	0
Equity		
Common stock	4,000	0
Retained earnings	765	0
Total liabilities & equity	$6,965	$0

changes in cash took place. It also confirms that the cash reported on the balance sheet is accurate. Figure 2.13 outlines this process in the form of a GAAP cash flow statement, the starting point for DDI's cash flow statement.

As the accountant began to list each activity in the cash flow statement for DDI (Figure 2.14), she explained to Barry and his friend that when an activity of a company results in a cash inflow, it is classified as a *source of cash*. If the activity results in a cash outflow, it is classified as a *use of cash*. She began with the *cash flows from operating activities*. This section lists all the uses and sources of cash from producing, selling, and delivering the products of the company. It begins with the net income from the income statement. But net income is not the same as cash, as we discussed earlier. Remember all the rules that were applied to make sure that revenues were matched to expenses? These have to be undone to convert net income into a net cash flow amount.

There are two primary areas in which the accountant must make adjustments to reconcile net income and arrive at net cash flow: depreciation and net increases

FIGURE 2.13. BASIC STRUCTURE OF A GAAP CASH FLOW STATEMENT FOR ONE YEAR.

Cash flows from operating activities	$xxx
Cash flows from investing activities	xxx
Cash flows from financing activities	xxx
Change in cash	xxx
Beginning cash balance	xxx
Ending cash balance	$xxx

FIGURE 2.14. DDI GAAP CASH FLOW STATEMENT: YEAR 0 TO YEAR 1.

Cash flows from operating activities	
Net income	$765
Adjustment to reconcile net income to net cash	
Depreciation	650
Net (increase) decrease in working capital	(2,800)
Net cash provided (used) by operating activities	(1,385)
Cash flows from investing activities	
Decrease (increase) in long-term assets	(4,000)
Net cash provided (used) by investing activities	(4,000)
Cash flows from financing activities	
Issue (repurchase) of equity	4,000
Issue (repayment) of debt	2,000
Dividends distributed	0
Net cash provided (used) by financing activities	6,000
Change in cash	615
Beginning cash balance	0
Ending cash balance	$615

or decreases in working capital. Depreciation is not actually a cash expenditure because the company paid for the assets at the time of purchase or development, so the amount for depreciation is added back into the cash flow statement as a use of cash, a positive amount. Working capital is the cash tied up in operating the business from day to day. It is calculated by subtracting current liabilities from current assets. Current assets are investments in the company that should result in cash during the year. Current liabilities are obligation that will have to be paid within the year. The difference between current assets and current liabilities is the net amount of cash available for the business. Or, if this difference is negative, it shows the business's need for cash. Increases or decreases in this net amount from year to year result in a use or source of cash.

In the case of DDI, the balance sheet (Figure 2.11) showed current assets were $1,000 in accounts receivable, and $2,000 in inventory for a total of $3,000. All these current assets were uses of cash because they deferred the conversion of the asset into cash that could be used to operate or invest in the business. Inventory consisted of goods that had not been sold, and accounts receivable was cash that had not been collected. Current liabilities were $200 in accounts payable. This was a source of cash because it was cash owed that had not been paid out yet. So working capital equaled $3,000 minus $200, or $2,800. The amount of working capital for the previous year was $0. The net increase in working capital was $2,800. This net amount was a use of cash so it was recorded as a negative number (in parentheses) on the cash flow statement. Adding depreciation of $650 to net income of $765 and subtracting the $2,800 change in working capital, revealed that the net cash used by operating activities was $1,385.

Cash is listed under current assets on the balance sheet, but it is not included in the calculation of changes in working capital. Instead it is entered into the cash flow on the last line as *ending cash balance* to be compared to the *beginning cash balance* taken from the balance sheet at the beginning of the year. Net cash flow should equal the difference between the ending and the beginning cash balance.

Compared to the section showing cash flows from operating activities, the rest of DDI's cash flow statement was relatively easy to complete. The *cash flows from investing activities* section tracks increases or decreases in long-term assets. This item records the cash spent at the time of purchase of these assets and ignores depreciation, which was recorded in the cash flows from operating activities section. For DDI, long-term assets included property, plant, and equipment for $2,000 and the operations system software code for $2,000 (from the balance sheet, Figure 2.11). Because these figures were both $0 at the beginning of the period, the increase in long-term assets was $4,000. This was the *net cash used by investing activities.*

The final section, *cash flows from financing activities,* records the transactions that took place during the financing and returning phases of the cash cycle. It includes the issue or repurchase of equity, the issue or repayment of debt, and any dividends distributed. That is, this section records the sources and uses of cash from and to outside sources. During its first year, DDI relied heavily on outside sources of financing. It issued $4,000 in stock and took out a bank loan for $2,000. It did not pay out any dividends.

It was apparent to Barry that his new company had a long way to go. For the first year the operations of the company did not have a positive cash flow. They were a use of cash. He had expected that they were going to be a source of cash.

After all, he had made a net profit. However, he had not realized that the need for working capital to support inventory and accounts receivable would outweigh the cash generated by the rest of the operating activities. He began to realize that reducing inventory and getting the Computer Company to pay its bills faster would help to increase sources of cash. He also began to think about how he could wait longer to pay his bills as well. This would be another way to increase sources of cash. The accountant showed Barry how to recalculate the GAAP cash flow statement so that it would be a more useful managerial tool, a free cash flow statement. *Free cash flow* is the cash left over at the end of each year after operating and investing activities. The formula for free cash flow is Cash Flows from Operating Activities – Cash Flows from Investing Activities = Free Cash Flow. This form of cash flow statement shows whether there will be cash available to pay down debt, repurchase stock, or pay dividends or whether lack of cash will require the issuing of new stock or debt. In the case of DDI, free cash flow was a negative $1,385 from operations and a negative $4,000 from investing for a total negative free cash flow of $5,385. That is why the company needed $6,000 in financing for its first year of operations.

Barry began to build a model of what he thought was going to happen next year. He started with a model, or pro forma, income statement containing the revenues and expenses he expected to occur during the next year of operations. From this he also developed a pro forma balance sheet and free cash flow statement. Now he had a good idea whether he would be able to pay off his bank debt and issue a dividend or whether he was going to have to seek new loans or issue new stock. For project managers, this ability to model the cash flows for a project and the project outcome lifecycle is very important for working with upper management in project evaluation and selection. It is also very important in managing the project as a total enterprise. By managing from a business model as well as the project plan, project managers will be able to make or suggest decisions during the project that will better take into account the larger long-term picture of net profit and free cash flow. These figures are the essential building blocks for shareholder value.

This chapter has provided the foundation for a critical set of competencies for a project management entrepreneur. We will build on this foundation throughout the remainder of this book.

Examples and Using the Business Systems Calculator

The Newprod and Newsys projects that we began describing in Chapter One offer examples of treating financial information for projects like financial information for independent business enterprises.

Newprod Project

One section of the on-line business systems calculator output shows monthly financial results that are based on an income statement. In this section we look at data from the calculator output for the first four months of the Newprod Project (Figure 2.15), to show that project net income can be developed in the same way as the net income for an independent company. The calculator is designed for projects in which the major costs are salaries for the project team members. As salaries represent current expense, this example assumes that the project outcome will not be capitalized but rather expensed. The calculator also allows for depreciation charges that may come from outside the project for the use of plant and equipment. These depreciation charges are shown as an expense for the calculation of project net income. However, they are not actual cash outlays for the project. Therefore, as explained earlier, the depreciation charges are added back to the net income to get the figure for cash flow.

While your Newprod project is in progress, there is no revenue, only expenses. Thus the cash flow is negative during project execution. To fund this negative cash flow the project "borrows" money for working capital from the larger organization. The project must pay this loan by way of a *capital charge*. The capital charge

FIGURE 2.15. NEWPROD PROJECT DATA, MONTHS 1 THROUGH 4.

Month	1	2	3	4
Project costs	250,000	250,000	250,000	250,000
Demand	0	0	0	0
Price	300	300	300	300
Units sold	0	0	0	0
Revenues	0	0	0	0
Cost of production per unit	240	240	240	240
Cost of goods sold	0	0	0	0
Net from sales	0	0	0	0
Gross margin	−250,000	−250,000	−250,000	−250,000
SG&A	0	0	0	0
Depreciation	0	0	0	0
Other expense	0	0	0	0
Operating income	−250,000	−250,000	−250,000	−250,000
Tax	−82,500	−82,500	−82,500	−82,500
Net income	−167,500	−167,500	−167,500	−167,500
Cash flow	−167,500	−167,500	−167,500	−167,500
Discounted cash flow	−165,926	−164,366	−162,821	−161,291
Cash flow with capital charge	−169,089	−339,783	−512,097	−686,045
Capital charge	1,589	3,194	4,814	6,449
NOPAT	−167,500	−167,500	−167,500	−167,500
EVA	−169,089	−170,694	−172,314	−173,949

is based on the total capital on loan to the project multiplied by the finance rate charged by the organization. In this example, we assume this finance rate is equivalent to the cost of capital for the overall organization. This is called the *weighted average cost of capital* (WACC). The WACC is discussed in detail in Chapter Seven; for now consider WACC as the interest rate the project pays to the larger organization for use of capital. WACC is an input variable to the calculator. The capital charge is calculated each month with this formula: Amount of Capital on Loan to the Project × (WACC / 12). The capital charge is added to the cash flow to show the total cash needs of the project, given by the line *cash flow with capital charge.*

Once a project is completed, the project outcome begins to generate revenue and (the company hopes) subsequent positive cash flow. This cash flow is used to pay back the loan and the capital charges to the company. This will take some time so capital charges will continue to be levied on the declining balance of the loan until it is paid completely.

Figure 2.15, then, shows the income statement and cash flow calculations for the first four months of your Newprod project. Your net income and cash flow at this early stage are negative. NOPAT (net operating profit after taxes) and EVA (economic value added) are explained in Chapter Seven. Until we get to that chapter, we examine the effect of adding the new feature to Newprod, as discussed in Chapter One, by examining the effect on cash flow.

Newsys Project

Things have not changed much for the internal project Newsys. You have found out from accounting that the cost of the new phone system will be depreciated over the five-year expected life of the project. Once the project is over the total cost will be entered into the balance sheet as equipment. Because we are depreciating the phone system, an income statement for this project will be different from Newprod because it will have no tax credits during the life of the project (see Figure 2.16). So taxes are 0 in year zero. Based on the five-year depreciation, we will spread the tax credits over the five-year life of the asset.

FIGURE 2.16. NEWSYS INCOME STATEMENT.

Revenue	$0
Operating expense	350,000
Operating income	(350,000)
Taxes	0
Net income	$(350,000)

FIGURE 3.1. BUSINESS SYSTEMS DIAGRAM.

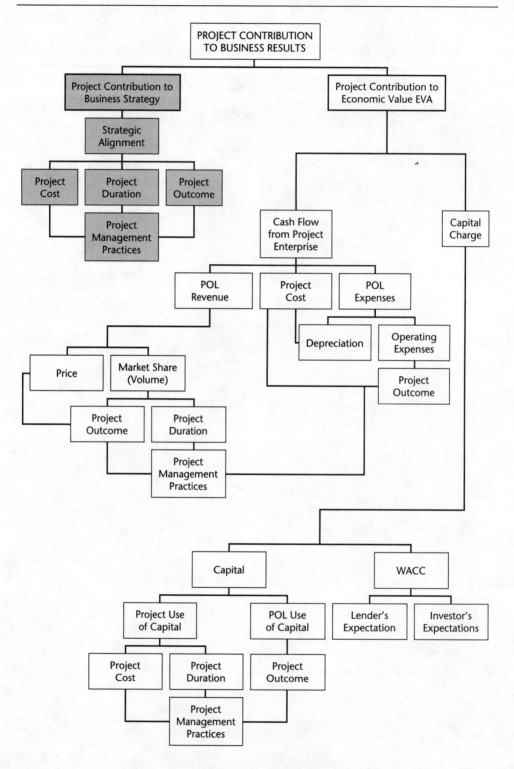

CHAPTER THREE

BUSINESS STRATEGY

Where Are We Going and How Are We Going to Get There?

Without strategy, you fail. Without strategy in a rapidly changing industry, you fail rapidly.

LOUIS J. GERSTNER, CEO OF IBM, 1999

All organizations have a strategy, explicit or implied, that upper management uses to guide decision making. Most project managers, however, are too involved in day-to-day problem solving and managing their projects to pay much attention to that strategy. Even when they do have time to look up and view the broader long-term horizon, strategy does not seem very important to them. After all, upper managers who are supposed to be the champions of strategy frequently do not seem to take it all that seriously. Most of the time, strategy is like the weather—everyone may talk a lot about it, but no one seems to do very much about it. At other times, upper management may seem to contradict the principles of the strategy it espouses. It is rare for a project manager to be called on the carpet for some decision made or action taken that violated a strategic principle or interfered with the strategic direction of the company. There are many decisions and actions project managers can take that they know will result in negative feedback. These are often referred to as career-limiting moves. However, they usually do not involve strategic issues. They are much more likely to involve some form of failing to deliver a fast, good, and cheap project or some other result expected by an influential upper manager.

So, why should project managers care about strategy? Because there is a revolution going on in companies that we believe will continue. Upper-management behavior is changing to match the changing business environment. In the past upper management acted as if strategy and strategic planning were a ritual rain dance. Every year there was a strategic planning process during which layers of management scanned the environment to identify threats and opportunities, looked internally to analyze strengths and weaknesses, set a direction, and formulated a strategic plan. The strategic plan document was then locked in a drawer, and the planning experience ignored along with it, until the next year, when it was reviewed and revised through the same process. The fact that the planning process did not change behavior did not really matter very much when organizational environments were more placid and predictable. Planning of any kind could be a ritual when the road traveled by the company changed so little from year to year. Take IBM as an example. Its mainframe strategy lasted through two generations of Watsons. That strategy stopped being successful only when two teenagers started fooling around with personal computers in a garage and eventually turned the industry upside down. A lack of emphasis on strategic planning at the upper levels of many corporations generated one of the major reasons that upper managers used to interfere with or not support the need for extensive project planning. Based on the experience of these managers, planning was not very important. Moreover, in the early post–World War II period almost any form of planning was suspect because planning was what communists did ("the five-year plan").

Environments are no longer placid and stable. They have become turbulent. Change is happening more often, at a faster pace, and in less predictable ways. Because of this, management behavior and focus must change rapidly, and these changes need strategic direction. As a result, strategic planning has become a much more active process of setting a strategy and direction for the company, formulating priorities, guiding managerial action, and evaluating results so that the business can stay aligned with the environment. Under conditions of environmental turbulence it becomes very important for all managers to understand and internalize strategy because decisions must often be made where the action is happening. Checking decisions "up the line" often takes too much time. Things are happening too fast. And making decisions according to an authoritative set of specifications is no longer practical because everything is so unpredictable. The managers implementing the corporate strategy must be able to react to change as they go along. These reactions must be based on a sound awareness of and alignment with the strategy. Project managers are especially subject to this requirement because of the important role of projects in strategy implementation.

More and more the project portfolio is the driving engine for strategy implementation (Cleland, 1999). And of course project managers are the ones who must manage the projects that make up the portfolio that drives the strategy. Now that upper management is finally taking planning more seriously, is there any reason to doubt that project managers will be held more and more accountable for keeping their projects aligned with strategy? If this increasing accountability is indeed the case, then project managers must understand what the strategy is and how their projects fit into the strategic picture. "The road to capital productivity begins with a tight link between capital spending and business strategy. It is paramount that companies understand at the outset a capital project's impact on cost structure, profitability, and competitive position" (Koyama and Van Tassel, 1998, p. 145).

Project managers need to understand strategy and how to align their projects with it for the following reasons as well.

Be prepared for evaluation. Very soon now companies will be evaluating project managers on implementation of strategy. If you bring your project in on time, under budget, and exactly to specifications but it fails to support the strategy of the company, it will not be considered a success, and you will not be considered a successful and skilled project manager. Remember, specifications from upper management become less reliable as the environment becomes less predictable. Project management used to be like conducting a marching band. You were given a set score and you and your team played it. Now project management is more like playing in a jazz ensemble. Keeping the original melody (the strategy) in mind, you have to improvise on it as you go along (see Eisenhardt, 1997, for a discussion of jazz as a paradigm for strategic decision making). This kind of project management is becoming especially important for e-commerce organizations. With profitability in the distant future for many Internet companies, the immediate criteria for success must focus on a project's support for ongoing strategy.

Make more appropriate decisions. Understanding your company's strategy will help you make decisions during the project. For example, if the company's strategy is best implemented by being first to market with the project outcome, you will know to focus more on maintaining the schedule and cycle time. However, if the company's strategy emphasizes efficient operations and low costs, you will know to focus on budget and efficiency in your project.

Foster team building. Knowledge of company strategy will help you develop your team because it will help you clarify project goals for the team. Having a common goal is the first step in developing a group of individuals into a well-functioning team. Studies of project failure often cite the lack of a clear goal as a factor in the failure. Aligning a project with company strategy also makes the goals of the project more relevant to every department in the organization and this helps in developing a cross-functional team.

Resist project cancellation (for the right reasons). Aligning your project with company strategy will also help protect it from being canceled, unless the organizational strategy is changed. You will be able to demonstrate how important and relevant your project is in supporting the strategy of the company whenever someone comes gunning for that project.

Accept or recommend project cancellation (for the right reasons). Conversely, your project may have moved down the list of strategic priorities. After you present the consequences of project delay or cancellation, it is the job of upper management to manage the company's project portfolio and cancel projects that have been superceded by other strategic priorities. If you realize that your project cannot meet current strategic goals, you should recommend that it be cancelled. Chevron's project management process promotes project cancellation when a project cannot meet strategic or financial goals.

Stay on track. Alignment with strategy will help you and your team resist all kinds of organizational pressures to serve parochial and short-term interests with the project instead of staying the course and serving the long-term interests of the company. Cleland (1999, p. 99) lists a series of questions about projects that upper managers should ask to determine strategic fit. These questions translate into a series of questions that project managers need to ask to stay on track and stay aligned: Will the project continue to focus on the customer? Will the outcome be superior to the competition's outcome? Will the project support the design and execution of organizational strategy? Will it stay within organizational risk tolerance levels? Will it optimize meeting the goals of cost, duration, and outcome (the old triple constraints)? Will the project outcome provide high value for the customer? Will the outcome ultimately provide a satisfactory return on investment to the organization? Does the outcome fit into the ongoing portfolio of projects and support the company strategy?

You can do all these things better by understanding the purpose of strategy in a company and the importance of maintaining a strategic focus while managing your project. This is the first core process that you must master to become a project management entrepreneur, *aligning to achieve strategic fit.* If you do not master this core process your project will probably fall victim to one of these wasteful practices (Deschamps, 1999, pp. 64–65):

- Overemphasizing technology as an end in and of itself, resulting in projects that wander off pursuing a technology that does not fit the strategy or a customer need
- Focusing on problems or solutions that have a low priority strategically
- Focusing only on the immediate customer rather than on the whole marketplace and the value chain (described later in this chapter)
- Trying to solve every customer issue with a product or service rather than focusing on the 20 percent with 80 percent of the value

- Engaging in a never-ending search for perfection that no one except the project team really cares about

The Purpose of Strategy

In its most basic form, strategy is simply the way in which a company orients itself toward the market in which it operates and toward the other companies in the marketplace against which it competes. Strategy answers the question of how a company will position itself against competition in the market over the long run to secure a sustainable competitive advantage. A sustained competitive advantage means that the company has developed not only the means to win against the competition today but also the means to continue winning into the future. Assuming that the planned strategy is based on sound principles for sustaining competitive advantage, it will succeed in maintaining that advantage when everyone in the company agrees on those principles and implements them in concert as they operate the company. A successful strategy adds value for the targeted customers over the long run by consistently meeting their needs better than the competition does.

To better appreciate the importance of strategy, managers need to see how it functions in the larger business system, a system of value creation. Why do companies exist? What is their purpose? We have heard people respond to these questions with a wide variety of answers: to provide self-aggrandizement for the owner and top management, to create jobs, to advance technology, to provide community, to make money, to satisfy customers. These have all been offered as answers in various settings, and they all have something in common. They describe the creation of value for someone or some group stated or implied. The central purpose of most businesses is to add value for their stakeholders, anyone who has an actual or potential stake in the business. The most important stakeholders are shareholders who own the business, employees who work for the business, and clients or customers who purchase goods and services from the business. A successful company adds value for each of these stakeholder groups. In addition, value added for each stakeholder group becomes the means to add value for other stakeholder groups. The value creation process is systemic and interactive (Ghoshal, Bartlett, and Moran, 1999). Figure 3.2 illustrates how the major groups interact. Shareholders invest their money in the company expecting a return on that investment. People who work in and with the company use that money to create products and services to meet customer demands. A sound strategy helps them to do this better than the competition and to continue to do it *over the long run*. Customers create cash flow for the company by buying products or services. They do this because the product or service meets their needs better as a total value proposition than

FIGURE 3.2. THE PROCESS OF VALUE CREATION.

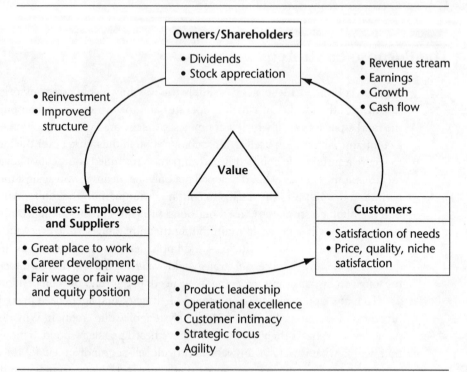

Source: Strategic Management Group. Used by permission.

other available products or services do. If the company is successful in meeting customer demands, this cash flow will provide the expected returns to shareholders. This completes the cycle. Companies can be successful over the long run only if they develop a way to consistently meet customer demands better than the competitors who are also trying to respond to these demands. A sound strategy enables this success.

As was discussed in Chapter Two, shareholders provide money needed to start and sustain the business. This money (shareholders' equity), plus any debt, constitutes the working capital and assets needed to run the business. As owners of the company, shareholders have rights to the profits of the company. When they leave profits in the company to be used to generate more profits, these retained earnings becomes additional shareholders' equity. In return for leaving the profits in the company, shareholders expect to earn a return on their investment. Their expectations are influenced by economic conditions. In general this return consists of two things: any dividends paid out by the company and appreciation of the price of the stock that they own.

People working in the company make decisions on how to invest the shareholders' money to produce greater returns in the future. They work for the company because it adds value for them as well. In most cases they are looking for fair wages (based on their labor market value), a good place to work (in terms of environment and culture and so forth), and development of their skills to maintain and increase their labor market value. They may also become shareholders and play a dual role in the business systems process. In return for the value added they receive as employees, they put forth their best efforts to add value for customers. They do this primarily by following a strategy and converting it to tactics and operations that meet customer needs better than the competition does today and by ensuring the company has the ability to meet those needs over the long run. This process comes down to decisions and actions that are enabled by the money that shareholders have invested in the company. It should result in net cash flow that is at a minimum great enough to provide expected returns to shareholders.

Customers produce this cash flow by buying goods or services from the company. What are customers looking for? In general they are looking for value in what they purchase. How well the product or service meets their expectations over the short and the long run determines this value. Even more important is how well the product or service meets their expectations in relation to the competition, the similar products and services of the other companies in the industry. A good strategy begins with a plan that is successfully implemented to position a company to meet targeted customer needs better than the competition does. It further enables this to happen again and again over time.

Strategy is a major driver of the overall creation of value that lies at the center of the company's purpose. More than positioning the company in the marketplace, in its broadest sense strategy is the process by which the organization establishes and when necessary changes its basic orientation, the process by which the organization "makes up its collective mind" (Mintzberg, 1989, p. 25). It is a mental model of how to run the business for the long term. The most important function of strategy as a planning process is to develop this collective mind and transfer the knowledge to managers who will be engaged in implementing the strategy. Project managers need to internalize this mental model in order to reproduce the strategic process within their projects and ensure that project results align with the strategy. Strategy should provide both the basic orientation for a project and the basic foundation for decision making as that project progresses. As we said earlier, this is the first major process and goal for the project management entrepreneur—aligning to achieve strategic fit.

Strategy as Process

One of the reasons strategy sometimes seems difficult to deal with is that a number of different things in organizational life are called strategy. As the strategic planning process has evolved in most companies to actively provide direction over the long run, strategy must function in at least the following three ways:

- *Planning process, or directed strategy.* First and foremost, strategy is a planning process that aligns the members of the organization toward achieving organizational goals. At this point, strategy is intention only. It is what upper management says that the company is going to do.
- *Management process or emergent strategy.* Strategy starts to become reality in emergent strategy. Emergent strategy is what middle and project managers actually do as they try to implement directed, planned strategy.
- *Priority-setting process, or realized strategy.* Once strategy functions to set priorities that align the organization for coordinated and focused action, it produces results over time. Realized strategy is what gets done, the results.

The key to understanding strategy as a management process and the role of project managers in that process is to understand the difference between directed strategy and emergent strategy. Directed strategy is what upper management says the company should do and will do. Emergent strategy is what the company really does. Why are they different? Because middle managers and project managers have to translate directed strategy into action. It loses some things but gains others in the process. There is always a gap between directed strategy and emergent strategy, but when the strategic process works well, they serve together to steer the company along a focused, consistent, and successful path (Floyd and Wooldridge, 1996).

Directed Strategy

When people in organizations first think of strategy, they most often think about what upper management does to develop and facilitate a vision and a strategic plan. The results of this process is directed strategy, or planned strategy. It represents the intention of upper management. When the people in the company are aligned with the directed strategy, so that everyone understands and agrees with it, then it should represent the intention of the whole organization. Upper managers develop directed strategy through a process of setting direction and communicating it to middle managers who are in charge of making it happen. They do this by, first, establishing a vision of where they want the company to be in the future. Then they assess where it is in the present and the threats and opportunities that face it. The strategy is a road map for how the company will get from where it is now to where it wants to be. The strategy also points toward a set of aligned and coordinated actions that should take the company to where everyone wants it to go, as long as everything goes according to plan. In most companies, however, this planning and alignment is not a neat linear process. It is more often a chaotic, interactive, imperfect process. Nevertheless, in the end, for the company to be successful, it must set a viable direction in the marketplace.

One of the most concrete expressions of strategy as intention is the composition of the portfolio of projects that the company is executing as a result of the strategy. This is where the rubber meets the road, where intentions take the first step toward becoming actions. This begins the process whereby planned strategy is converted into realized strategy. Think about the kinds of things projects accomplish for a company. Projects are the engines of change. They produce the new products and services. They build the new plants and install the new equipment. Projects improve infrastructure, install new systems, and enable new processes. They even serve customers directly by providing custom products or services. Any significant changes that must take place in an organization to implement an evolving strategy usually take the form of some kind of project.

Therefore upper managers must develop the project portfolio so that it supports the strategic plan. First, the portfolio must match the capacity of the company to do projects. If the portfolio has too many projects, either none of them will be done very well or some will be done well as others will fail miserably. If the size of the portfolio matches organizational capacity and the projects in the portfolio represent major milestones on the route to getting the company where it wants to be strategically, then upper management has done its job to express intentionality through planned strategy (Graham and Englund, 1997, chap. 2).

However, until project managers plan, execute, and close out these projects, strategy will not be realized. If they finish the projects but do it without understanding the projects' strategic purpose, a strategy may emerge, but it may bear little resemblance to the intended strategy. The realized strategy (results) is always a combination of directed strategy (upper management's plan) and emergent strategy (middle managers' and project managers' action). Both are essential to business success.

Emergent Strategy

Are the strategic plans and the results they give rise to ever exactly the same? No, they usually are not. As we said, things do not usually go entirely as planned. A strategic plan is not much different from a project plan in this respect. The only thing that anyone knows for sure about a plan is that reality will be different. The major reason managers, or any other people, make a plan is to have an idealized vision of where they want to go and how they want to get there. This vision helps them set a direction and suggests the kinds of milestones that will tell where they are. Having a goal and a map, however, does not mean that they will get to their exact destination or that there will be no problems on the way.

First, companies face the very common problem that directed strategy is often not communicated or if it is communicated it is not taken seriously. During a consulting intervention that Dennis Cohen conducted at a well-respected engineering firm a number of years ago, the subject of strategy came up for discussion, and one manager complained that a major problem for the firm was that it had no strategy. Another manager jumped up to exclaim that the company did have a strategy. He possessed a numbered copy of the top-secret strategic plan. The executive team had passed it out to a small group of top managers who were sworn to secrecy. He kept that plan under lock and key in his desk drawer. The executive team had spent months working on developing the strategic plan but felt that restricting circulation of the plan was necessary to prevent competitors from knowing what the company was up to. The sad part was that the company's competitors probably knew more about what it was trying to accomplish in the marketplace than its own people did. Even project managers had no idea of how their projects fit into an overall strategy.

Ironically, this company had its final undoing as the result of a failed project. It tried to apply its existing technical competence in a new market to solve a new problem. It had been quite successful at building boilers, power plants, and nuclear plants. Its managers now thought they could apply the company's technical competency in a new area, trash-to-steam plants. This idea looked like a slam-dunk, but it was not. It did not fit their existing patterns of business (it does not seem right to say existing strategy because the strategy was hidden from view rather than functional), which was to apply tried and tested technology in engineering projects. Trash-to-steam was brand-new technology, untested and untried. The company's first project ran into giant cost overruns, which is not unusual when working with brand-new technology. However, because the company was used to predictable technology and projects that came in consistently on time, at budget, and to specifications, project managers did not know how to handle the cost overruns. The one thing they did know was that if upper managers found out about the overruns, they would not understand. In other words, letting them find out would be a career-limiting move. So, the cost overruns remained unreported and hidden from the company president until after he had assured the board that the firm was expecting a profitable quarter. Between that meeting with the board and the final closing of the books for the quarter, the cost overruns finally surfaced. Things were never quite the same after that. The president left after six months to pursue other interests. The company was sold to a European firm. All this because no one took strategy seriously or, more accurately, because they took it too seriously as a plan but not seriously enough as a guide to action.

A second problem occurs when companies overload the project system. Strategy is taken seriously, but managers select too many promising projects and it becomes impossible to carry out all of them. One financial services firm that Dennis Cohen worked with put its largest projects through a strict screening process to match them to strategic intent and available resources. The firm did not do this, however, for all its smaller projects. Needless to say, there were constant complaints from managers of the smaller projects that resources were constantly shifting from project to project, with consequent stops and starts. Many of these projects never die but only because no one dares to put them out of their misery by canceling them. Instead they just fade away. It is difficult for these projects to support any long-term strategy because project managers and teams are so busy putting out the daily fires. Setting priorities for these smaller projects too would result in fewer projects being initiated but more projects producing their intended results.

Even when strategy is formulated elegantly, communicated well, and supported strongly by the project portfolio, there will still be many bumps in the road that can push a company or a project off the planned route. Following even the best-formulated and -articulated strategy must still be balanced against the exigencies of project implementation, countermoves by the competition, unanticipated internal and external events and trends, and unexpected emerging opportunities or threats of many kinds. This is why it is very important for you, the project manager, to be aware of planned strategy and how your project fits that plan. It is also important for you to be aware of how your project is contributing to results throughout both the project lifecycle and the project outcome lifecycle. The way that you manage your project is your contribution to strategy. Project management should be the process of applying the planned strategy of the company in the light of the dynamics of the internal and external environment as the project unfolds.

Finally, it is important for you to be aware that strategy is evolving to become a more interactive process in most companies. The plan used to be the end of the process. Now it is only the beginning. This means that you have more responsibility to interpret the strategy, scan the environment, and make changes as necessary according to your judgment. "In a fluid, volatile environment, the best approach may be to allow strategy to evolve through the discovery of what works and what doesn't" (Wall and Wall, 1995, p. 15). To make such strategic changes, you need to fully understand the strategic principles driving the company, to focus on customers and markets, and to be able to respond to environmental changes when necessary.

Realized Strategy

Then there are the results from the project. If you and the organization have done your jobs well strategically, projects will contribute significantly to your company's ability to sustain a competitive advantage over the long run. This is realized strategy, the results. How do companies attain realized strategy? They apply the directed strategy through the project portfolio and through each project intelligently and most of all with focus.

Think back to the problem of the overloaded project portfolio. How and why does this miscalculation happen? The basic process is very simple. There are always an infinite number of things that any company might do to satisfy the customer, meet the competition, solve problems, and take advantage of opportunities. However, there is always a finite amount of resources to do these things. In many organizations managers find it easy to say yes to new projects. They always seem to know how to use strategy to tell them what they ought to do. Conversely, they find it difficult to say no to new opportunities or to put a badly failing project out of its misery. However, a good strategy should be used as a tool for both deciding what to do and, even more important, deciding what *not* to do.

Approaches to Company Strategy

Successful companies are companies that focus their efforts strategically. First, they target a group of customers (often called a *market segment* or *niche*) and figure out what these customers value in the marketplace. Then they figure out how to focus their efforts on delivering that value. To continue delivering the value they must continuously develop the organizational capabilities that support delivering the value. These include the organizational structure, systems, culture, people, work patterns, competencies, and skills.

Strategy Through Market Disciplines

According to Treacy and Wiersema (1995) companies will do well to consider three market disciplines. In concentrating their efforts strategically, companies should adopt one of these disciplines as their major focus. The first is *customer intimacy*, a focus on the segment of customers who demand extreme responsiveness to their specialized needs. The second is *operational excellence*, a focus on the market segment that is looking for the best possible value for the total cost of ownership. The third is *product leadership*, a focus on the market segment that needs or just wants the latest and greatest product or service available and that has the money to pay for it. Because each of these disciplines aligns with a large group of potential customers, the companies that serve one discipline especially well will tend to capture the business from that group of customers. Companies that do not specialize do not dominate any of the customer niches because they lose out to the companies that do have focus.

A company with focus can compete with even a very large company that lacks a focus. Consider Compaq competing with IBM in personal computers; the decline of Sears against more focused retailers; and the rise of Japanese car companies, successfully challenging U.S. car companies and luxury-car makers such as Mercedes and BMW. A large unfocused company is like an elephant crashing through the forest. Competing companies hunt the unfocused company in much the same way as the people of the Ituri Forest in Africa used to hunt elephants. Each hunter concentrated on only one leg of the elephant and cut it with a knife. Down crashed the elephant, and everyone in the hunting party jumped on the crippled elephant to finish it off (Turnbull, 1987). Companies have three legs that focused competitors can attack one by one: customer intimacy, operational excellence, and product leadership.

Of course when we say that a company must focus primarily on one discipline that does not mean it should ignore the other two. As we illustrate in the following more detailed discussion of these disciplines in relation to strategy, even the discipline least important to a company cannot be ignored without dire consequences. Furthermore, the process of focus is never neat and clean. It often involves resolving conflicts between disciplines. Marketing and sales usually speak for customer intimacy. Engineering and research and development typically speak for product leadership, and production often speaks for operational excellence. Thus choosing to focus primarily on one discipline also means that the functional groups representing that discipline will often prevail over other functions when there is a disagreement.

Customer Intimacy. When a company elects to make customer intimacy its major marketing focus, the members of the organization concentrate on the market niche populated by customers who demand extreme responsiveness to their specialized needs. These customers want tailored products and services that provide a total solution to their problem, and they are willing to pay for this solution. Firms that focus on meeting customers' needs at this level place a very strong emphasis on making the client a winner. They develop an extensive line of products and services so they can offer their customers many choices. When this variety is not enough, they are willing to tailor solutions for individual clients. They must have a broad expertise in order to be adaptive to client needs and must be willing to use that capability to respond to those needs when asked. To support this discipline, they promote and build a network of specialized skills internally and with strategic partners. They attract a workforce that possesses a broad spectrum of industry experience and skills. Customer intimate companies provide the structure, process, and incentives that encourage everyone in the firm to share knowledge about meeting customer needs.

Companies with a major emphasis on customer intimacy think of their business as the management of a lifetime profit stream from each customer. This means that they have to choose their clients very carefully. They must be willing to forgo business that does not have long-term potential. They thrive on deep and long relationships with clients and are much more interested in a smaller group of loyal customers than in a larger group of fickle customers. Their share of a client's wallet (a term used by many consulting firms) is much more important to them than overall market share.

Classic examples of companies that have focused this way include Nordstrom (department stores), Home Depot (hardware and building supply centers), and Airborne Express (an overnight delivery company). If you are not in corporate shipping, you may not have heard of Airborne Express. Unlike Federal Express and United Parcel Service, it does not advertise. Yet it has become quite successful by targeting corporate customers who have special scheduling and shipping needs. A crucial point is that these customers are also willing to pay extra for the special service. Both Nordstrom and Home Depot provide total solutions to their customers by training employees to be focused and knowledgeable. Home Depot not only sells you hardware but also provides you with the tools, know-how, and materials to complete your home project. Nordstrom combines personal shoppers, a surplus of salespeople on the floor to help customers, and a "no questions" return policy to support its strategy. When Dennis Cohen's son was in high school, he got a summer job at a Nordstrom department store. His friend who got a summer job at another retail chain received no training at all, but Dennis's son went to training for three days. The goal of this training was to focus these new salespeople on giving the customer whatever he or she wanted. They were told not to call in a supervisor to approve a return or a difficult decision because the supervisor would simply give the customer what he or she asked for and make them look foolish. That is strategic focus. Recently, however, Nordstrom has lost a bit of its focus. Neglecting to take advantage of technology to improve its ability to respond to customers' needs, Nordstrom has allowed its competitors to surpass it at its own game (Browder, 1999).

Operational Excellence. Organizations that focus on operational excellence focus on the customer segment that is looking for the best possible value for the total cost of ownership. They focus on making their operations and processes as efficient as possible to serve their customers' needs. They are intent on delivering the lowest total cost of ownership. This requires that they concentrate on a narrow line of products or services or both. Too much variety gets in the way of operationalizing and routinizing processes. These companies will sacrifice sales rather than deviate from standard operations because they are engaged in a relentless pursuit of optimizing their internal processes. When these companies invest in technology, it is not to deliver the latest and greatest products. Rather it is to reduce costs or to make their operations more effective at delivering lowest total costs of ownership to the customer.

Because high volume is necessary to sustain an operationally excellent enterprise, these companies focus on market share and the efficient use of their assets. Because of their push toward uniformity, they are characterized by standardized operating procedures and centralized decision making. They have a functionally oriented workforce with teams organized to improve departmental efficiency. Cross-functional teams are not as common as they are in companies that focus on greater product variety. In general these companies constantly seek simplicity everywhere in their value chain.

The most recent examples of companies that focus on operations are found among the Internet retail success stories such as Amazon.com and Buy.com. They offer low prices and an efficient buying process that translates into a low cost of ownership and a short transaction time. One reason they can offer these benefits is that they have eliminated much of the "bricks and mortar" required by retail stores, placing it with "clicks and orders," and they have developed highly efficient processes of shipping and distribution. A more traditional example is McDonald's. Here is an operation that has lowered the price of fast food and maintained uniform reliability through the development of controlled processes. When you walk into a McDonald's anywhere in the world, you know right away where you are and that the product will have only minor variations from the product sold in McDonald's stores elsewhere. This is what McDonald's customers expect, and this is what they get. They get it because the company is organized to promote standard parts, standard procedures, standard structure, standard processes, and even standard uniforms. The general form of the code of any company with a focus on operations comes down to us from Henry Ford: "A customer can have a car painted any color he wants so long as it's black" (or any hamburger so long as it's a Big Mac). The possibilities opened up by the Internet, however, may be changing this limitation and leading a transformation in the operational excellence focus from mass production to mass customization. For project managers this change brings the customer deeper into the project process.

Product Leadership. Whereas companies that emphasize their operations for strategic advantage must focus on uniformity to promote efficiency and reliability, companies that practice product leadership must do almost the opposite. These companies deal in creativity and variety. They target the market segment populated by the early adopters, those users who need or just want the latest and greatest product or service available and have the money to pay for it. These companies focus on the benefits that unique product features can offer to their target customers. They are continuously experimenting with the latest concepts and technologies. Companies that focus on product leadership are willing to develop new products that will cannibalize their existing products, knowing that if they do not do this their competition will.

Companies with this strategy are characterized by open communications across functions. In product leadership companies, new product development is almost always carried out by integrated cross-functional teams. These companies focus on creating the future and support their creative processes through major investments in technology. They demand technically proficient workers and value the individual contributor highly. They also feature a wide dispersal of power rather than centralized decision making. All of these traits enable the delivery of premium value through innovation.

Classic examples of companies that focus mainly on product leadership are Intel and Microsoft. Intel has dominated the microprocessor market by continuously introducing a new more powerful processor before the previous model begins to fail to meet customer needs. Microsoft has constantly upgraded its products with new features to take advantage of the increased capacity of the latest Intel processor. In fact the combination of Intel on the processor hardware side and Microsoft on the software side has tended to drive the computer market and has almost forced customers to buy the new model before they are ready for it. Together Intel and Microsoft have enticed the early adopters to upgrade their machines and software quite often so they will have the latest and greatest computing capability available. This kind of strategy works especially well in new markets but becomes more difficult to sustain as markets mature. This has become evident for both Microsoft and Intel in recent years. First, Intel had to respond to market pressures to lower the cost of processors in general. It did this well by producing the Celeron chip, a low-cost alternative to its top-end Pentium chips. Now, however, it is coming under increasing competition from AMD, which has produced a high-end processor with better specifications than Intel's Pentium III top-of-the line product. In early March 2000, AMD announced the introduction of its gigahertz Athlon chip, leaving Intel scrambling to release a gigahertz Pentium III (Lewis, 2000, p. 1).

Another example of a product leadership company is 3M corporation, which has promoted innovation as a key corporate value. Employees are encouraged to spend 15 percent of their time working on whatever creative endeavor they desire. The company is famous for developing innovative products such as Post-It notes; the "yellow stickies" that have become a necessity of business life were developed by accident by a 3M researcher who was looking for a better glue. Sony Corporation's long history of innovative products is chronicled in the corporate museum at Sony headquarters in Tokyo. Of course its most famous product is the Walkman. An even more recent example of a product leader is the Palm Pilot. It was first introduced by Palm computing as the Zoomer, a handheld device to replace the personal computer. By failing miserably with the Zoomer, the company found out that customers wanted something that was smaller and that communicated with their computer rather than replaced it. Thus the Palm Pilot was born in the spring of 1994 (Dillon, 1988; Rae-Dupree, 1997).

Balancing the Disciplines. Although a company should focus on one of these three market disciplines, customer intimacy, operational excellence, or product leadership, it should still make sure that it practices the other two disciplines at a level that meets the industry average, or the threshold of customer tolerance. In this way it can dominate the market segment that contains the customers who most value what is offered by the chosen focus and avoid distracting these customers by deep deficiencies in the other two areas. We call the threshold of customer tolerance a type of industry average because it is relative to the performance of the competition. If an industry is characterized by abysmal service and no company moves to improve that service, the tolerance threshold will be very low. Let one company improve service even slightly, however, and the tolerance level will move up quickly.

There are feasible variations on this pattern. For example an industrial equipment company that Dennis Cohen works with has product leadership as its primary focus. This company has dominated its market by being on the cutting edge of technology and developing equipment that allows its clients to produce the most advanced products in their field. Everyone in that company understands that a product focus must come first to support company success over the long run. However, the focus on customers is a close second, and the company works with its customers in a manner that fits a customer intimacy emphasis. This is required given the nature of the industry and the limited number of potential customers. Industrial equipment is not a mass market. Operational excellence as a focus, however, is a distant third, and the company has had to "fix" its operations again and again. Its operational excellence was below the industry average, and it was beginning to lose customers to competitors because problems with quality and process began to draw customers' attention away from the value added by the company's strengths in product leadership and focus on the customer. However, like all focused companies, it has not let its efforts to fix operations get in the way of leading with products.

Other Approaches

The market discipline approach to strategy is only one framework that companies have adopted to interpret their environment and frame their destiny. Treacy and Wiersema (1995) based their work on an earlier body of work by Michael Porter (see especially Porter, [1985] 1998) that stresses a focus on the value chain. Many high-tech companies use an ecological approach to define what strategy to pursue (Moore, 1993). Another approach that came out recently is called the Delta Model. And e-commerce is producing yet another paradigm that companies in that industry are trying to invent and follow at the same time. We look at each of these four approaches briefly here.

According to Porter ([1985] 1998) a company needs to compete on cost or on differentiation or on both. For it to do so, management must understand the *value chain* within the industry and within the company. The industry value chain is made up of all the processes that go into a product or service, from the extraction of basic raw materials to the use of the final product or service by the customer. Along the way each process adds value for the customer and adds cost to the end product. The successful company is the one that adds the most value for an equivalent cost in relation to its competitors.

The company value chain includes all the processes involved from taking in materials and services from suppliers to transforming these resources to value-added products and services for customers. To understand the chain from raw materials to R&D to manufacturing to marketing to distribution to service (or in whatever form it takes for your company and industry) is to understand the interdependence of company and industry processes on one another. No process adds value (or cost for that matter) in isolation. The most important implication of this for project managers is that they must understand the position of their projects in the value chain. How can the project add more value for the customer than the competition can and at an equivalent cost, either directly in the project itself or indirectly through another link in the value chain? An example of adding value directly is designing in a new feature while keeping the cost of the product constant. An example of adding value indirectly is designing a product so that it can be manufactured more efficiently and thus at a lower cost. Trade-offs may also occur within the value chain, inadvertently as well as intentionally. If the product with the new feature is designed so that it is very difficult to manufacture, the resulting defect rate could easily wipe out the added value of the feature. The concept of the value chain emphasizes how important it is for the project manager to always think beyond the end of the project and to view the triple constraints as a means for value chain management rather than as ends in themselves.

The *ecological* approach to strategy views groups of complementary businesses as the units of competition. In some ways it is a supplement to the product leadership market discipline. A good example of an ecosystem is Apple Computer and its cluster of suppliers, a group that defined a particular approach to personal computing. At first this cluster of companies was in competition with a cluster led by Tandy, over which it prevailed. Then it was in competition with another ecosystem led by Digital Research and Micropro, over which it also prevailed. It met its match against the IBM-led ecosystem that eventually became the Microsoft and Intel-led ecosystem of personal computers. Another good example is Palm, which we mentioned earlier as a company that failed with its first product. It had tried to be an ecosystem leader of a group of companies that would build various components of the first personal digital assistant (PDA). Palm was to provide only the software. No one remembers how miserably this first product failed because it came out late, beaten by Apple's Newton, which failed even more miserably. In its second try, fueled by what it had learned from its earlier disaster, Palm developed the design of the hardware itself and subcontracted with outside suppliers to build it. Once the Palm Pilot was a success, it then attracted hundreds of software companies to write programs to expand its usefulness (Rae-Dupree, 1997).

The ecological approach typically takes companies through four evolutionary stages:

Birth. In this first stage the product leader must work with customers and suppliers to define the new product offering and make the technical innovation a viable commercial product. Competitively, the company must protect its proprietary technology and when possible keep critical suppliers as sole sources to make it more difficult for competitors to emerge. Problems are technological: get the sucker to do anything; just get the thing to hum. The customer as the first user of the new technology is often sympathetic and understanding of problems. At this stage projects focus on technological issues and problems.

Expansion. In this second stage it is critical to boost market demand and also expand the ecosystem fast enough to supply the demand. Competitively, it is important to provide a better product than the competition can in order to stay in the leadership position. Operations come more into play as the company needs to supply the growing demand. It begins to set up relations with other companies. The customer base no longer consists of early adopters, and the customer becomes more demanding. Now projects must be more customer and market focused.

Leadership. In this third stage the lead companies' leaders must bring the members of the ecosystem together with a compelling vision of the future to bind them in cooperation and to secure a balance of power that prevents them from taking over the lead position. The "Intel inside" campaign is a good example of maintaining customers' focus on the lead company. In addition the customer becomes the primary focus. Late adopters need products that are intuitive and that they can understand through common sense. They do not have the technical knowledge characteristic of early adopters. Project managers should remember how Intel reacted at first to publicity about a bug in the Pentium chip. Its initial announcement that it would not replace the chips and that few users would notice any problems anyway were appropriate for the birth stage or even the expansion stage, but Intel had already entered the leadership stage, and customers were no longer understanding about technical flaws. At this stage the project team must be totally immersed in the customer's point of view and think and act accordingly.

Self-renewal or death. In this final stage the leader must bring new innovations to the ecosystem and stay ahead of competitors or go the way of the dodo bird (Moore, 1993). At this point, projects should reemphasize technical innovation.

Another strategic framework that has recently emerged is the Delta model (Hax and Wilde, 1999). This point of view classifies the universe of strategic possibilities into three positions: *best product, customer solutions,* and *system lock-in.* The customer solutions position is quite similar to the customer intimacy market discipline. The best product position combines aspects of product leadership and operational excellence. The system lock-in position is reminiscent of the evolutionary patterns found in the ecological approach. This strategy locks customers into a product or service by making the price of switching to a competitor high enough to be ordinarily prohibitive. We cannot do justice to this framework here, but be forewarned. The upper manager who was talking about market disciplines yesterday and predators and prey today will probably be talking about the Delta model tomorrow.

Finally, there is the new strategy associated with the Internet. What is it? It is developing so fast that what it is today will be different from what it is tomorrow. It is just a blur. Any snapshot we describe now will probably be ancient history by the time you are reading this book. One thing is for sure, however; you should hang on to your seat and get ready for a wild ride. Strategy in the world of e-commerce is the perfect example of responding to the new conditions we described at the beginning of this chapter. This world is the turbulent environment taken to its logical next step—more change at a faster pace that is less predictable and thus presents a higher risk. "The impact on planning is revolutionary. Net-speeds force all sorts of cultural changes. Hierarchies flatten out. Budgeting cycles get compressed. Decision-making gets pushed out to the front lines. And customer expectations, not the executive board, guide the next big project" (Stepanek, 1999, p. EB52). The value chain is compressed so that suppliers and customers fold into the project in more intimate ways. They should be made regulars on the core team rather than being treated as mere stakeholders (Prahalad and Ramaswamy, 2000).

The emergent theme for projects in this environment is speed, speed, and more speed. However, even the Internet has not suspended the principle of front-end loading. Project managers in e-commerce are finding that it is best to get the product or service on-line and working as fast as possible, without waiting until it is perfect, but that even these on-line activities need the up-front planning and design work of sound project management. They just need this planning and work done faster.

Whatever the directed strategy may be, the influence of emergent strategy is growing to determine the final result. What you do and how you do it as a project manager is becoming a crucial element in the long-term success of your company.

Implications for Projects and Project Managers

Whether it is one of the more classic strategic frameworks or a new one evolving in a brand-new industry, directed strategy should drive project portfolio selection. Which projects best serve the needs of the company's top market disciplines? What must be done to maintain parity with the industry in the lowest-ranked discipline? In making the business case and setting project specifications and scope, the project manager will do a better job if he or she can align these things with the directed broader business strategy.

Englund and Graham (1999) noted that companies that excel in creating an environment for successful projects often exhibit a well-defined process for selecting projects and managing the project portfolio with strategy in mind. This finding has been supported by further research in which the Project Environment Assessment Tool (PEAT) was administered to project managers and their managers at eight best practices companies: Chevron, IBM, 3M, Boeing, NCR, Hewlett-Packard, Motorola, and Lucent Technologies. The managers were asked to rank seventy-two items, drawn from the initial research done by Graham and Englund, to indicate their importance in an environment for successful projects. The highest-ranked item was, "I understand how this project will add value to the organization" (norm of 5.76 on a 7-point scale). The seventh highest was, "The project goal is/was clearly linked to business strategy" (norm of 5.26 on a 7-point scale) (Graham, Englund, and Cohen, 2000).

This emerging emphasis on strategy by the best organizations indicates that the project manager should take strategy into consideration when developing a business case to submit for project approval. Questions that need to be answered by this case include these:

- How does the proposed project outcome support the ongoing strategy of the company?
- How does the project itself set priorities consistent with the company's strategy?
- What are the risks in the project that might push it off its strategic course?
- What are the contingency plans to address these risks if they occur?

We suggest that the project manager think first of the three areas of strategic focus, the three market disciplines, that we have emphasized here. From your company's strategic planning and communications, it should be clear what its strategic priorities are. If they are not clear, your first priority should be to find out what they are. If upper management cannot tell you, you should tell your manager what you think the priorities are. This should lead to a dialogue that ends in an agreement about what the priorities are. It is best to get them in writing. Once you know what the strategic priorities are, your job is to align your project with those priorities. The most concrete way that you can do this is to think about the way your project performance outcome could contribute to each of the possible areas of emphasis. Given the fact that you have finite resources, you will probably have to limit the number and type of contributions the outcome will be able to make. So, make sure that you focus on delivering as much as you possibly can in the primary area of emphasis. For instance, if the primary strategic emphasis of the company is on product leadership, then using the latest technology and methods is probably de rigueur. Time to market will also be very important. However, features that allow customization and flexibility might be sacrificed, given limited resources. So might processes that drove down costs at the expense of time to market or using the latest technology.

Also remember that you will be making these decisions in a dynamic project environment that cannot be totally locked into project specifications and plans. No one can anticipate all the contingencies that may arise during a project. So to maintain alignment throughout the project, it is extremely important for you to be clear on the strategic priorities as they relate to the planning, execution, controlling, and closing of the project. In each of these project phases the strategic priorities should point the way for setting project priorities. First, however, you will need a process to implement the strategic alignment. The process should proceed through the following steps:

1. Note the strategic market discipline (customer intimacy, operational excellence, or product leadership, or some other strategy, depending on the strategy framework in use) that your company ranks first, and brainstorm all the ways that your project can support and contribute to this emphasis.

2. Note the strategic market discipline that your company ranks second. Brainstorm all the ways that your project can support and contribute to this emphasis.
3. Note the third-ranked strategic market discipline and brainstorm all the ways that your project can support and contribute to it.
4. Look at your list of supports and contributions for the third-ranked emphasis. Eliminate any item that would interfere with supports and contributions listed for the first- or second-ranked strategic emphasis.
5. Look at your list of supports and contributions from the second-ranked emphasis. Eliminate any item that would interfere with supports and contributions listed for the first-ranked emphasis.
6. Rank the supports and contributions left on all the lists by order of the value they add within their strategic emphasis and then incorporate all the support and contribution ideas into your project as long as you have the resources (including time) to execute them all. If you are short of resources, you will need to eliminate some ideas, usually starting with the lowest-ranked item in the third group. However, if the company has fallen way below industry par in fulfilling a particular market strategy, you may have to adjust your priorities to boost that strategy, even though it is ranked low in the company.

Without a process and without vigilance on the part of the project manager, projects do drift off course and out of alignment with strategy. As we commented earlier, each department has a bias in favor of one of the disciplines. For the overall organization, strategy is often kept on track by upper management through budget decisions. Such decisions will also be reflected in the selection process for the project portfolio. However, within the project, the project manager should recognize that core team members might reflect the bias of their functional area. You may have to periodically remind the team of the strategy to prevent the project from drifting from the strategic path. And when people make suggestions from their functional bias, your response should be, How will that help us to follow our strategy?

We have seen this functional bias in a number of financial service companies that we have observed. Systems designers and software engineers have tended to drift away from the directed strategy of customer intimacy because of the demands of their technical discipline. They are oriented toward product leadership. They focus on the biggest, fastest, most advanced solution even if it does not contribute to staying close to the customer. Unless a business manager is in charge, the projects seem to produce outcomes that are sound technically but that do not meet the strategic needs of the business. Because the management of information is a core function of the financial service industry, such project failure has dire consequences for strategy implementation. In discussions among the various employees in these companies, the technical requirements generated by systems engineers and business requirements generated by operating unit managers often came into conflict. We have read a number of similar accounts, along with suggestions that the technical project members should report to a project owner who is responsible for the strategic business implementation (Johann, Macesich, and Massoudi, 1998). Another example of this functional bias comes from a process improvement project in the plant of a semiconductor manufacturer that had adopted a strategic initiative of greater customer intimacy. The plant manager assigned the project to a project manager and team of process engineers. As they got deeper and deeper into the project, however, they focused more on the technological advances that would allow them to produce semiconductors more efficiently and with fewer defects. And they lost their focus on greater customer intimacy. The new process they developed made it more difficult for the division to respond to custom requirements from each customer, a capability that they had been successfully promoting in order to renew their sagging business. Somewhere along the line someone lost track of this strategy. Regardless of whose fault it might have been, everyone considered the project a failure. It certainly did not advance the career of the project manager.

The different types of projects will make different contributions to a directed strategy. In general, a new product development project will make its contribution by developing a product that attracts the same customer niche that is defined by the company's strategy. Such a project would not be aligned with strategy if it developed a mass-produced product to be sold to a customer segment looking for custom products. Internal projects are not tied directly to the market, but they do produce outcomes that should support and enhance the ability of the company to pursue its primary market discipline. A process reengineering project at McDonald's to provide customers with a wide variety of foods on demand would be an anomaly. A client engagement project also needs to conform to strategic requirements. If the customer is expecting a tailored application of a process or product and what he or she gets is obviously off the shelf, that customer will not be satisfied. The project will not have supported the strategy.

There are a number of ways that projects can support customer intimacy. In general the focus should be on an outcome crafted to customer expectations. First, the marketing data should be broken into micro-segments to make sure that every targeted customer need is met by the project design. The project outcome should be made as flexible as possible so that it can be tailored to fit each individual customer's need for a value-added custom solution. If the project is an internal project its outcome should contribute to the company's ability to be flexible and responsive to customer needs. Project team members should have extensive experience in working with clients or very close contact with clients in order to supply insight into their unique needs. When the product design is being developed, marketing team members should have significant influence over technical designers because they represent the customers or clients that are now lifelong partners or are targeted to become such. In this strategy, retaining loyal customers is more valuable than attracting new ones. There should be coordination between the project and the existing portfolio of products or services to enhance the company's capacity to provide total solutions for specific customer groups. There should be no hesitation about charging a premium price to deliver exactly what the customer wants.

To support operational excellence a project should focus on the general issue of efficiency. It should deliver the outcome for the lowest cost possible while meeting customer needs, which in this case are for the lowest cost of total ownership of the outcome. Instead of a broad portfolio of products and services to meet any specialized need of any customer, a very narrow line of products and services is now the focus. If an individual client has special needs, just say no. The project will contribute by focusing on the general customer need for low cost for the highest value possible. Whatever the project outcome, it should be compatible with the need to optimize process for greatest efficiency. This means close attention to manufacturability and reliability. Internal projects should focus on optimization of internal processes, efficient asset utilization, and cost reduction. Customer engagements should be based on well-designed repeatable processes. Within the constraints of the low-cost to high-value ratio, increasing market share should be an important goal.

Support of and contributions to product leadership focus in general on time and outcome. The emphasis should be on producing unique product or service features. Any product development project and client engagement project should maintain this focus. Internal projects should enhance the ability of the firm to produce such product or service features. This means that as the project progresses, there should be a willingness to experiment with leading-edge concepts, even if they will render existing products obsolete. The project should focus on the customer who wants to live tomorrow today, is willing to pay for it, and understands that sometimes reliability must be sacrificed on the altar of using the latest in technology. Given competitive forces in the marketplace, firms with a strategic focus on product leadership are very sensitive to time-to-market issues. Anything a project can do to enhance the ability to be innovative, creative, and produce quantum leaps in performance will support a strategic focus on products.

We have discussed project phases from the cash flow standpoint. From the standpoint of getting the project work done, one can think of a project as having these stages: initiating, planning, executing, controlling, and closing (Project

Management Institute, 1996). A focus on strategy at each stage of the project will help to keep it aligned. During the initiating phase, strategic alignment, as we have said, is an important criterion for project selection, and it should enter into the development of a business case for the project. As the initiating phase is completed, make sure that you have established what the strategic priorities are as you take on the project.

During the planning phase, make sure that the team understands what the strategy and strategic priorities are. Maintain strategic alignment throughout planning by referring to the company's strategy and strategic plan. Keep asking team members how different ideas will contribute to the strategy during planning and design.

During executing and controlling, midcourse corrections should be aligned with strategic considerations. Project managers should bear in mind which strategy factor is most important. Think of *Star Trek* and Mr. Spock saying to Captain Kirk, "Jim, remember the prime directive"; focus on the most important strategic issues and ask the right questions. Continue to watch out for drift among your core team members.

Finally, during closing make sure that part of the evaluation and determination of lessons learned focuses on how the project outcome contributed to the strategy of the company. Make sure that others monitor the project outcome lifecycle to answer this question over a longer period.

Examples

In our continuing examples, the project managers must also answer the questions, Where are we going? and, How are we going to get there?

Newprod Project

One of the first questions to ask regarding any new feature proposal is does it align with strategy? Does the new feature support, for example, a strategy of customer intimacy, operational excellence, or product leadership? Your company has stated that it wants Newprod to be the product leader in the market, so you have assumed that product leadership is the dominant strategic focus. You make further inquiries and find out that customer intimacy is a secondary focus and that operational excellence is a distant third. This suggests to you that product performance and project schedule are the most important of the triple constraints, with costs being less important. Therefore, if the new feature that a team member thinks it might be good to add to the project does not add increased product performance but does lower product costs and does cause a project delay, it should be rejected as not aligned with strategy. However, if the new feature does add increased performance to the product and also increases product costs and has an uncertain effect on the schedule, it should not be rejected at this point as it does align with the dominant strategic foci. You and your team decide that the new feature will add increased performance and therefore you do not reject the new feature proposal at this point but rather subject it to further analysis (which we will discuss in subsequent chapters).

Newsys Project

Now things get interesting for the Newsys project. In selecting the new phone system you and your team find there are a number of choices that fit the project specifications. With choice A, the project can save some money. It meets the basic specifications of being digital and able to handle the projected growth of the company. Its only additional feature is a system that automatically chooses the cheapest long distance provider for each call. Choice B is also within the budget but has an added feature set that will give anyone who communicates with a customer the ability to instantly link the phone to computer records and have the customer profile at their fingertips as they speak. Choice C is also within budget but has an added feature set that uses the latest technology to help R&D staff collaborate and brainstorm the latest concepts to devise the latest technological breakthroughs.

Which system should you and your team choose? It depends on the strategy of your company. If its strategy focuses on operational excellence, choice A is the best. Choice A emphasizes efficiency. If the focus is on customer intimacy, Choice B is the best. Choice B emphasizes service to the customer. If the focus is on product leadership, choice C is the best. Choice C emphasizes support for innovation.

FIGURE 4.1. BUSINESS SYSTEMS DIAGRAM.

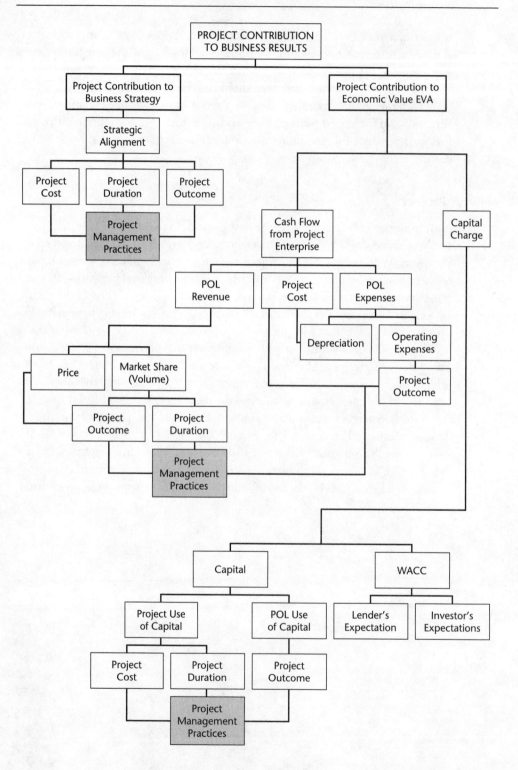

CHAPTER FOUR

PROJECT MANAGEMENT PROCESSES FOR BUSINESS RESULTS

Folly (or perversity)—the pursuit of policy contrary to the self-interest of the constituency or state involved.

BARBARA TUCHMAN, *THE MARCH OF FOLLY,* 1984

This chapter examines the effect of project management processes (Figure 4.1) on the creation of economic value. In particular it looks at the link between project management practices and project cycle time. *Project cycle time* is the time elapsed between the beginning of the project and the end of the project, when the project outcome is ready. We believe that the way the project is managed and led determines when the project will be done and thus when the project outcome will be completed. The date that the project outcome is ready can have an enormous effect on the project outcome's contribution to economic value. The sooner the outcome is ready, the sooner it can begin to produce its value and begin to pay back the investment used to produce it. Thus reduced cycle time adds to cash flow, reduces the project capital charge, and subsequently, increases economic value.

Most examples of the value of reducing cycle time come from new project development projects, where the end of the project defines the date that the project outcome is ready for the market. Many of these examples show the benefits of investing in a higher budget for good management practices in order to reduce project cycle time. For example, according to an often-quoted McKinsey & Company study (Dumaine, 1989), if a project is late for an amount of time equal to 10 percent of the projected life of the product, there will be a loss of around 30 percent of the potential profit. However, if the project goes 50 percent over budget but is delivered on time, there will be a loss of only about 3 percent of the potential profit. The McKinsey study made many restrictive assumptions, so these numbers should not be taken as absolute projections for the results of reducing cycle times on all types of projects. However, the study findings do indicate that companies can often gain a significant amount of profit by being fast to market and that this profit often outweighs by several times any extra costs that might be incurred to achieve that speed. From studies like this, managers can see that even though features, quality, performance, and customer value are important variables in project success, one of the more important variables for increasing economic value may be the ability to get the project done quickly. Therefore this chapter examines management practices that reduce cycle time.

Of course those management practices that reduce cycle time often increase project costs, and there's the rub. The need for extra project investment in order to reduce cycle time has often caused friction between project managers and financial managers. Project managers argue for best management practices in order to decrease time, and financial managers ask what the cost is for the additional investment needed. That is, one stresses time, whereas the other stresses cost. This conflict has often led to folly in that the organization ends up pursuing practices contrary to its self-interest. This chapter is an attempt to alleviate organizational folly and answer cycle-time questions in a way that will allow project managers to show financial managers the benefits of good management in financial terms. Once project managers begin to answer financial managers' questions *in their language,* a new world of understanding will emerge.

Experienced project managers may feel they already know well the practices that lead to reduced cycle time and so may want to skip this chapter. However, even readers with considerable experience may gain helpful insights from reading through quickly to see how these practices are linked to financial performance and from paying close attention to the last section, which explains using the business systems calculator to show the benefits of best practices in financial terms.

Cycle-Time Practices

At first glance the answer to reducing cycle time may seem to be to work team members harder and micromanage them until they "get it done, fast!" Most project managers have experienced projects where upper management put enormous pressure on to get the work done quickly, where project activities were *crashed* through rapidly adding extra manpower and working people overtime until they dropped. Most project managers know that these practices rarely work. In addition they are very poor project management and leadership practices. This chapter addresses the learning and growth part of the balanced scorecard (Chapter

One), the people side of the project management, thus it examines better project management processes, those that reduce cycle time without the crash.

As we mentioned, most of what is known about reducing cycle time comes from experience with new product development projects, and we draw heavily on that knowledge for this chapter. However, the lessons learned are easily transferred and seem to be beneficial to all types of projects. Getting internal projects done faster means the benefits of the project outcome will be enjoyed by the company that much sooner. In addition, project team members will be available sooner for the new projects that are constantly arising. A shorter cycle time for client engagement projects will probably be welcomed, or even required, by the client. In addition, with a shorter cycle time you can bill the client that much faster and thus help the company manage its working capital and increase its cash flow.

Some managers argue that decreasing cycle time may not be necessary on all projects, even new project development projects. They point out that the project outcome may enter the market before the market is ready for it. For example, as we described in the last chapter, Apple Computer's handheld Newton computer failed because the market was not ready for it and because it was not ready for the market (it was too big to fit in a shirt pocket). The Palm Pilot, which came later, now dominates the market (Rae-Dupree, 1997). However, the problem of getting to the market too early does not prove a need for longer cycle times but rather points to the need for the project manager to understand the market thoroughly. The start of a project may be delayed so the manager can gain this better market understanding, but once begun, the project should be completed quickly. Having said that, we add that managers should not delay a new product only because no one else seems to be making a competitive product. History is full of examples of similar new products from independently working researchers or companies being ready at the same time (the telephone is just one example), with market success going to the group that got the product to market first.

Project Management Processes and Economic Value

Throughout this chapter we show the business results of various project management practices. In later chapters we look at costs, finance, and post-project revenue in relation to economic value. We go into considerable detail so that project managers and financial managers can see how support for best practices actually pays off in increased economic value. The business results will show the positive total effects of following best practices and "doing the project right."

Project managers will be able to use our on-line business systems calculator to perform the same calculations we show here and to obtain the business results for their own projects that can support good decision making and help them convince financial managers that good practices pay off in the end. Even though many of the best practices to reduce cycle time are expensive, they are often expensive only in the short run. That is, these practices will increase project costs per month, but because the project will run for fewer months, total costs may actually decrease. And if as a result the project outcome gets to market faster, still more financial benefit may accrue from the investment in best practices. Using the results of the business systems calculator will show the possible long-term benefits of best practices and show how good management makes money. This should warm the heart of even the most skeptical financial manager.

One of the reasons that project managers and financial managers have not always agreed about best practices is that from the financial managers' point of view, projects represent expense without any matching income. The income statement, as we discussed in Chapter Two, is designed to match expenses with associated income, but until the project outcome is completed, the project has no income. As a result, financial managers tend to concentrate on project expenses, making an assumption that less expense is better than more expense. Added to that is the problem that forgone income, income that might have flowed to the company if more cash had been invested in the project, never shows up on the income statement at all. So financial managers have often viewed the argument that a project should spend more money now in order to increase income in the future with skepticism, particularly during the project when there is no income at all. Presenting the results of management decisions in financial terms, as we show in this and later chapters, terms that financial managers can best understand, can help project managers make their case.

Another reason to have financial managers see the business results of a decision is to help them develop a project point of view, to see that some decisions that look good on the ledger now actually cost more money in the long run. For example, Robert Graham remembers when he was the manager of a project to change the method by which student billing was done at a college, switching from an accounting machine to a computer. He planned to run the two machines in parallel to ensure proper functioning while he was working out the computer bugs. That was sound management practice. However, the financial manager forced him to give up the accounting machine early and skip the step of running in parallel in order to save one month's rent on the accounting machine. That decision looked good on the ledger, but caused Graham a lot of problems, caused many students much grief, and delayed the implementation of the new billing system by three months. The total costs to the college far outweighed the month's rent that was saved, but these costs were never tallied; they were never compared to the rental savings. The decision looked good on the ledger, and so it came to pass. If Robert could have shown the potential costs of that decision, perhaps he could have changed it. But the decision was made to save expenses as the financial manager saw them, not to avoid potential costs a project manager could not fully explain. It is situations like these that lead most project managers to conclude that a good financial decision is rarely a good project management decision.

When project managers can present the consequences of decisions in financial format, it is possible that financial managers will move beyond their short-term fixation on expenses and begin to make decisions that are good for the organization. In fact there are some indications that financial managers are already beginning to listen and are moving "beyond bean-counting" as a *Business Week* article put it (Zweig, 1996). The article noted, for example, that "thanks in part to quantum leaps in computer hardware and software technology in the past few years, [Johnson &] Johnson's finance department is no longer preoccupied with transaction systems, reporting and cost efficiency, but is concentrating on analyzing information to boost revenues" (p. 130).

When the project manager can speak the same language as the financial manager, and when the financial manager is willing to take the long-term view and concentrate on profit rather than cost, it is possible that good project management practices will be allowed. Let us proceed toward that brave new world.

Project Management Practices for Reducing Cycle Time

There are many good management and leadership practices that are a part of successful project management. Some of these are providing training for project managers and encouraging their enthusiasm, establishing a full-time core team for each project, setting project goals with the core team, leading team development, colocating the members of the project team (or at least of the core team), establishing good customer–end-user relationships, working with project stakeholders, ensuring upper-management support, understanding how to deal with a recalcitrant boss or team members, and so on. We focus here on six practices that we believe to be most influential in decreasing the total duration of a project while increasing quality and most likely decreasing total costs:

- Have one well-trained project manager.
- Develop a rapid prototyping process.
- Establish a core team for the duration of the project.
- Have core team and other team members work full time on one project.

- Co-locate core team and other team members, especially on new product development projects.
- Develop upper-management support.

Of course this is a dream list; not all these practices are likely to be attainable on most projects. However, the general concept is that cycle time will be reduced to the degree that these practices are attained. Thus there may be some benefit, even though not the maximum benefit, if a practice that cannot be fully attained can be approximated. In our discussion of these practices to reduce cycle time, we will also describe approximate processes. Before we turn to these practices, however, we think it is necessary for managers to understand why projects take as long as they often do. Projects ordinarily take longer than they have to owing to some combination of the following problems:

Lack of team direction. Lack of direction can come from either of two sources. When a project has a manager who is what we call an *accidental project manager,* someone who is not trained as a project manager and for whom the project is an addition to his or her usual duties, the team is less likely to function with focus, and the project is likely to take longer. Also, when a project has an unclear goal, the team is likely to experience confusion about its tasks. Unclear goals are often cited as the number one cause of project failure.

Lack of continuity. When project team members come and go, handing off work or receiving handed-off work, it adds to project duration because the handoffs are seldom smooth and often create situations in which rework is necessary, or at least believed necessary. It is the rare professional who can take someone else's work and say, "Wow, this is great! I can use it as is." The usual response is more like, "This is junk. I'll have to start from scratch!"

Lack of focus. When project team members work on many projects rather than working full time on one project, their focus will suffer. Everyone knows that achieving difficult goals requires focus, focus, and focus. When project team members' focus is diffused, it adds duration to every project they are working on.

Lack of team spirit. When team members are scattered around, rarely see each other, and do not participate in team-building activities, it is often unclear to them exactly who is on the team and thus difficult to build any team spirit.

Lack of commitment. When upper managers and other stakeholders are not truly committed to making a project happen, the upper managers often pull team members away for other tasks, reduce available funds, assign their lowest-level people to the project, and otherwise interfere with it in ways that increase its duration.

Most projects seem to suffer from one or more of these problems. We call these projects the ones where people "do it as usual." To alleviate these problems, to "do it right" and thus to reap the benefits of shorter cycle time, we suggest the following project management practices.

Have One Well-Trained Project Manager

Start the project off in the right direction. Select the project leader judiciously. He or she should be someone who is enthusiastic from the beginning and trained to manage projects. It often seems that project leaders are appointed because they are good technical contributors, they are good functional managers, or they are simply available at the time. However, people should be appointed as project managers only after they have shown that they want to do the job. Hewlett-Packard, for example, helps employees find out if they want to be project managers. They take a "transitions" course (Graham and Englund, 1997, chap. 9) in which current project managers "tell it like it is" in order to ensure that these job candidates know the job they are being asked to do. If they are still enthusiastic about the job, they are then thoroughly trained in the Hewlett-Packard techniques for managing projects and reducing cycle time. Cycle time reductions should not be expected from accidental project managers.

Kopelman and Voegtli (1998, p. 136) advise further that it is best to have one project manager on a project, so that team members report to only one leader. Appoint one leader and ensure there are no de facto extra leaders, such as executives who countermand decisions behind the scenes. When there is a single project leader, it is clear to everyone who has the authority to make decisions, resolve differences, and direct the project.

Some organizations appoint two project managers to a project with the intention that one will manage the beginning, or more creative part, of the project and the other will manage the ending, or production part, of the project. They often take this step after having poor experiences with letting their more creative people try to manage the detailed aspects of production and operations. However, we suggest that the best solution to this problem is to place the creative person and the operations person on the core team, as described later. When this is not possible, two project managers can be appointed but it must be clear that each is being appointed for a specific part of the project, so that one manages the first phases and the other manages the completion. In that way, although there are two project managers on the team, only one is managing the project at any given time.

Develop a Rapid Prototyping Process

An essential tool for clarifying the goal of a project as well as decreasing project cycle time is *rapid prototyping*. Developing prototypes allows project team members to develop a much clearer image of the end product than they would otherwise and thus helps clarify the project goal. Because lack of goal clarity is so often cited as a factor in increasing cycle time, prototyping becomes the first step in cycle-time reduction.

In addition to generating increased technical momentum, prototyping is also important for the human interaction it facilitates, an essential aspect of project team building. Schrange (1999) explains that such human interaction has become increasingly important in cycle-time reduction because of the profound shift in methods of design that is currently taking hold in modern industry. In the past it was common practice for companies to gather detailed specifications from customers before building the first prototype. However, the current trend is to use a rapid sequence of prototypes to elicit specifications from customers. That is, as Schrange points out, innovation is shifting from spec-driven prototypes to prototype-driven specs. The result is a final product that the customer has actually co-designed, rather than just described.

Using rapid prototypes may seem expensive to upper managers used to the old design methods. Smith (1999) tells of an instance in which managers questioned the expense of early rapid prototypes that revealed design mistakes. In response, the developer deferred making any prototypes until it was certain the design was perfect. Of course, that reaction increased the project cycle time and negated the value of the rapid prototyping program. Project managers must stress that rapid prototyping is a technique to decrease cycle time, not to show excellence in design.

Cisco Systems is an example of a company that embraces the rapid prototyping philosophy. Cisco customers can customize their routers and switches by playing with prototypes and simulations on-line rather than just listing specifications. "Prototypes," says Cisco CIO Peter Solvik, "are far less ambiguous than words" (Schrange, 1999, p. 10).

Establish a Core Team

Another essential management practice for cycle-time reduction is the creation of an interdisciplinary core team of people from important departments who will stick with the project from beginning to the end. The core team members will represent the ideas of and direct the work of people in their home departments. Core team members typically come from these functions and groups:

- Engineering, information technology, and so forth, that is, whatever departments will design and create the project outcome
- Marketing (or, for in-house projects, the department that will use the project outcome)
- Customers or end-users (or the core team may have access to customers through interviews, prototyping sessions, or focus groups)
- Production or operations, or whatever departments will produce and maintain the project outcome
- Customer and technical support
- Quality assurance
- Finance

The function of the finance member of the core team is to watch over the financial side of the decisions and trade-offs that are made during the project and to cost out various options. Throughout the project this person should help the team determine what it would cost to add new features, use new technology, buy new equipment, or make whatever other change the team is considering. When the numbers come from this person, they will be much more believable to financial and other upper managers. Some veteran project managers may feel that putting a financial manager on the core team is akin to inviting the devil to dinner. After all, why invite trouble? However, in the light of the spirit of cooperation between project and financial managers that is becoming more and more necessary if companies are to succeed, this is an important move as it supplies the financial manager with a project point of view.

Core teams were once thought to be an expensive extravagance pushed by those who emphasized the people side of project management (for example, Graham, 1989). However, because many benefits from these teams have been experienced over the years now, core teams have become de rigueur in many organizations. Smith (1999) points out that in his experience, "the biggest schedule compression opportunities happen to be in cross-functional areas, such as jointly developed product specification, the fuzzy front end, and transition to manufacturing" (p. 226). The following sections look more closely at some benefits of using core teams.

Core Teams Reduce Cycle Times. Some may argue that having people from many departments involved from the beginning of the project seems like wasting money. However, when the core team helps to reduce project cycle time, it does not waste money—it generates money in the form of the potential for additional profit. For example, the Cadillac Motor Company (1991) found that by using interdepartmental teams in a *simultaneous engineering* process, it could reduce the time it took to make styling changes in Cadillac automobiles. A process that previously took 175 weeks can now be completed in 90 to 150 weeks, allowing the new models to be on the market much faster.

Core Teams Increase Quality. In addition, it seems that because core teams cut cycle time, they add to product quality. Faster product development through faster learning has improved not only cycle times but also product capabilities and quality. Motorola, for example, discovered that "one of the fastest ways to improve quality is to focus on reducing cycle time. They found that when they focused on cycle time, defects were reduced at a much faster rate than when they focused on defect reduction alone" (Schmidt and Finnigan, 1992, p. 311). This improvement is attributed to the fact that with a core team there is less handoff of work from one department to another and thus less loss of information and less chance that quality will decrease due to information loss.

Cores teams also improve outcome quality by helping the project do a better job of meeting customer expectations. Because the team is involved from *concept to customer,* it usually contains a representative from the marketing area who can expose other team members to marketing concepts and heighten their customer awareness. Two other approaches with similar results are to place a customer or customer representative on the core team as a permanent member or to give the whole team access to people representative of the targeted customers.

Core Teams Develop Better Project Plans. The core team refines the project objectives, develops strategies for meeting those objectives, identifies critical resources, and develops the plan for the project. That plan becomes the daily guide to action for members of the project team. The core team should always be involved with the project manager in the planning process. Core team participation may mean planning takes longer, but there are benefits.

Core team participation in planning helps members understand the goal of the project. A common, well-understood goal is part of the team-building process as well as part of a successful project. A well-understood goal reduces cycle time. In addition, core team participation in the planning process allows members to experience working with each other before the project begins. It allows them to develop trust in each other as the planning process proceeds.

Core team participation in the planning process also helps to ensure that all needed parts of the project will be considered up front, reducing the chance that some significant part will be overlooked and its lack not discovered until near the end of the project. After participating in the planning, core team members should know when to schedule help in their areas. They also should know when to schedule outside experts to work on the project.

Core Teams Encourage Creativity. Core teams are also important for increasing creativity. With members coming from different departments and having different points of view, core teams embody the concept of *requisite variety.* This concept states that creativity is encouraged when a variety of points of view attack a particular problem. This does not mean that teams composed of people from one department cannot be creative, but rather that cross-departmental teams are likely to be even more creative in finding solutions

Core Teams Access a Range of Technical Expertise. Any successful team needs to be able to use the technical expertise in the organization that is necessary to produce the final product. The project manager may not have this technical expertise, so it must reside in the core team or be accessible by the core team. It is becoming apparent that companies need people who can do two things effectively: serve as interdepartmental team members and lead an effort within their own functions. Core team members serve exactly that function as they are responsible both for working with the core team and for directing the work of project team members from their departments. Core team membership is thus a pivotal position and should be highly regarded in the functional departments.

Core Teams Minimize Handoff Problems. Members of the core team should be involved in handing off the project outcome to manufacturing or operating departments. We do not expect this team to stay with the project outcome for its entire lifecycle. However, team members should stay together for some percentage of the expected product life in order to assist with making any changes needed at this stage. Then the original core team can hand off to the core team members of the operating departments. The original core team and the operating departments' team should run in parallel while handoff is made, like runners in a relay race.

Have Team Members Work Full Time on the Project

In the most productive project situation, almost all people on the project team work full time on one project only. This was the case with the Boeing 777 project, for example, but overall it seems to be a rare situation. When other people join the team for a temporary period of time, they too should work on that project only. At a minimum, the core team members should work full time on one project.

The fastest way to get anything done is with full-time focus (Kopelman and Voegtli, 1998, p. 137). One of the central arguments of the landmark book *The*

Mythical Man-Month (Brooks, 1975) is that a person cannot be partitioned without loss of output. That is, when you start to partition people's effort across several projects, the idea that those people will produce the same output in a month that they would if they were working on one project is a myth. Asking people to work on multiple projects, often called *multitasking*, is a technique for decreasing focus, decreasing output, and subsequently increasing cycle times, a loser on all fronts. However, despite the fact that multitasking is well known to negate efforts to reduce cycle time, it remains a popular organizational phenomenon.

A numerical example can show the folly of multitasking. Assume that a person, Joe, is assigned to Project X, has a 400-hour task, Task A, works 40 hours per week, and earns $1,000 per week. Task A can thus be done in 10 weeks for $10,000. Suppose a new 80-hour task, Task B, from another project, Project Y, is then assigned to Joe, giving him 480 hours of work. The people on Project Y are in a hurry, of course, and say they "can't wait" for Joe to complete Task A before beginning Task B. The people on Project X do not want their project delayed while Joe works on Task B. Upper management, typically, does not want to do the right thing, which would be to assign a new resource for this new task. So Joe is told to work on both tasks at the same time, thirty-two hours per week on Task A and eight hours per week on Task B. The folly of this assignment is the assumption that adding Task B will push the completion of Task A out only to twelve weeks (480/40 = 12) and that after those 12 weeks both tasks will be completed for a total of $12,000. But the reality is that people are not divisible that easily. Things happen during the hours or days they are away from one project to work on another project, and then they must catch up when they return. In addition, it takes time for them to change their mind-set from one project to another, to focus on different goals, different procedures, different team members, and a different timeline. Both these factors add to the duration of both Task A and Task B for Joe. He could easily lose 2 hours in catching up on each project, taking a total of one-half day a week for the switch from one project to the other and back again (4 hours). So now Joe has 36 hours per week of actual working time, to complete 480 hours worth of tasks, which will take 13.3 weeks, costing $13,300, not to mention the delay to the original Project X of which Task A was a part.

In this example, neither task is finished until the end of 13.3 weeks. However, if they were done sequentially, with Joe working on one task and then the other, the first would be done in 10 weeks and the second in the 2 subsequent weeks, and therefore both would have been done in 12 weeks for a total of $12,000. Such are the "savings" for this effort at multitasking; it took Joe 1.3 weeks longer and cost the company $1,300 more. Remember moreover that this multitasking was done because the people on Project Y said they "can't wait" for Joe to complete Task A before beginning Task B. So because they couldn't wait to get Task B done in 12 weeks, they got it done in 13.3 weeks instead. Such is the result of the typical organizational folly regarding multitasking.

The waste of this folly continues exponentially when more tasks are added. Adding an 80-hour task increased the finish time approximately 10 percent, from 12 weeks to 13.3 weeks. If the company now gives Joe another concurrent 80-hour task, Task C from Project Z, the assumption may be this will push his work on all three project tasks only from 12 weeks to 14 weeks $(560/40 = 14)$. However, adding another half day lost in switching from Task C to Task A or B, leaves Joe with only 32 hours per week to complete 560 hours of work, which will then be completed in 17.5 weeks, a 25 percent increase over the assumed 14-week completion. Of course if the tasks were done in sequence, they would be done in fourteen weeks, so one-quarter of Joe's time is wasted due to three-way multitasking. Because employee output has been cut, the organization may decide to hire 25 percent more people to get the work done, but they will all be multitasked, which slows things down even more, and so it goes on and on. So although two-way multitasking is a minor folly, asking people to work on three or more tasks borders on absurdity. Despite this knowledge, three-way multitasking is a common organizational practice.

Clearly, companies save time and money by single-tasking. Smith and Reinertsen (1991) argue that "spreading available resources across multiple projects insures that none of the projects will get done as quickly as it could if it was staffed full-time" (p. 128). Kopelman and Voegtli (1998) further point out that when people work full time on one project, companies will avoid many misunderstandings and instances of dropped information, notorious time wasters on any project. Because less information is lost due to loss of focus, companies get a bonus in increased quality when they single-task. So it seems that single-tasking decreases time, decreases total cost, and increases quality. A winner! So why is it such an anathema to many organizations? One problem is that it looks expensive, so it is often resisted by upper managers. A person may finish Task A on Wednesday and not be able to start Task B until Monday and so have two days unassigned. That is two days of salary with no task, which looks like a waste of money. From a financial viewpoint it seems that if the person had been assigned another task on another project, the company would not be wasting this money. As a result, people are multitasked, and things slow down, but that slowdown does not show up on the ledger. The crux of the problem seems to be that single-tasking increases the rate of expense, which does show up on the ledger, in order to decrease the total time, which does not show up on the ledger. In most organizations, what gets counted is what counts, and because cost is usually counted more than time, the cost argument usually wins. Now it may be that because the higher expense for single-tasking is for fewer months, the total costs are less than they would be for multitasking. But even if the total costs are less, this practice still looks more expensive as the costs are incurred, and for seemingly no good reason because saving time does not count. Therefore, to the financial manager without the long-term view, single-tasking looks like a loser, and it is resisted. Once again, another good management principle is sacrificed due to a short-term financial focus.

In addition to misplaced financial values, the realities of organizational life often seem to dictate poor management practices. Organizational veterans point out that the downside of single-tasking is the possibility of not getting some projects done at all. Organizational dynamics dictate that it often is better to get started, get something going, show some results, and then add people later as the project attracts more resources. This process increases time and decreases quality, but at least it gets something done. To get started under these circumstances typically requires multitasking people who are on other projects. Multitasking can thus be seen as a device to get around poor management of the organization as a whole, and because so many organizations are so poorly managed, it has become a popular technique.

Despite the popularity of and apparent necessity for poor management practices, the project manager interested in reducing cycle time should continue to argue for full-time team members. When this really cannot be done, the next best option is to have temporary team members who work on the one project only. The most practical and workable approximation is to have full-time core team members directing temporary project team members who are working on that project only.

Co-Locate Team Members

The project team is a multifunctional team whose members are not used to working together. They require much communication among themselves in order to develop as a team. Presumably, the more communication they have, the faster they will develop as a team, and the shorter the project will be. Co-location increases communication and thus decreases project duration.

The usual citation for this result is the Allen (1977) study showing that colleagues sitting forty meters apart had only a 5 percent probability of communicating at least once a week. The percentage did not increase until the distance was reduced to eight meters. Co-located team members overhear conversations, join in, and end up collaborating more closely.

Many organizations have benefited from co-locating project team members. For example, Intel employees working on the same product are purposely placed at the same office location (Kopelman and Voegtli, 1998). Smith (1999) relates that "Chrysler spent over $1 billion on a new development center that allows them to co-locate their development teams, a potent tool to accelerate decision making" (p. 225). General Motors has built a facility to co-locate four engineering groups that previously had been separated by fifty miles, making meetings difficult to schedule. Decisions that once took six weeks to resolve can now be settled in a few minutes, solved on the way to lunch, with a time savings of 99.99 percent (Smith and Reinertsen, 1991).

The need for co-location increases when the project outcome is new to the organization. Research by Kessler and Chakrabarti (1999) points out that team member proximity is more important for radical development projects than for incremental development projects. It indicates that more frequent face-to-face communication enables more rapid feedback, decoding, and synthesis of complex information. Information synthesis is particularly needed during the "fuzzy front end" of radical development projects. Frequent face-to-face communication is less important for the more familiar tasks of incremental development projects. Thus most of the benefits of co-location seem to be realized in those projects with a high degree of uncertainty concerning the nature of the final project outcome.

When co-location is not possible, its benefits can be approximated by having a team meeting room, regular core team meetings, and rapid prototyping. All of these practices encourage face-to-face communication and can help in reducing cycle time.

Develop Upper-Management Support

An important cause of project failure is lack of upper-management support. Upper managers and departmental managers must commit continual support or project leadership will unravel. Leadership is always at its best at the beginning, as upper managers make their commitments for the good of the project. However, as the project proceeds, upper-management support often begins to disintegrate. Upper managers may change the project manager, yank people off the core team, renege on full-time commitments, take away meeting space or budget or both, and so forth. Slowly, almost imperceptibly, one by one, decisions are made that negate the project manager's ability to create a project outcome that will increase shareholder value. Each upper manager will have perfectly valid reasons for making his or her one little change. Each manager will argue that the change will not affect the project outcome "that much." It may well be that each individual decision will not effect the project "that much," but the sum total of the changes is often a disaster, a disaster caused by upper managers but usually blamed on the project manager.

Project managers have difficulty fighting off these incursions as the assailants are, by definition, higher in the organization. Thus the most important leadership factor is the presence of an upper-level project champion, an upper manager who is committed to project success and who can stop others from endangering that success.

Implementation of Best Practices for Reducing Cycle Time

The best practices for reducing cycle time are so well understood and so well known that you would think they would be common practices in most organizations. However, that is not the case. For example, a recent survey by the Bourton Group (1999) on a cross-section of British companies found that *project management* tends to be weak, with little monitoring or measurement: Teaming is accepted as inherently essential, but there is no trend toward co-located multifunctional teams. Likewise, less than 10 percent of respondents "always" use a dedicated resource. Another study done of some of the premier firms in the United States, firms known to have good project management practices, revealed that use of most of the best practices for reducing cycle time scored below the average usage of all the project management practices employed in those firms (Graham, Englund, and Cohen, 2000). The practice of having a core team scored the highest and above the average. However, even in these best practice organizations, lower-than-average usage scores were found for co-location, full-time team members, formally trained project managers, and upper-management understanding of project management processes. The lowest score regarded the practice of multitasking, and project team members routinely reported they were working on too many projects. Smith (1999) laments that even if a company does implement some of these practices, "all too often [it] places great emphasis on one project, gets its glamour story written up in a prominent trade magazine, then falls back to its former ways" (p. 222). This is behavior contradictory to the best interests of the organization, a sure sign of folly.

What could cause such behavior? According to Tuchman's analysis of folly (1984, p. 386), this type of behavior reveals that senior people in an organization are too busy attending to too many tasks, so that they cannot see clearly the right thing to do. Tuchman feels the modern leader deals with too many subjects and problems in too many areas to have a solid understanding of any of them. She sees that bureaucracy, "safely repeating today what it did yesterday, rolls on as ineluctably as some vast computer, which, once penetrated by error, duplicates it forever." Therefore it is imperative that project managers present the benefits of best practices in a way that upper managers will clearly and easily understand, and that means presenting them with the business results of those practices. Otherwise, the folly will continue.

Financial Results of Best Practices

In many industries, companies have been able to remove roughly half the time formerly needed for product development projects by using many of the project management practices we discuss here (Smith and Reinertsen, 1991, p. 2). Boeing used all these best practices and saved one-third of the time it would otherwise have taken to build its 777 aircraft. Hewlett-Packard reported saving half the time it would otherwise have taken for a new printer product, and Ingersoll-Rand (Kleinfeld, 1990) had a similar experience. Of course, part of these time savings were due to using new technology rather than to better management practices. However, even if we split the difference between better management practices and better technology, management practices can still be said to account for reducing cycle time by one-fourth.

The specific amount of time saved by successful organizations is not the most important number here. What is more important is for managers to realize that time can be saved with better management practices and to estimate for their own projects how much time they could save if they followed those practices and "did it right." In our experience project managers generally say they could cut a third to a half off of project duration if they were allowed to "do it right." That is, we ask them to estimate how long their project will take and then to estimate to what degree they have implemented the factors discussed here. If a project manager says that on a 16-month project he or she has 50 percent of the project best practices in place, that means he or she has already achieved one-half of the possible one-third to one-half time savings. Therefore, if this project manager were allowed to "do it right," he or she could reduce duration an additional one-sixth to one-fourth, another 2.65 to 4 months.

Of course, these time savings do not come without some costs. So next the project manager needs an estimate on cost: What would it cost in cash terms right now to "do it right"? This cost estimate will be used to compare the total project costs to "do it right" with the total project costs to "do it as usual" in order to see whether the time savings are worth the costs. In this comparison we emphasize the *total* project costs, as the costs per month will be higher for better management practices. The cost savings arise from the reduction in the duration of the project.

A quick decision aid can be derived by finding the *indifference point* between the higher costs–faster duration project and the lower cost–slower duration project. This is the point at which the total project costs for the faster project equals the total project costs for the slower project. As an example, consider, as Case 1, a 16-month project that costs X per month for total project cost of $16X$. For Case 2, double the cost per month to save one-fourth of that time, or 4 months. Case 2 is then a 12-month project, and each month costs $2X$, for a total cost of $12(2X) = 24X$. This second case is not desirable from a cost standpoint, as both the monthly project costs and the total project costs are higher than the costs for the first case. Now consider a third case in which there is only a one-third increase in monthly project costs to get the 4-month reduction. In this case each month now costs $4/3X$ and the project lasts for 12 months, so the total project costs will be the same as for the first case, namely $12((4/3)X) = 16X$. This indifference point indicates if "doing it right" costs less than a third more per month, the project will not only get done faster but will cost less. Of course this does not take into account the possible sales increase or other value attained by getting done faster, which will be covered in next chapter. In this chapter we concentrate solely on the project investment.

To find the general formula for all projects, let monthly project costs, PC, start at \$$X$ per month. Further, let the length of the project, PN, start at N months. The formula for total project costs, TPC, then is $TPC = PC \times PN = N \times X$. Now assume you know you can apply best practices to save one-fourth of the project duration, so that the length of the project, PN, is now $3/4N$. How much more should you be willing to spend per month for that duration reduction? Let's try the one-third cost increase illustrated earlier.

In this new case, $PC = 4/3X$ and $PN = 3/4N$, so the total project costs will be $TPC = PC \times PN = (4/3X) \times (3/4N) = NX$, the same as the first case. Thus the general indifference point formula is that in order to save a percentage of time, P, such that new project duration is now $(1-P)N$, you are willing to spend at least $1/(1-P)$ more per month. At that cost per month, the old total project cost was NX, and the new project cost is also NX.

As an example of using this formula, determine how much more you should be willing to spend per month in order to reduce cycle time by one-third. Let $P = 1/3$. Then to save one-third of the time you should be willing to spend $1/(1-(1/3)) = 3/2$, or half again as much, so that $TPC = (2/3N) \times (3/2X) = NX$. Similarly, assume you want to reduce cycle time 20 percent. With $P = 0.2$, the cost factor is equal to $1/(1-0.2) = 1.25$. Thus you should be willing to spend 25 percent more per month to get the same total cost as $TPC = (0.8N) \times (1.25X) = NX$.

The indifference point formula gives you a quick estimate of the relationships between time and cost. However, completing a project faster may be worthwhile even if the cost is above the indifference point. This is because there are additional benefits to faster cycle time.

Business Systems Example for Project Cost Analysis

In this section we examine some of the effects of faster cycle time, of "doing it right," on project costs. Continuing our earlier examples, assume that you are managing a 16-month project that has 50 percent of the good management practices in place. So you already have one-half of the one-third to one-half time savings that you think are possible. If you are allowed to "do it right," you can reduce duration another one-sixth to one-fourth, or another 2.65 to 4 months. Now let's say that in Case 1 you would conduct this project with 5 core team members and 25 project team members, each person being paid \$100,000 per year and working three-quarters time on the project for 16 months. The total cost per month would be $187,500, with a total project cost of $3,000,000. In Case 2, you have the same people at the same salaries, but you suggest putting everyone in one building and on full time to get the project done in 12 months. With everyone working on the project full time, you increase the monthly project cost to $250,000 per month for salaries, which is the indifference point in order to get the one-quarter time reduction, as total salaries are still $3,000,000. In addition, let's say the company imposes a "moving charge" on the project of $20,000.

Now you might no doubt get stern looks from your accountant both for increasing monthly project costs and spending $20,000 unnecessarily. However, even from a financial standpoint this is a good deal. In Chapter Seven we will explain in more detail about the capital charge, what the company charges the project for the use of money based on the company's cost of capital. In the "do it right" case, Case 2, you will be using more money but for less time, so the finance charge may be less than it would have been. Assume a yearly finance rate of 12 percent. This equals a monthly charge of 1 percent. In Case 1, the capital charge for the first month would be $187,500 \times .01 = $1,875. In Case 2, the capital charge would be $250,000 \times .01 = $2,500. In addition, because the cost of the project is not repaid until the project outcome brings in enough net cash to pay back the cost of the project, the capital charge must be paid on a cumulative basis. That is, every month you pay a capital charge for the money "on loan" that month, but the money on loan includes not only that month's costs but all the costs of the months before, because that money is still on loan to your project. Figure 4.2 shows the charges for the first three months of Case 1.

The first month you are charged for salaries plus the capital charge for that month. The second month the principle amount outstanding includes this month's salaries plus the salaries and capital charge from the first month, so the monthly charge increases. The third month the principle outstanding includes this month's salaries plus the salaries and capital charges from the first two months, so

FIGURE 4.2. PROJECT COSTS AND CAPITAL CHARGES FOR CASE 1.

	Principle	Finance at 1%/Month	Monthly Charge	Cumulative Charge
Month 1	$187,500	$1,875	$189,375	$189,375
Month 2	187,500+189,375= 376,875	3,768.75	191,268.75	380,643.75
Month 3	187,500+380,643.75= 568,143.75	5,681.44	193,181.44	573,825.19

the monthly charge increases again. The charges continue on in this way until the project is over. If this were a three-month project, the total amount the organization would have paid out for the project would be the last entry in the cumulative column, $573,825. Continuing on this way for 16 months (see the business systems calculator output in Figure 4.4), Case 1 will cost a total of $3,268,208, whereas Case 2, running only 12 months, will cost only $3,202,332. This represents a saving of $65,876, more than enough to pay for that $20,000 move.

This should make the accountant happy as you have saved at least $45,000. An additional savings will happen during the period from the end of the project until breakeven as well, but we will discuss that in a later chapter. You have more than enough to convince the accountant to be happy. However, accountants are not normally given to merriment, so she or he will no doubt point out that the $20,000 moving charge must itself be financed. This represents an additional charge of $20,000 \times .01 = $200 per month, reducing your savings by $2,400 ($200 \times 12$), yielding a net saving of $43,476. Still, it's a good deal.

This example shows the basic idea of taking a business systems approach to evaluating alternatives. From a cost standpoint it looked like the idea of moving people together and having them work full-time was not cost effective due to the $20,000 moving charge. In an organization that maintained tight budget control, this good management idea could have been rejected out of hand as too costly and "not in the budget," another good management idea sacrificed to short-term financial considerations. However, when considering the capital charge, this idea becomes a cost saving as well as a good time-saving idea.

As we discussed at the beginning of this chapter, project managers have often thought arguing good project management principles to financial managers akin to casting pearls before swine. However, if you can show that these principles also save money, there is a better chance they will be adopted. Many times we have heard project managers say, "Oh, if they would only let me do my job," after financial considerations have stopped good project management. Taking the business systems approach allows project managers to show the benefits of good management to financial managers using their numbers and their system, in essence beating them at their own game. The accountants are finally hoist on their own petard, and good management can prevail.

Using the Calculator for Project Cost Analysis

To this point we have developed Case 1 and Case 2 as shown in Figure 4.3. Figure 4.4 shows the input-output screen of the on-line calculator as it would look after calculating costs for Case 1.

To use the calculator for this case, you would go first to the *project* section of the screen and key in $3,000,000 for *project salaries* and 16 for *project duration*. Fur-

FIGURE 4.3. PROJECT INVESTMENT WITH CAPITAL CHARGES FOR TWO CASES.

	Case 1	Case 2*
Total project investment	$3,000,000	$3,020,000
Project duration	16 months	12 months
Project investment with capital charge	$3,268,208	$3,225,030
Difference from Case 1		$45,178

*The total investment for Case 2 now includes the $20,000 moving charge, and the investment with capital charge reflects the added capital charge for that amount.

FIGURE 4.4. CALCULATION OF COSTS FOR CASE 1.

Project

Project duration		16
Total project salaries		$3,000,000
Total project investment (including other expenses)		$3,000,000
Project investment with capital charge		$3,268,208

Market demand

Length of time until the market for this product begins	(months)	12
Length of time after introduction to peak of market	(months)	24
Length of time after peak of market ends	(months)	20
Sales volume at market maturity	(units/month)	20,000

Revenues

Price	($/unit)	$300.00
Price deterioration	(%/year)	5%
Expected market share if first to market	(%)	30%
Expected market share otherwise	(%)	20%

Costs

Costs of goods sold	($/unit)	$240.00
Cost reduction	(%/year)	8%
Selling, general and administration (variable)	(% of revenues)	0%
Selling, general and administration (fixed)	($/month)	
Depreciation	($/month)	—
Other expenses	($/month)	—
Tax rate	(%)	0%
Company WACC	(%/year)	12%

Breakeven

Approximate time to breakeven	(months)	36

Net cash flow (NCF)

Period of time to be considered in NCF calculation	(months)	55
Net cash flow without capital charges		$2,307,564
Net cash flow with capital charges		$1,542,988
Net present value		$991,587

ther down, under *costs*, ensure that the WACC entry is set at 12, for a 12 percent finance rate. Also ensure that selling, general and administration, depreciation, other expenses, and the tax rate are set to zero. We are not considering tax consequences in these examples.

Looking back to the project section you will see the result $3,268,208 in the box labeled *project investment with capital charge*. The shaded boxes on the input-output screen are output, the results of the input numbers. Thus the project investment with capital charge box shows the result of the continuation for sixteen months of the calculations shown in Figure 4.2. The numbers in Figure 4.3 for Case 2 were also obtained from the calculator. (In this chapter we are concerned only with the project section of the calculator. The other sections are covered in subsequent chapters.)

At this point, Case 1 is somewhat more expensive than Case 2, so the move does look worthwhile from a cost standpoint. However, before accepting the move we should first consider the effect of the move on potential income. We turn to that topic in Chapter Five.

Examples

The Newprod and Newsys projects also begin looking at the benefits of best practices.

Newprod Project

You and your Newprod team members examine options for adding the new feature a team member had suggested. Then the team meets and decides to add the feature, even though it will require a one-month delay in completing the product. This will cost $250,000 more in salaries plus an extra month's capital charge, for a total project cost with capital charge of $3,401,000. You and the team arrive at this figure by using the business systems calculator, putting in 13 for the number of months and $3,250,000 for salary costs. Because the original project cost with capital charge was $3,128,400, this new feature represents a cost increase of $272,600. Alternatively, the feature could be developed by an outside firm for a cost of $500,000 and then integrated into the final product with no delay. But from a cost standpoint it looks like the current team should work on the new feature, and the financial manager favors that. However, as schedule is more important than costs due to strategic focus, you favor the outside firm. The marketing manager on the core team thinks it might be a disaster to delay one month. At a standstill, you delay the decision until you and the team have looked at market factors (as covered in the next chapter).

Newsys Project

You and your Newsys project team feel the project is already using all the best project management practices, so you continue on to estimating revenue (as covered in the next chapter).

FIGURE 5.1. BUSINESS SYSTEMS DIAGRAM.

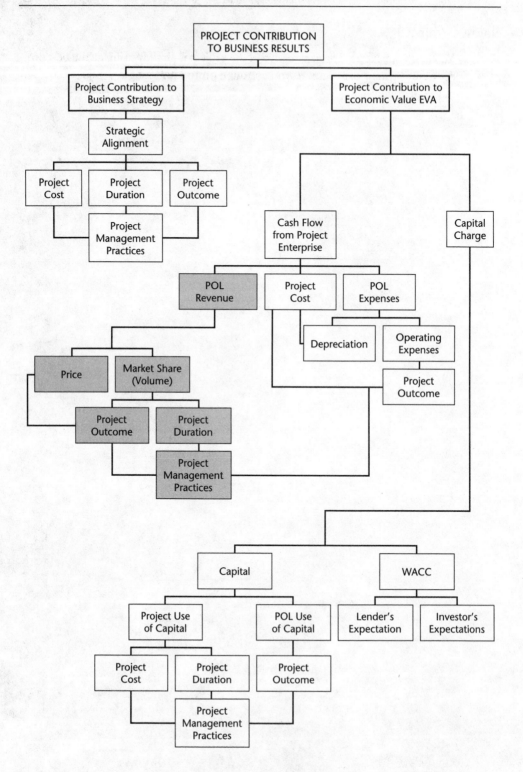

CHAPTER FIVE

MARKETING AND
THE PROJECT MANAGER

Understanding the Customer
and the Competition Too

For my thoughts are not your thoughts,
neither are your ways my ways

ISAIAH, 55:8

In this chapter we examine the revenue side the project, the cash flow that will be generated by the project outcome, along with the decisions that project managers may make during the project that can affect that revenue. The major themes of the chapter are crafting the project outcome for market performance and timing that outcome for maximum cash flow. That is, we will examine the process for developing a project outcome that solves problems for and meets the needs of the intended users and that delivers that outcome when the intended users are ready for it. As discussed in Chapter One, these themes take the place of the outcome and schedule constraints that were prevalent when project management had a more technical emphasis. These new themes move project management toward a market and business emphasis, which we reflect in this chapter. The dual emphasis is essential because a business orientation emphasizes cash flow, and all cash income comes from the sale or use of the project outcome in a market.

The contents of this chapter will help the project manager to better understand that marketplace and positively influence the cash flow resulting from the project outcome. New product development projects are clearly linked to the market. However, all project outcomes from all types of projects ultimately end up in the market. For internal projects the immediate customer may be another department in the same organization, but the end-user, the person who ultimately benefits from the project outcome, will be the customer of the organization. The same is true for client engagement projects. The immediate customer is the client, but the ultimate end-user will be the customers of that client. The results of all projects end up competing in a marketplace.

Crafting an outcome for market performance is a process of understanding the customer and developing an outcome that the customer wants and will purchase. Crafting for market performance implies an intimate knowledge of the customer and of the market for the project outcome. Understanding the competitive forces in the market is an important aspect of this knowledge. In the past, caught up in technical features of projects, project managers often neglected to focus on the combination of customer, competition, and market dynamics. The shift to emphasizing market performance thus opens up a new and crucial area for project manager knowledge. This chapter focuses on marketing issues most important to the project manager: determining who the potential customers are and what they want; learning who the competitors are and what they offer; understanding the trade-offs among the product performance attributes of benefits, features, and price; and determining the timing for market introduction. We define these important functions and show how project decisions (made with the assistance of the business systems calculator) can affect both the project outcome and the ultimate economic profit.

The shaded portions of Figure 5.1 indicate the marketing areas in the business systems diagram. The first step to generating revenue is to design products, services, or processes that help customers solve problems (the project outcome benefits) and that meet or exceed customers' expectations. As we have mentioned, these results are what we call the features of the project outcome. Project outcomes that solve problems better than the competition's project outcomes do influence customer demand, or market share. Customer demand is also influenced by the total market demand, and a company's share of that market is influenced by both the project outcome and the project duration. Normally, although not always, the faster a project is completed, the better position a company is in to capture market share. When this is the case, the market share of the project outcome is very sensitive to project duration. Customer demand and price determine revenue, a source of cash for cash flow. Features of the product outcome affect project costs, the cost of producing the project outcome, and the cost of goods sold, all of which are uses of cash. Sources of cash and uses of cash, as we explained in Chapter Two, are important factors in determining the cash flow that is the project's contribution to economic value.

Marketing Considerations for Project Managers

Project managers have often had a nebulous view of marketing and have often equated marketing with sales. The project manager's emphasis was usually on producing the final product, not selling it, and his or her reward was based on that production work too. If the project outcome needed to be marketed and sold, that was someone else's problem. The design for the product often came from some internal assumptions about what would sell. One implicit assumption was often "if we build it they will buy it." This assumption has often proved false, however. One example of such a failure was the Iridium project, which intended to use satellite technology to provide global telephone service. Although there were several reasons for the failure of this project, Lohr (2000) feels that a fundamental problem was that "Iridium had the old mentality—build it and we will force people to use it—as opposed to—is there a market for this anyway" (p. Bu-4).

When these "if we build it they will come" assumptions proved faulty on many projects, it became clear that more thought had to be given to marketing. One early solution was to put a marketing person on the core team. This does serve to increase the team's knowledge and understanding of customer and market issues. However, because marketing processes are now so tightly intertwined with the project outcome, and because the results of marketing are so important in the new definition of project success, the project manager too needs a greater understanding of marketing.

This does not mean that the project manager takes over all marketing functions connected with the project outcome but rather that the project manager becomes involved in those marketing functions we identified earlier as important to project managers: identifying what the customer or end-user really wants, understanding the competition, making trade-offs between features and price or cost, and determining the timing of project completion (product introduction). The project manager must understand these functions because the project team must make decisions in these areas during the course of the project, and these decisions will affect the success of the project outcome.

For our purposes, then, we define marketing as those procedures that help the project manager get to know the market. The market consists of those customers that may buy the final product, the end-users that will use it, the problems these people are trying to solve, and the competitors who are offering solutions to the same problems for the same customers and end-users. The processes of marketing increase the project manager's ability to craft a project outcome that solves customer problems better than the competition's product can. If this can be done, the final outcome will have the competitive advantage, and that advantage will increase the potential for sales or use of that outcome.

Marketing is necessary for all types of projects. The need for it may be most obvious in new product development projects. However, for client engagement projects too, marketing knowledge will help ensure that the final product meets the needs of the end-user in the client organization. What the client does with the product is no longer "their problem" but rather "your problem." For internal projects, marketing processes help ensure adoption and use of the project outcome within the organization. In a broader sense, good marketing should also help both client engagement and internal projects to focus on the ultimate market and the competition. This will help the client produce its own best outcome in turn to sustain its competitive advantage and ensure that internal projects are enabling the organization to be competitive.

In short, marketing savvy is important to project managers because

- Sales and sources of cash are an important component of the cash flow that will be used to determine project success.
- Market performance will soon be, if it is not already, considered in the project manager's evaluation.
- Market knowledge can help with decision making during the project; potential product features can be evaluated in light of market considerations and the features' likely effect on cash flow.
- Market knowledge can improve the functioning of the project team as team members learn how customers will use the product.
- Projects may attract more resources when the project manager can show the potential size of the market.
- Market knowledge can help define product quality; knowledge of customer expectations can help the project manager identify and argue against management decisions that are detrimental to quality.

Crafting for Market Performance: Market Segments and Competition

One of the first questions that must be asked in any project is, What is the market? We suggest thinking of the market as a set of customer needs or problems that you can satisfy or solve, along with a set of competitors who are trying to do the same thing. A project outcome is crafted for *market performance* when that outcome enables the company to solve customer problems better than the competition can (cheaper, faster, more effectively or efficiently, and so forth). Size, segmentation, and competition can further describe the market.

Size

How big is the market? For new product projects the size of the market is the total annual sales of this type of product to all market segments. For in-house projects the size of the market could be considered the total number of end-users, that is, organizational customers who will be affected by the project results. For client engagement projects the size of the market is the number of client customers who will be affected by the project outcome.

Segmentation

What part of the market is the target? All markets are composed of various segments. These segments are usually defined by customer attributes. For example, the market for clothing can be divided into such segments as male or female, young or old, high fashion or casual, and so on. When crafting for market performance, the project manager should understand which segment the project is aimed at and work to ensure the project outcome is aligned with that segment. A common cause of project scope creep is the attempt to have one product serve many segments. However, managers should pick one segment and stick to it. Experience shows that projects that try to be all things to all people end up being nothing to nobody.

Most markets can be segmented by price sensitivity coupled with the quality and performance expectations of the customers in that segment. For example, the market for hotel rooms is highly segmented. At the high end are luxury hotels and resorts catering to customers with low price sensitivity but high expectations for quality and performance. Midrange hotels cater to business travelers and those to whom price is less important than quality and performance. Low-range hotels cater to the budget traveler. Each segment requires a differentiated product, and no one product will appeal to all segments. Therefore management must choose the segment of the market your project will address and you must stick to it, remembering that a hotel designed to appeal to all three of the major hotel market segments will probably sell in none.

In addition, the segment chosen should match the organizational strategy. Using the hotel segmentation of high-end, middle, and low-end, it seems that it would be difficult to compete in a high-end segment with an operational excellence strategy. High-end customers will most likely require a customer intimacy strategy, whereas the low-end customers may be reachable only with an operational excellence strategy. This is a further illustration of why knowledge of strategy is so important to project managers. Matching project outcome features to strategy allow them to segment the market and focus on that segment. They then follow the advice of Treacy and Wiersema (1995) to choose your customers, narrow your focus, and dominate your market.

Once you determine the relevant market segment, the next step is to determine the potential overall size of that segment and the potential total sales volume per year for it. To determine the potential sales volume, you need to determine your project outcome's potential share of that total market segment. That determination requires knowledge of the competition for that segment.

Competition

Who is in pursuit of the same segment? The relevant competition consists of organizations that are aiming at the same segment with a similar strategy and with solutions to the same problems. Knowledge of these competitors is essential in determining the outcome feature set, price, and potential volume. The idea of competitive advantage requires that you know the competition, that you can rate how your solution to customers' problems compares to competitors' solutions, and that you can explain this difference to potential customers. In addition, knowledge of competitors' prices can help you set your estimated price as prices are normally set—by market conditions rather than by the cost to create and produce the product. Price and volume estimates are essential for estimating cash flow (and for using the business systems calculator).

The potential volume, your share of the market segment chosen, will also be determined in part by competitor actions. Thus you need knowledge of your competitors to begin to predict their actions and reactions. Of course, competitor actions and reactions cannot be predicted exactly, but you can gain insight by analysis. Chance does favor the prepared mind.

The first step in competitive analysis is to draw up a list of competitors. The contents of this list will depend on how you define the market in the first place. For example, if a car company were to define its market as American-made automobiles, then its competitors would be the big three U.S. automakers. If it defines its market as automobiles in general, a host of foreign automakers enter the competitor list. And if it defines its market as transportation vehicles in general, competitors abound. Coca-Cola is an example of a company that has broadened the horizon of its product teams by defining competitors as producers of all types of drinks, not just Pepsi.

In the next step in competitive analysis, the core team members agree on who the competitors are and assign individuals to monitor specific competitors' actions. Agreeing on competitors will solidify an image of the marketplace in the minds of core team members. Assigning individuals to monitor the actions of specific competitors will further solidify this image. It may also turn up some interesting information that might otherwise have been overlooked. When a person has a specific organization to monitor, it is amazing how much news he or she notices about that firm. It is similar to the way investors will notice company information once they own that company's stock. They read articles that they would have missed before, see information that they would have overlooked before, and study advertisements that they would have ignored before to see what the company or its rivals are saying. Similar close attention can yield a wealth of information about the potential actions and reactions of a project's competitors.

It is also important to keep up with competitors' technological developments and new products that may be substitutes for your product. The failure of Iridium is again instructive. Lohr (2000, p. Bu-4) posits that Iridium failed partially because it was blindsided by the rapid growth in ground-based competition. While the Iridium project sputtered with delays, ground-based wireless phone service grew at an astonishing rate. Business travelers, the main market segment for Iridium's service, found they could use their cell phones in most major cities around the world. An understanding of this development could have led to a product redesign and perhaps a more successful project. This shows how understanding competitors' developments can be important to project success.

Finally, it is important to try to identify what new competitors might look like, competitors unknown to your company at this time, as Amazon.com was to Barnes and Noble. How easy is it to become a competitor? What are the barriers to entry? Are those barriers changing? Most important, try to think like a new competitor. If you were going to start a new firm to compete with your project outcome, what would you do? The principle of relentless competition indicates that if it is possible for someone to start a firm to compete with your project outcome, then there is someone doing that right now. Whatever you would do to compete is probably what some other firm is doing. Assign someone on the core team to look for signs of someone doing that. As Intel chairman Andrew Grove (1996) says, "Only the paranoid survive."

With all this information you can begin to monitor competitors' actions and reactions and to build a model of their behavior. Your core team marketing member will be most important here. What is each competitor's strategy? What does it see as its competitive advantage? Will it try to beat you on price, service, features, or some other issue? How do you think the competitor will respond to your combination of price and features? Again, the principle of relentless competition indicates that whatever price-feature combination you offer will be immediately matched by the competition. The way airlines match each other's fares is a good example of this phenomenon. You have to be ready to match whatever competitors offer if you feel it is of value to people in your market segment. So competitor information is obviously important to know as you and your team make decisions that affect the price and features of the project outcome.

Crafting for Market Performance: Understanding the Customer

Information about customers and end-users is also important in defining the appropriate price-feature combination for the project outcome. Unfortunately, managers of technical projects and also project team members often seem to have a sort of love-hate relationship with customers and end-users of the project outcome. On the one hand they love them because they ultimately pay the bill for the outcome, not to mention the team members' salaries. On the other hand we have heard many team members complain, and one of us remembers complaining himself in his youth, that customers are such a pain. They do not really know what they want. They are forever changing their minds. They do not know the latest technology; they do not appreciate the wizardry of our solutions. Jeez, they are just so dumb!

The business-oriented project manager needs to change this type of thinking when it exists in the core team and the project team. Crafting for market performance requires understanding, not disdain. You should assume that most of the assumptions just stated about customers are true, except the last one—they are not dumb. Yes, they don't know what they want, but that's why you are there, to show them solutions to their problems. Yes, they change their minds, but don't we all? This characteristic is actually in your favor as your job is to change their minds in your direction. And, yes, they do not know the latest technology or appreciate the wizardry of your solutions. But expect technical kudos from your colleagues, not your customers. Customers care most about how well their problem has been solved and only secondarily about the technology used to solve it.

Disdain for the customer does not appear just among people working on new product development projects. People working on internal projects often display ample disdain for people in other departments of the same organization. And people working on client projects often think the client is not too bright. This is an important problem that the project manager must tackle. The project manager must change any feeling of disdain to one of understanding of and empathy for the problems of the customer.

Kotter (1990) gives an example of how important team member participation in understanding the customer is in project success. He tells of Jim Adamson, a project manager who turned around the NCR ATM plant in Dundee, Scotland, moving it from a facility near closing to a world leader in the manufacture of ATMs and other self-service equipment. Adamson stressed that a key to new product success was "knowing the marketplace." He felt that groups of engineers should spend time visiting customers and potential customers. Visiting customers was not a normal activity for engineers, but with Adamson himself setting the pace on this issue, the engineers followed. The lesson for project managers is clear—for team members to develop empathy for the problems of the customer, they must get to know many customers, and the project manager must lead the way.

Who Is the Customer?

The *customer* is the person or organization that purchases the product outcome. Normally this is the person who is paying the bill for the outcome. For new product development projects the customers are the people who will buy the end product. For internal projects the customer may be another department in the organization or the organization itself. For client engagement projects the customer is the client who requests the engagement.

Because the people paying the bill are the customers, it is normally through them that the project manager is introduced to the problems to be solved. The customers represent the first level of people who must be satisfied with the project outcome. Sometimes these customers work in groups to make buying decisions. The person who makes the ultimate decision to buy may rely on a gatekeeper to screen prospects. There may be an additional economic customer who concentrates on price and value and a technical customer who has veto power over technical issues. However, all these customers usually define their needs based on the needs of another group of people, the end-users.

Who Is the End-User?

Often the person paying the bill is not the person who will actually use the project outcome. For example, in the market for low- to medium-priced canned condensed soup, most is purchased to give to someone else. Most soup is given to children or to elderly parents or used in a dish to feed the family. The purchasers do not usually intend to eat the soup themselves, at least not directly as soup. Thus there is often a big difference between the customer and the *end-user.*

The person who uses or benefits from the project outcome is the end-user. Ultimately, this is the person who must be satisfied with the project outcome. Although it is important to know and to please the customer, it is even more important to know and to please the end-user. This is an important distinction that project managers may miss. Concentrating on the customer gives one point of view about problems to be solved, but the end-user has another point of view. Listening only to customers and solving their problems may not necessarily solve the problems of the end-users, yet those are the most important problems to be solved.

What Are Their Problems?

Customers and end-users gain value when using product features to solve problems. When determining a feature set, it is often a mistake to focus only on features as though they existed in a vacuum. The project manager should focus on the benefits and value that arise when the features solve problems. For every feature ask, What is the purpose of this feature? What is the overall value proposition for the customer? How would customers define this feature in a solution to a problem?

Customers and end-users may assume they want a certain feature, but it may be that another approach or another feature would be even better for their purpose. The project manager may not think of that approach or that feature because of customer input or may reject the approach because of a focus on feature. But a focus on problems and the way customers and end-users gain value may reveal an important feature. The core team should line up features with problems and experiment with various features that may solve problems differently and better. You may be able to avoid problems if you set up a matrix with features as one dimension and benefits as the other and place an X in the intersection of benefits supported by features. If any feature lacks a cell with an X showing that it supports a benefit, it is probably unnecessary. If any benefit lacks a cell with an X showing that a feature supports it, you and your team have probably missed something. Figure 5.2 is an example of such a matrix for a project to develop a new camera.

Always remember when dealing with new products with new features and new benefits, just because customers or end-users say that something is so does not mean it necessarily is so. For example, some of the first answering machines had no query feature for picking up messages remotely because initially the majority of people did not like answering machines at all. When most people first encountered answering machines, they were uncomfortable and would hang up and call again later. (Although we have now come full circle. Now some people are irritated when a real person answers!) Because they did not like the machine itself, they did not want the remote query feature, and some initial versions of the machine did not have it. But once people saw how the query feature solved problems, how they could get messages when they were on the road, everyone wanted the remote query feature. So sometimes the project team needs to build a prototype feature and put it into end-users' hands in order to get an accurate reading on the end-users' problems and the real benefits of a particular feature.

Relying on market research to define end-users' problems can also lead to misperceptions. A major chemical company, for example, built a useless fertilizer plant because it did not understand the problems of the end-user (Cohen and Kuehn, 1996). The kind of fertilizer the company made was the kind least preferred by farmers, but it was selling well at the time the company did its market research because there was a fertilizer shortage. But by the time the company was ready to enter this market, there was a fertilizer surplus, and farmers were no longer buying this type of fertilizer. The company would not have made this error if it had

FIGURE 5.2. NEW CAMERA PROJECT: BENEFITS AND FEATURES.

Benefits	Features		
	Automatic Exposure	High-Fashion Case (*feature without a benefit*)	High-Quality Lens
Easy to use	X		
Can take it anywhere (*benefit without a feature*)			
Takes great pictures	X		X

truly understood the needs of the end-user. Relying on market research is not enough. The project core team should be ready to become very familiar with real live end-users.

What Are Their Requirements?

Determining customers' and end-users' problems is one thing, and determining the product requirements that fit those problems is quite another. Project team members tend to jump to solutions before really understanding customer and end-user requirements. A major reason they do this is that the process of determining requirements is ambiguous and fuzzy at best. Technical project team members in particular are often repelled by fuzzy situations and want to get on with the project. As a result the process of determining requirements is not given the time it deserves.

The main cause of the fuzziness is that team members need to get requirements from customers and end-users, but these customers and end-users do not always know what they want. Gauss and Weinberg (1989, p. 24) have identified these sources of ambiguity among customers and end-users:

- Observation: variations in what people see or hear
- Recall: variations in what people remember
- Interpretation: variations in how people interpret important happenings
- Problem understanding: variations in how people interpret in their own minds the problem to be solved

Adding to this individual ambiguity is the typical organizational problem of involving people serially in problem definition. This source of ambiguity is epitomized by the game of Whisper Down the Lane. Robert Graham experienced an example of it at A Tremendous Telephone Company (call it ATT for short). The problems to be solved were those of a group of end-users at a Gigantic Motor Company (GMC) who wanted better telephone service. These end-users told their problems to an information manager at GMC. This person became the customer, and interpreted the end-user problems to a sales representative from ATT. This salesperson then explained his own interpretation of the information manager's interpretation of the problems to someone from engineering, who then reinterpreted the end-users' problems to the designers, who went to work to develop the requirements for a solution.

This process was rife with opportunities for ambiguity. To begin with, the end-users experienced the typical observation, recall, interpretation, and problem understanding variations in identifying their problems. Then there were four handoffs—to the customer, to sales, to engineering, and to design. At each step, people added interpretation ambiguity as they passed along requirements. To estimate how much information is lost in this kind of serial involvement, assume that the initial problem statement is only 80 percent accurate, and that you lose 20 percent of that information on each handoff. Then this formula determines the amount of the necessary information actually passed on through the chain: $(0.8)(0.8)(0.8)(0.8)(0.8) = 33\%$. No wonder designs so rarely match end-user needs. The needs of the end-user are lost in the process. Part of the solution is for the core team to get together directly with customers and end-users. This helps eliminate Whisper Down the Lane problem. In many organizations, however, having engineers sit down directly with customers and end-users is simply not done. There is no organizational protocol for it. The project team needs to get past this problem.

How to Get to End-Users

To begin, it is best to have the entire core team talk to customers and end-users, not just the marketing member. This way you get different points of view on what end-users are doing, what they need. Having everyone participate is also good for team building and for getting buy-in from all departmental representatives. A good example of this process comes from an Hewlett-Packard printer plant that sent only people from marketing to talk with end-users about printer functions (Graham and Englund, 1997). The marketing team discovered ten end-user needs, but the engineers rejected many of them. It was only when the engineers went to end-users together with the people from marketing that the engineers accepted that all the needs had to be met.

Here are four typical ways to get direct end-user input:

Put customers and end-users on the core team. New organizations today, especially with Web-based e-businesses, are partnering with end-users, customers, and suppliers in ways unheard of earlier. Organizations must be willing to bring representatives of these groups deep into their processes. This requires a degree of openness and transparency that is new to most commercial organizations. Many companies are reluctant to take on this level of involvement, release proprietary information, or show dirty laundry, but you have to be ready to open in order to develop a true understanding of end-user problems. Smith and Reinertsen (1991) identify an additional benefit of involving customers and end-users in writing project specifications. These people can often identify future trends. They can help project teams find lead users, the innovators who are eager for new products. They are the most demanding and have the best knowledge of existing solutions. Put these lead users on the core team.

Directly observe end-users' problems. It is amazing what you see when you look from the end-users' point of view. Direct observation allows the team to see what end-users are doing and also to see the problems. Again consider the NCR example from Kotter (1990). Because the ATMs the plant produced were failing, the project manager sent engineers out to observe people actually using ATMs. It was an important part of the turnaround that brought the plant from near bankruptcy to being a dominant player in the ATM market.

Another benefit of direct contact with end-users and customers is an increased ability to resist bad product ideas from other managers in the organization. In the case of the NCR ATM plant (Kotter, 1990), when people at headquarters felt they knew better about product design, the project manager could point to his market data and say, "What customer did you get your idea from? Mine comes from talking to these 50 customers" (p. 26). The project manager could show that he had become the expert on the market and design squabbles were minimized.

Develop focus groups to explain problems. Focus groups of end-users, working with a facilitator, can describe problems and evaluate feature solutions in ways that are very useful to core teams. Focus groups are normally discussion groups, so participants often are not actually using the product when they discuss features. These groups are good for evaluating ideas before they get into the production stage.

Develop prototypes to give end-users experience. To get true end-user evaluation there is nothing like putting a prototype product in end-users' hands. Lesch's law of product development is that "you never know what is going to sell until you try to sell it" (Smith and Reinertsen, 1991, p. 72). This law is often at odds with the designer or engineering mind-set. Designers and engineers may think they know what the customer *should* want, or feel that the customer should want it because they designed it. They may fall in love with their design and take offense when changes are suggested. To change this mind-set often requires designing prototypes for some end-users to try and then putting the entire core team in touch with these end-users. Sometimes a failed attempt acts like a prototype, as the Zoomer did for Palm computing, which went on to develop the Palm Pilot.

Understanding the Dynamics of Price in Relation to Features and Value

A good understanding of the market will help the core team not only to understand demand but also to help set the price. The price of a project outcome that is a product is not set by project costs but by the dynamics of the market. Some of the important factors are the type of project, project outcome features (which confer benefits), competitors, and time of market entry.

Type of Project

The price of the project outcome is set differently for different types of project. The client often sets the price paid for the project outcome of a client engagement project. When this is the case project costs become relatively more important as cash flow will be determined by revenue minus costs. However, the potential for additional benefits may be discovered as the project continues, and including these benefits may bring an increase in price and subsequent cash flow. A focus on costs alone may cause the core team to miss these benefits and cash flow opportunities. So the focus should be on cash flow.

For internal projects the price of the project outcome is essentially the project cost, with the cash flow being determined by the use of the project outcome within the organization. Again, additional benefits may be discovered as the project continues, and including these benefits may bring an increase in price but also increased cash flow to the organization. A focus on costs alone may cause the core team to miss these benefits and cash flow opportunities. So the focus should be on cash flow.

For new product development projects, price depends on the benefits yielded by the features (or *feature set*), the competition, and the time of market entry.

Benefits

One of the first determinants of price is the feature set, which yields benefits, or value, for which customers will pay. One important result of knowing customers and end-users well is learning what they will pay for various features. When determining an initial feature set or when evaluating an additional feature, one of the first questions should be, How much is the customer willing to pay for this? Of course a feature may be added for competitive reasons even if the customer is not willing to pay for it. However, in most cases project managers should be able to determine the price customers are willing to pay for various features. Project managers can do this when they know the benefits the customers and end-users will get because they know the problems customers and end-users are trying to solve.

Another way to think about pricing for a feature set is in terms of the supply and demand dynamics of the marketplace. When you raise the price of a product, it will lower the volume of sales, and vice versa. How will this affect the total revenue?

Here are some trade-offs between features and price. The cost of a feature is based on project uses of cash to develop it, production uses of cash to produce it, and possible lost sales from customers who are not willing to pay for it. This cost also includes the uses of cash to market the feature, service it, and maintain it. The sources of cash from a feature are the additional revenue from customers who are willing to pay for the feature (not only new customers attracted to a new feature but also customers who would buy whether the feature was available or not) and from preventing loss of sales to a competitor who has the feature. The decision to add a feature should begin by looking at these trade-offs. The first question should not be, Can we do it? but rather, Will it produce additional cash or prevent loss of cash? We show some more detailed examples of this at the end of this chapter.

Competitors

An important benefit of knowing your competitors is the ability to predict more accurately what they will offer in terms of price and feature set. Moreover, you can expect the price to decline over time due to competition, not only from other firms but also from other technologies or product concepts.

Market Entry Timing

It is well known that being first to market usually commands a premium price. As competitors enter the market, either the price decreases or the price stays constant as features increase. This has certainly been the experience in the personal computer market. If you are first to market, you can often set a premium price, and this premium alone is often enough to cover any additional expense incurred in producing the project outcome quickly. If you are following the leader with a similar feature set, the price will have been set for you, particularly if your strategy is operational excellence. If you have unique features, you may still be able to charge a premium price, until the competition follows your lead.

Some argue, however, that the cost of being first is exceedingly and increasingly expensive and that the cost cannot be covered by a premium price and longer sales life, so it is better to be a follower. As discussed later, the project manager must decide if being first to market is worth it. The decision will depend greatly on the strategic focus of the project. For customer intimacy or operational excellence strategies, the cost of being first may not pay off in increased economic value. However, if you have a product leadership strategy, you had better be first in order to cover the increased costs of being a market leader.

Also, because unit production costs are likely to decrease as more is learned about production of the product and because the longer the company produces the product the more these costs decrease, being first to market is also likely to result in a greater reduction of production costs.

Determining Market and Product Lifecycles

The *market potential* of a project outcome estimates how much of the total market the outcome will get and how much cash flow it will generate. This estimate depends in part on determining the "right" time for the project to be done or the product to be introduced. This time is a function of the concept lifecycle and project outcome lifecycle and also of your strategy and competitor reactions as they operate within those lifecycles.

Concept Lifecycle

Every product fits into a certain concept for solving a problem or achieving a result. For example, printing on paper has gone through a series of concepts for achieving that result. This series has included the scribe using a pen, the Gutenberg-style press with movable type, the Linotype, offset printing, the typewriter, the IBM Selectric, the daisy wheel printer, the impact (dot matrix) printer, the ink jet printer, and the laser printer. Each one of those concepts for printing has had a lifecycle and those organizations that introduced each concept and introduced products that fit the concept at the beginning of the lifecycle, had much more market potential than those introducing products at the end of the cycle. For example, anyone introducing a new dot matrix printer at this time would have essentially no market potential. In other words, the concept lifecycle defines the window of opportunity for the project outcome.

When a new concept, the laser printer for example, emerges for a given operation, sales are slow in the beginning as people do not know much about the new concept. As awareness increases, more people buy. Nevertheless, sales are still held up by Luddites, like Robert Graham, who cling to old dot matrix technology. Over time even Robert gives in and sales reach their maximum. But then a new concept emerges, page-at-a-time printing, and sales decrease. Given this pattern, end-users can be classified as innovators, early adopters, early majority, late majority, and laggards, as shown in Figure 5.3.

Innovators. The innovators are the first group of people to purchase any product and often seek it out before it is formally introduced. This is particularly true of new technology products, which innovators may buy to explore a device's properties, whether or not it solves any problem they have. This is a small group but important for establishing a beachhead for further product expansion. Without these innovators' endorsement there is little chance that later groups will buy. Consider, for example, the segment of early adopters for new electronic devices in the $500 price range. Members of this segment are primarily male and have an income of over $100,000 per year. They buy the device, and if they do not like it, they throw it away and tell no one. If they do like it, they use it and show all their friends. If you fail with these innovators in the electronic devices market in this price range, your product is dead.

Early adopters. The early adopters are not as enticed by new technology in itself but quickly see the benefits of the new product and understand how that product can help solve a problem. They base their buying decisions on how well the

FIGURE 5.3. CONCEPT ADOPTION CURVE.

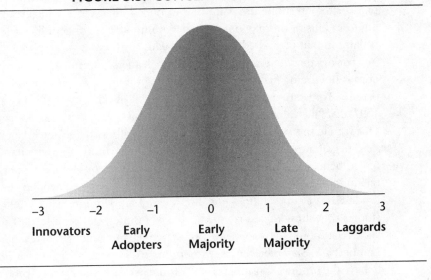

−3	−2	−1	0	1	2	3
Innovators		Early Adopters	Early Majority	Late Majority	Laggards	

product solves that problem rather than on endorsement by other users. This group shows the way for product application. The core team should remain intact at least until this stage is completed before handing the product over to the production manager, who has been on the team all along (Moore, 1999).

Early majority. Those adopters who are among the early majority also understand how the product can help solve a problem they have but will wait and see how others are making out before they buy themselves. This group likes to see an endorsement from others that the product does indeed work. This group comprises the buyers for about one-third of the product lifecycle.

Late majority. Buyers in the late majority need even more assurance than those in the early majority and will normally not buy until the product is established with support and experience. These people like all the bugs to be worked out of any product and support from those who have experienced the product and so tend to buy from large, experienced companies. Although product price starts decreasing with this group, so do production and selling expenses. This group also contains the buyers for about one third of the product lifecycle.

Laggards. These make up the group of people (often Luddites) who won't buy a product until everyone else has one. When this group starts to buy, the concept lifecycle is just about over, and the organization should be ramping up a new product.

Once you are familiar with the concept lifecycle idea, you can time the completion of your project within its concept lifecycle so that project outcome revenue is maximized. This timing replaces the old project deadline constraint. The technique is to determine the point in the concept lifecycle at which revenue will be highest. This point may be at the beginning of the concept lifecycle, or it may be later in that lifecycle. It depends on your strategy.

For organizations following a product leadership strategy, the traditional wisdom is that being first to market at the beginning of the concept lifecycle is imperative. For example, the Project Management Institute claims (Toney and Powers, 1997) that "the value of reducing time to market by one day is phenomenal" (p. 92). One firm in this study reduced cycle time from fifty-two to eighteen months so that sales began almost three years earlier than they would otherwise have. The estimated benefit was incremental sales of approximately $1.4 billion per year or $4 billion for the thirty-four months. Recent research has revealed, however, that the product first to market does not always win. Lambert and Slater (1999) cite many studies that show mixed results for market pioneers. Some studies show an inverse relationship between being first to market and gaining market share or profit. Lambert and Slater feel a more important goal is to be the first to *mindshare*, that is, to have the product consumers think of first in order to solve their problems. Lambert and Slater thus argue for market-focused project management that stresses understanding the customer and the market rather than being first. The Iridium project shows what can happen to organizations following a project leadership strategy and not paying enough attention to market conditions.

For projects with a customer intimacy strategy, the project outcome will be targeted to the high end of the market, and it may be more important to "get it right" and show value to customer rather than to "get it fast." It is probably best to introduce this outcome toward the beginning of the concept cycle, after the innovators have been exposed to it, in order to maximize value to customers. A good example here is Airborne Express. Federal Express invented the business of overnight delivery. It was the product leader. United Parcel Service (UPS) came in as the operational excellence company, and as the industry matured, FedEx was forced to compete on price. Airborne Express came into the fray as a customer intimate firm. Now it tailors its service to individual corporate needs; each customer engagement is a project.

For organizations pursuing an operational excellence strategy, the project outcome will be aimed at the middle and the low end of the market, so it may be best to follow the leader, minimize cost, cut price, and go for volume at the heart of the lifecycle, after the innovators and early adopters have bought. Some corporate examples of this approach include Royal PDA, which sells a cheaper version of the Palm Pilot; eMachines, which sells dirt-cheap PCs; and AMD, which has been chasing Intel with clones of processors. UPS is another good example. It has been able to take advantage of the tremendous increase in volume in overnight delivery resulting from e-commerce sales. By concentrating on costs and processes to keep prices low, it can respond as the industry matures and the market is made up of everyone rather than just a select few.

Project Outcome Lifecycle

Your project outcome will have a lifecycle of its own, the project outcome lifecycle (POL). When the outcome of the project is a product, the POL is more commonly referred to as the product lifecycle. The POL is embedded in the concept lifecycle. Figure 5.4 illustrates the concept lifecycle as the total market for a product type. Within that lifecycle is a single specific product's lifecycle; let's say it is your product. In this example the market demand for the product type is shown as starting sixteen months from now, reaching a maximum twenty months later (thirty-six months from now), and declining twenty months later (fifty-six months from now). Your product will be ready sixteen months from now and achieve a 30 percent market share for maximum sales of 6,000 units. (This figure is taken from the output of the business systems calculator.)

Remember that the end of a project is the beginning of its POL. However, the concept lifecycle will proceed no matter when you introduce your product. When you do introduce your new product, sales will be slow in the beginning, as few will realize that your product exists. As awareness grows, sales will grow and then decline, in lifecycle fashion. If you introduce your product at the beginning of the concept lifecycle (Figure 5.4), you can expect your sales to rise and fall with the total market. However, if you introduce it later in the concept lifecycle (say, six months later, as shown in Figure 5.5), its sales potential will be much less because, first, your POL will start later due to the later introduction, and second, that POL will be cut off sooner than it would have been if you had been earlier to market, due to the ending of the concept lifecycle. The net result is that your sales and market share will be reduced.

Figure 5.6 summarizes the marketing tasks we have discussed so far.

Using the Business Systems Calculator

Project managers must estimate project outcome and concept lifecycles for the business systems calculator. What we have emphasized in this chapter for these lifecycles is determining sales volume over time, price behavior over time, the number of months or years the project outcome will exist, and the subsequent revenue over time.

Estimating sales and revenue is different for the different types of projects: new product development, internal, or client engagement. For internal projects, it is necessary to put a dollar value on the increased organizational efficiency or effectiveness that results from the project and itself results in increased sales or savings

FIGURE 5.4. PRODUCT LIFECYCLE WITHIN CONCEPT LIFECYCLE.

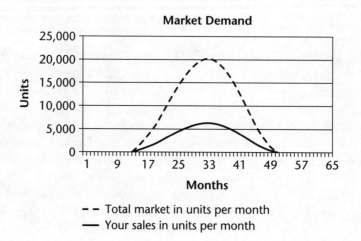

Market Demand

- - Total market in units per month
— Your sales in units per month

FIGURE 5.5. LATE PRODUCT LIFECYCLE WITHIN CONCEPT LIFECYCLE.

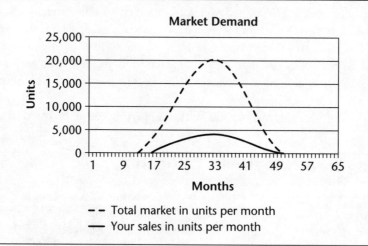

Market Demand

- - Total market in units per month
— Your sales in units per month

FIGURE 5.6. MARKETING TASKS FOR THE PROJECT MANAGER.

Initiating the Project

1. Talk to customers and end-users.
2. Determine initial definitions of final product specifications and functions.
3. Define market and market size and potential sales volume.
4. Define competitors and their reactions.
5. Define concept lifecycle and product lifecycle.
6. For internal projects, think through to the market, and determine how the project supports adding value to the company.
7. If possible, use rapid prototyping to get more accurate end-user input on what end-users need, want, don't need, and don't want.

Planning the Project

1. Talk to customers and end-users.
2. Determine initial product specifications.
3. Estimate competitor moves.
4. Evaluate customer demand.
5. Estimate market share and sales volume.
6. Determine price points.
7. Refine product lifecycle.

Executing and Controlling the Project

1. Talk to customers and end-users.
2. Change product specifications as needed.
3. Monitor competitor reactions.
4. Determine price.

Closing the Project

1. Talk to customers and end-users.
2. Launch product.
3. Operate and evaluate.
4. Support marketing and sales to promote and sell the project outcome.
5. Look for opportunities to upgrade and improve the outcome.
6. Record what you learn to be incorporated into the next project.

of some kind over the project outcome lifecycle. An internal project may look like a new product project if it affects a particular product. If it is a client engagement project, revenue is the payment stream that comes from the client.

For new product or service development projects, estimating sales and revenue is complicated. You can begin by estimating, on the basis of the market knowledge you have gained from learning about customers, end-users, and competitors, when the market for this product will be ready, that is, when the concept lifecycle will begin. You can then estimate how long this market will last and what the sales volume might be at the peak of the total market. From this you can construct a market lifecycle curve. Next assume a first-to-market position. Estimate your market share if you *make the market*. Then assume you *miss the market* and are not ready until later. In that case your market share may drop, depending on the type of market, so estimate your market share if you are not first to market. From this information the calculator generates a sales lifecycle and volume for the project outcome.

The calculator now needs estimates of price and costs. The price also changes over time. Therefore you start with an estimate of the initial price if you make the market, and you assume that price will erode by a particular percentage each year. You make similar estimates for production costs (explained further in the next chapter). From these figures, the calculator generates estimated revenue.

Consider two examples. Assume in both examples that market will be ready in twelve months, will peak in twenty-four months after it begins, with peak volume of twenty thousand units per month, and will end twenty months after that. Assume the initial price is $300 per unit, with an erosion of 5 percent per month and an initial cost of $240 per unit, with costs decreasing 8 percent per year. Assume a 25 percent market share if you make the market and 20 percent if you do not. The first example assumes a $3,000,000 project. The project duration is sixteen months, and thus the project outcome misses the market. (This is Case 1 from Chapter Four, as shown in Figure 4.3.) For the second example, the project duration is twelve months and the investment is $3,020,000. In this instance, the project outcome makes the market. (This is Case 2 from Chapter Four.)

For the first example the cash flow with capital charge is $1,542,988. For the second example the cash flow with capital charge is $4,897,356. Obviously, the second case is the better deal, as sales are higher due to having the project outcome ready at the start of the market. This example illustrates the price of delay for this particular product in this market. Due to the four-month delay for Case 1, sales were much lower. The revenue difference between the first and the second example is $3,354,368. That is, for the one-hundred-and-twenty-day delay, the price is $27,953.06 per day. This is thus an illustration that the price of delay is often indeed dear, more so than most people realize.

The second example here is the continuation of Case 2 in Figure 4.3. In Chapter Four, Case 2 was originally rejected because it looked too expensive. The case looked better after considering capital charges. Now it can be seen as a feasible alternative in terms of the results of the project outcome. This illustrates another advantage of the business systems approach. Project approaches that might on first examination have faced a managerial veto due to costs may be shown to be viable options when you examine the entire system from start to finish.

A better understanding of concept and product lifecycles can help project managers make better decisions about whether or not to include more features. More features cost more and may delay the project. The effect of the delay depends on when the product can be introduced relative to the start of the market for that product. Of course the effect of this delay must be weighed against the possible effect of not meeting customer expectations. Either situation could result in a loss of market share, so the project manager must determine which would have more effect on cash flow. Examples of using the calculator for these types of decisions are given in the examples that close the chapter.

Examples

Now the Newprod and Newsys projects look at their markets from the point of view of estimating their revenue.

Newprod Project

When we left this example in Chapter Four, the financial member of the core team favored using the current team to add the new feature, as that approach would cost under $300,000 whereas using the outside group would cost $500,000. Using the current team, however, would also cause a one-month delay, so the team asked the marketing manager to examine the effect of that delay. The team members feel that the competitors' products will have the proposed feature, which means that customers will not pay extra for it. They also feel that only a small number of customers will be attracted by the feature, so having it will not increase the size of the market substantially. However, from talking to customers and end-users, they think their product will still lose some sales if competitors have the feature and their product does not. The product is still estimated to gain a 30 percent market share if it is on time and has the feature. It is estimated to gain a 27 percent market share if it is delivered on time but does not have the feature. It is likely to get a 20 percent share if it is late to market but has the feature. These estimates set up three runs for the calculator, and the results are summarized in Figure 5.7 (remember that net cash flows include the project costs).

It is clear that using the team and delaying one month is not your best answer. Given the results shown in Figure 5.7, you and the financial and marketing managers all agree that the best solution was to hire the outside firm. You and the other

FIGURE 5.7. CASH FLOW FOR THREE
NEWPROD FEATURE OPTIONS.

	Case 1: Use Outside Firm and Be On Time	Case 2: Use Team and Be One Month Late	Case 3: Have No New Feature and Be On Time
Project costs	$3,500,000	$3,250,000	$3,000,000
Duration	12 months	13 months	12 months
Market share	30%	20%	27%
Net cash flow with capital charge	$4,365,162	$1,554,395	$4,127,946

managers are ready to make this decision when the production manager says that using the outside firm will raise product production costs. The business systems approach requires that product production costs be taken into consideration, so no decision can be made yet. (We consider post-project costs in Chapter Six.)

Newsys Project

Revenues are more difficult to determine in an internal project. What are you going to use for the POL for this project, and how are you going to begin to talk about revenue? Obviously no product for an external market will come out of this project. In this case the POL is the new phone system and the process of everyone's using it to conduct business. If the outcome meets customer and end-user expectations so that everyone uses the system to its full potential, the results of this process should have an impact on company revenue or company costs or both.

As project manager you were smart and brought a marketing person onto the core team even though this was an internal project. The marketing team member began to interview end-users to find out what they needed in a new phone system and what was required to support them once the new system was in place. This was necessary to avoid the all-too-common outcome of a new system that no one uses or does not use up to its potential.

In addition the marketing team member knows the way to quantify value for internal projects when there is no direct revenue from the POL. It is to look at the difference between the projected cash flows that would occur if the project were not done and the cash flows likely to occur once the project is done. Working with finance you and your team determine that the customer-oriented features that you all have chosen are likely to increase sales by 0.10 percent. You enter this into your business case for the project as shown in Figure 5.8.

After considering costs (discussed in Chapter Six), you can next calculate a figure for gross margin.

FIGURE 5.8. PROJECTED REVENUE WITH AND WITHOUT NEWSYS PROJECT.

	Project Year 0	Production Year 1	Production Year 2	Production Year 3	Production Year 4	Production Year 5
Adjusted revenue with project	—	$412,078,334	$537,870,666	$731,330,600	$828,294,800	$952,539,020
Forecast revenue without project	—	411,666,667	537,333,333	730,600,000	827,467,333	951,587,433
Revenue increase each year	—	411,667	537,333	730,600	827,467	951,587

FIGURE 6.1. BUSINESS SYSTEMS DIAGRAM.

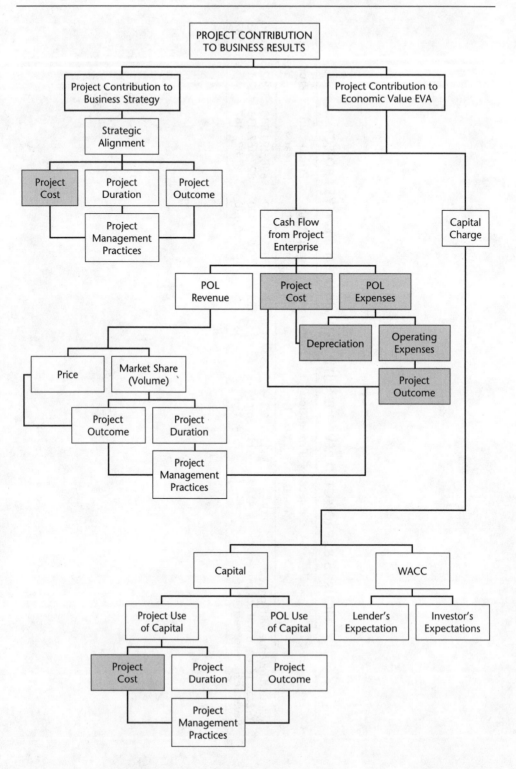

CHAPTER SIX

PROJECT AND POST-PROJECT COSTS

Expense, and great expense,
May be an essential part of true economy.

EDMUND BURKE, *LETTER TO A NOBLE LORD,* 1796

The previous chapter focused on revenue and the factors that influence the amount of revenue earned by a project outcome. This chapter focuses on costs and the factors that influence how much it costs for the project outcome to produce the revenue it earns. The income statement, as we explained in Chapter Two, records the revenue minus the expenses over a given time period for a business. A project can have an income statement also. However, in most cases it will not tell you a lot unless it covers the life of the project and the life of the project outcome: that is, the project must be viewed as comparable to a whole business enterprise. If it does not cover the life of the project outcome, the project income statement will show only expenses without any revenues. If it looks only at the project outcome, it may miss some of the expense incurred during the project itself. Thus in this chapter we develop a break-even chart that combines project costs, post-project costs, and project outcome revenue to model the project outcome lifecycle and show when the project outcome will begin to earn a profit and then how much profit can be expected over the project outcome lifecycle.

An exception to this general rule about what the project income statement must cover is the income statement for the client engagement project, work for hire. For this type of project, revenues are collected directly for the work performed during the project lifecycle. Revenue is booked during project execution or at completion or at both times. For all other projects, however, only by looking at both the project and the outcome lifecycle will the project manager be able to understand the full dynamics of the project as a business enterprise that contributes value to the whole company.

In addition to ensuring that revenues and expenses are examined over the life of the project and its outcome, project managers must understand the concept of cost, the different types of cost, how costs are measured, and how they are reported as expenses on the income statement or stored as capitalized costs on the balance sheet to be expensed at a later date. This knowledge will also help project managers to measure how much profit a project contributes to the company. In the next chapter we will discuss how to convert that profit into cash flow, a measure of economic value.

Cost Considerations for Project Managers

Cash flow, break-even analysis, and return to shareholders are important concepts for project managers. Profit equals revenue minus costs. The organization's economic value is increased only after the revenue from the project outcome exceeds the project costs, both the costs to create the outcome and the costs to produce and administer the project outcome. Understanding the effect of cost decisions on economic value is important as an increase in economic value is a measure of success.

This emphasis helps project managers focus on project decisions that affect both project and post-project costs. Project outcome features influence project costs as additional features take both time and resources. Features also affect production costs, as additional and more complicated features will normally be more costly to produce. Project management factors such as core teams, full-time team members, co-location of team members, and rapid access to customers and end-users represent additional project costs.

Understanding and using business concepts about costs for project decision making is the only way that project managers will escape the tyranny of the budget. In the past the project manager was often hobbled with a budget that focused on minimizing costs, often stifling creativity and effective decision making. This was done because upper managers did not believe that project managers could make decisions in the best interest of the organization. Most project managers were technical contributors and not used to thinking in terms of economic value. When project managers learn to make cost decisions that best return value to shareholders, then budgets will no longer be as necessary. The project manager will then be free to manage the project based on what is best for the organization rather than on what is best for the budget. This should result in greater project and business success, for it is rare that a good budget decision is also a good business decision. Thus, for the development of the project management position, it is important that the project manager understand how economic value is calculated and how project and post-project costs influence this measure.

The Concept of Cost

A formal definition of a *cost* is "a resource sacrificed or forgone to achieve a specific objective" (Horngren, Foster, and Datar, 1994, p. 26). For a project manager it is more practical to think of cost as simply the amount of cash that the company has to pay to acquire the goods and services that it uses to conduct business. This includes cash to develop assets, operate processes, market and sell company products and services, and generally manage and administer the business.

In some cases it may be simple to determine how much something costs. In our example in Chapter Two of the start-up company DDI, the founder, Barry, paid $200 to buy the materials to make one hundred copies of his operating system for computers. It was then a simple process to assign a cost of $2 to each product because each product used $2 worth of parts. It took $800 to pay the salary of the assistant who made the one hundred systems. It was also a straightforward process to calculate that each system then cost $8 for labor. The assistant did not record his time to make each system, but Barry assigned the cost of $8 per system on the assumption that each one took the same amount of time to make. It is not always such a simple process to determine how much something costs. When managers want to know how much something costs, cost accountants call the object of inquiry a *cost object*. They devise methods to measure the cost of the cost object. These methods along with the nature of the cost object and accounting conventions have led to a classification of different types of costs, all of which are important for a project manager to understand. This understanding will enable the project manager to plan and manage projects better.

Accounting conventions determine the difference between *cost* and *expense*—two terms that are often used interchangeably but should not be. We pointed out in Chapter Two that the income statement records expenses rather than costs. So what is the difference between a cost and an expense? Cost measures the value of the resource sacrificed. Expense adds the concept of timing. An expense is defined as occurring when the value of a resource or asset has been used up. It may cost a company $10 for the materials and labor to make a product. That cost is first recorded as work in progress inventory and then as finished goods inventory on the balance sheet. When the product is sold, that cost comes off the balance sheet and becomes an expense on the income statement. An expense is a cost that is matched to the associated revenue of that cost. Therefore a cost can be recorded as an asset (unused value) or as an expense (used value).

Cost Drivers and Cost Management

Project managers are interested in cost management when they are planning and executing their projects because decreasing costs is one way to increase profit. If a project manager can keep the revenue associated with his project constant while reducing costs, this will eventually increase profit. According to cost accountants, focusing on two key areas usually attains cost reduction: (1) "doing only *value-added activities,* that is, those activities that customers perceive as adding utility (usefulness) to the products or services they purchase, and (2) efficiently managing the use of the cost drivers in those value-added activities" (Horngren, Foster, and Datar, 1994, p. 29). A *cost driver* is any factor that influences the cost of a cost object. Any change in a cost driver will directly change the total cost of its cost object.

One set of cost drivers that project managers need to focus on relates to the cost of the project itself. These are the traditional cost drivers of the project budget. Another set relates to the project outcome. These are beyond the boundaries of the project. Project managers are more likely to overlook these cost drivers, yet they may be even more important than the project cost drivers in determining the total profit of the project enterprise. Examples of cost drivers for the project are such things as personnel hours, technical complexity, and the project management factors described in Chapter Four. Cost drivers for the project outcome lifecycle (POL) are factors in a number of business functions. In the design of a product, for example, the number of parts and the cost of materials used might drive the cost of making the product. So might the number of steps, the complexity of the assembly line, or the labor hours required to manufacture it. In distribution the weight of the product or the amount of packaging needed to ship it without breakage are examples of cost drivers. After the sale the number of service calls, the number of warranty repairs, and the amount of time required for each warranty repair are additional important cost drivers (Horngren, Foster, and Datar, 1994). For an internal project, post-project cost drivers might include the number of training days employees require to learn to use a new system or process, the process cycle time, or the number of person hours required to operate the system.

In general, "cost management is the set of actions that managers take to satisfy customers while continuously reducing and controlling costs" (Horngren, Foster, and Datar, 1994, p. 30). This cost management process for line or process managers should be the same for project managers. The only difference is that project managers must often make decisions during the project that will "satisfy customers while continuously reducing and controlling costs" in the future. Decisions project managers make during the project often have their most important consequences after the project manager has passed the baton on to other managers. This is why the project manager must always manage the project with the end in mind—not the end of the project but the end of the POL.

These considerations emphasize the need for a core team and for continuous membership on that team. The project manager cannot be expected to know all the cost effects due to product design decisions. The project manager must rely on the core team members for a full understanding of the cost implications of design decisions. Of course no one core team member will know all the cost implications either, as some team members concentrate mainly on project outcome creation and others concentrate on project outcome production. Thus the core team members who are concerned mainly with creating the project outcome—say, people from engineering or information technology (IT)—must work in close cooperation with those members concerned mainly with producing and administering the project outcome—say, people from production or operations. Only in this way can a project manager have a true cost management program.

Types of Costs

To implement cost management, project managers and core team members should understand the nature and dynamics not only of cost drivers but of the various kinds of costs as well. The basic types of costs defined by cost accountants are fixed, variable, direct, and indirect.

"A *fixed cost* is a cost that does not change *in total* despite changes of a cost driver" (Horngren, Foster, and Datar, 1994, p. 30). An example of a fixed cost is the cost to rent an office when the cost object is a project using the office space. No matter how many person hours are spent by the project team each month, the monthly cost of the office space remains the same. If the project manager reduces the work or the number of people on the project, the cost of the office space will remain fixed.

"A *variable cost* is a cost that *changes in total* in proportion to changes of a cost driver" (Horngren, Foster, and Datar, 1994, pp. 29–30). Labor costs on the projects are variable costs. They vary in proportion to the person-hours spent on the project.

Whereas the terms *fixed costs* and *variable costs* describe the behavior of costs, the terms *direct costs* and *indirect costs* describe how costs are measured.

Direct costs are costs that management can trace to a cost object in an economically workable way (Horngren, Foster, and Datar, 1994, p. 27). In other words a direct cost is something that can be measured in a way that will not cost more than the resulting cost information is worth. If a person has the sales slip for the materials he or she purchased for a project, it is easy to measure the costs from the receipt. If the person has records of the wages paid to the project personnel and the number of hours that they worked on the project, he or she again probably has the information needed to do *cost tracing*, "the assigning of direct costs to the chosen cost object" (Horngren, Foster, and Datar, 1994, p. 29).

Indirect costs, or allocated costs, occur when management cannot trace the costs associated with a chosen cost object or can do so only at great expense (Horngren, Foster, and Datar, p. 28). Project managers experience these allocated costs most often as overhead expenses or corporate charges. Such costs are often resented because they feel arbitrary and not directly attached to a concrete service received by the project. These are the expenses that are recorded most often under selling, general, and administrative (SG&A) costs on the income statement. They are allocated because there is not an economically expedient way to measure each individual cost object's use of these services. Project managers have very little influence over this overhead expense. It is usually governed by corporate policy.

A simple example is the cost of electricity for an office building. Each office contains different sorts of equipment requiring electrical power. Lights in each office are turned on and off at different times. The cost for each office could be traced if the electricity was metered at each office, but of course it is not. The cost of installing meters for each office is greater than the value of the information they would provide. Because the electricity is metered only for the building as a whole, cost accountants or management must figure out a method to allocate the costs for the whole building across the departments. The usual method in cases like this is to assume that each office uses about the same amount of electricity, divide by the number of offices, and charge each department based on the number of offices. A more accurate method might be to base the charge on square feet of occupancy. Whatever the allocation method, it should reflect the relationship between the cost driver and the cost object as closely as possible.

Given fixed and variable costs on the one hand and direct and indirect costs on the other, there are four possible combinations of these two sets of costs for project managers to consider, shown in the matrix in Figure 6.2.

First are the *variable direct costs*. An example is the cost of the parts used to make a product. This cost is usually easily captured through invoicing and knowledge of the number of parts needed to make each product. As the number of products increases, so does the number of parts needed. The cost varies with variation in the cost driver.

Second are the *variable indirect costs*. An example of this category is the electricity just described. It is a variable cost because the cost goes up with the use of equipment and lights. It is indirect because it cannot be measured and charged to each individual light fixture and piece of equipment; therefore it must be allocated.

FIGURE 6.2. TYPES OF COSTS.

	Variable	Fixed
Direct costs	1. Variable direct costs (example: cost of goods sold)	3. Fixed direct costs (example: building rent)
Indirect costs	2. Variable indirect costs (example: depreciation)	4. Fixed indirect costs (example: SG&A)

Third are the *fixed direct costs*. An example is the cost to lease the computers assigned to a project. These lease costs will not change, no matter how much or how little the project team members use their computers. These costs are direct because the cost is charged to the project by tracing the cost directly to the computers that the project is using.

Fourth are the *fixed indirect costs*. These are the classic SG&A charges. An example of this cost is the project's use of a company computer center. If the company does not measure the center's use by personnel from each project, management must allocate these costs in some way. For instance, the monthly cost of this center might be allocated to each project according to project size; hence the cost is indirect. The amount of use does not change the cost over time; hence the cost is fixed.

Other Cost Issues

Among the additional cost issues that concern project managers is the difference between a cost that is expensed right away and a cost that is capitalized. This often has serious budgetary consequences in the corporate game called Whose Expense Is It Anyhow?

Expensed costs are costs that are recorded immediately as expenses on the income statement. Project managers often experience these costs as the most important part of their budget. The line manager who has the project as part of his or her budget feels the most pressure to keep these costs down because they will directly affect results in the present reporting period.

Capitalized costs are costs that are first recorded as assets and then subsequently become expenses. Examples are costs incurred to purchase plant, equipment, and computers. (Some companies now expense computers because they have become so cheap, but this decision depends on the amount spent on computers in relation to other capital expenditures.) Project managers often experience less pressure in relation to capitalized costs. These costs are part of the capital budget, and they do not show up as expenses on any one manager's budget for the reporting period. In order to have more budget freedom, managers often play the game of trying to get as much of a project as possible considered a capitalized cost. Of course, over the life of the POL, the capitalized cost will be distributed as depreciation or some other form of expensing. Thus in most cases it does not make a big difference over the long term. This is because income statements do include costs that were initially recorded as capitalized costs but are now to be an expense for the period of the statement, such as depreciation for the period (Horngren, Foster, and Datar, 1994, p. 37).

The reason the difference between expensed and capitalized costs is important for the company as a whole is that, as we described in Chapter Two, an expense is recorded on the income statement during the period it is incurred. This has a direct effect on the amount of profit that the company reports for that time period. Because public companies are under so much pressure to show a certain level of performance every quarter to meet the expectations of Wall Street analysts and shareholders, too much expense can cause short-term problems for upper management. "The simplest, most visible, most merciless measure of corporate success in the 1990s has become this one: Did you make your earnings last quarter?" ("Learn to Play the Earnings Game," 1997, p. 77). However, if the expense is capitalized, it will not show up as an expense until later. Often this gets translated as not being directly charged to the project budget. A capitalized expense can feel like free money. Of course, over the long run, all things being equal, the same cash flows through to the bottom line (net income) either now or later. These kinds of games do not really add any value for shareholders. Whether project costs are expensed or capitalized, the consequences for cash flow and return on capital are very similar.

When all other things—such as tax laws, government regulations, and other factors—are not equal, companies treat expenses and depreciation very differently. In these cases there may be a real difference in contribution to cash flow from treating costs differently in the first place. In capital intensive enterprises such as oil companies this is definitely the case. The next chapter will look more closely at cash flow and return on capital. Whether project costs are expensed or capitalized, the consequences for cash flow and return on capital are very similar.

Another cost issue for project managers who are managing new product development is the nature of the following manufacturing costs, or the *cost of goods sold*. Project managers must consider these costs in building a model of the project outcome lifecycle.

Direct materials costs are all of the costs to purchase the materials that production will use in manufacturing the cost object and that can be measured and assigned to the project by management. They include any costs of materials acquisition and shipping.

Direct manufacturing labor costs are all of the costs associated with the labor to produce the product that management can directly trace to that product. They include costs for outside suppliers and subcontractors, fringe benefits for labor, and any other labor costs that can be directly assigned to the project.

Manufacturing overhead costs are the indirect costs allocated to the cost object because they cannot be traced to it in a sufficiently inexpensive way. They include power, supplies, indirect materials, indirect manufacturing labor, plant rent, plant insurance, property taxes on plants, plant depreciation, and the compensation of plant managers. Other terms for this cost category include indirect manufacturing costs, factory overhead costs, and factory burden costs. Manufacturing overhead costs are the costs most likely to be overlooked by project managers. It is important to include this cost category when modeling the project outcome lifecycle.

Yet another cost issue for project managers to understand is *sunk costs*, past costs that are unavoidable because they cannot be changed by any present or future action. When developing models for investment analysis, sunk costs should not be considered because they have already been incurred. For example, you develop a business case for a project and estimate that it will cost $100,000 and return $150,000 after one year. Six months into the project, after spending $50,000, you reevaluate the market and realize it will only return $90,000. Should you cancel the project? The concept of sunk costs says no. Because the first $50,000 is already gone, you should compare the $90,000 return to the $50,000 that you will invest for the return.

Sunk costs for an individual project may be irrelevant for analyzing the project as an investment, they are not irrelevant for the company as a whole. Any expenditure of funds in the company that does not contribute to a return dilutes profits, cash flow, and economic value. A project manager once told one of the authors about a game his fellow managers would play at his company. Misusing the concept of sunk costs, they would start a project without doing a business case. When they finally got around to doing the case, they would not include any cost that had been incurred by the project to date. These they called sunk costs and thus irrelevant to the analysis (firmly plant tongue in cheek). Without the burden of these early expenditures, every project looked like a wonderful investment and never got cancelled. As the performance of the company continued to go downhill owing to a series of lackluster products, no one seemed to make the connection between this faulty project selection process and poor performance.

Project Income Statements

In this section we discuss the project income statements for the different types of projects. Corporate reporting standards result in reports that do not necessarily present a clear picture of project and post-project costs in relation to project revenues. Different types of projects show up differently on the financial reports of a company. The way they show up depends on the project and the project outcome. A new product development project might be considered an R&D expense and be reported as part of the SG&A line on the corporate income statement, or it might be considered a capitalized cost and be reported as an asset on the corporate balance sheet. In many cases, as a result of accounting conventions, part of a new product development project's costs are expensed directly to SG&A and part are capitalized and incorporated into the balance sheet. This is also true for internal projects. An internal project might build a new plant or install a new telephone or computer system. The costs for such projects are likely to be treated as capitalized costs, assets on the balance sheet to be depreciated over their useful life span. Internal projects might also improve a process, fix a broken assembly line, or develop a new process. Such projects are more likely to be reported as SG&A expenses. However, in the third kind of project, a client engagement project, the company income statement is likely to incorporate the project costs and revenues in the same categories in which they might be reported on a project income statement. Because the client usually makes periodic payments during the project, with the final payment coming sometime after the project is completed to the client's satisfaction, the corporate reporting practices can have a more direct reflection of costs and revenues in the project.

The product development and internal projects have no direct revenue associated with them and so whatever contribution to revenue they make is not reported directly on a corporate statement. Their revenue is not the gross revenue of a client payment; rather it is the net revenue from the sale of a product, a cost savings from a more efficient plant, a cost savings from a more efficient process, or a marginal revenue increase from a more effective process. Whatever it is, it is tracked separately by the company from the project costs. What makes this revenue particularly difficult to track is that the revenue that can be directly attributed to the project is usually not received until well after the project itself is over. The project manager and team are already working on another project. Most people have forgotten the details of the project anyway. This makes cost and investment analysis (covered in the next chapter) difficult, but they are still important. It is up to management to connect what happens in the project and what happens in the project outcome lifecycle in order to understand each project's business and financial dynamics.

Regardless of corporate reporting standards, project managers can develop an income statement for each project. We have shown how to determine project investment and post-project revenues in previous chapters. Now a means of estimating post-project costs is needed. This can be accomplished by looking at three categories for each project: direct costs, such as cost of goods sold; indirect charges; and depreciation. Each of these is treated as a cost driver.

Costs for Product Development Projects

Direct costs: cost of goods sold, materials, labor, depreciation (if it applies directly to equipment being used), allocated factory overhead

Indirect costs: SG&A

Depreciation: general depreciation charges for plant and equipment used

Costs for Internal Projects

Direct costs: operating costs (probably mostly person-hours to operate the outcome), additional equipment and materials, training and hand-holding to help end-users use the result, fixing and fine-tuning (more person-hours), salaries of people doing training, maintenance, and so forth

Indirect costs: SG&A

Depreciation: any use of plant and equipment

Costs for Client Engagement Projects

Direct costs: cost of goods sold (cost of direct materials and labor) and any ongoing costs for the project outcome such as costs for warranty support, technical support, upgrades, and changes

Indirect costs: SG&A, perhaps assigned as a percentage of the contract price

Depreciation: probably included in SG&A

Figure 6.3 is an income statement for a hypothetical completed project, say, a client engagement project. A project income statement should cover the same categories as a business enterprise income statement (see Figure 2.10).

In Figure 6.3, *revenue* in the amount of $100,000 is the price that the company charged the client for the project.

The *cost of goods sold* is the cost of all the direct materials and labor that went into producing the project outcome for which the client is paying. It includes costs for outside suppliers, subcontractors, shipping and acquisition costs for materials, fringe benefits for labor, and any other cost that can be directly assigned to the project.

FIGURE 6.3. INCOME STATEMENT FOR COMPLETED CLIENT ENGAGEMENT PROJECT.

Revenue	**$100,000**
Cost of goods sold	55,000
Gross margin	**45,000**
Selling, general, & administrative	10,000
Depreciation	10,000
Operating income	**25,000**
Interest expense	10,000
Income before tax	**15,000**
Taxes	7,000
Net income	**$8,000**

The *selling, general, and administrative* costs are the allocated expenses from corporate for the project's share of corporate services, including a charge for the space occupied by the client engagement project, the utilities it consumed, and the human resources and IT services it used.

The *depreciation* expenses are based on the project's use of plant and equipment that is subject to depreciation. (Some companies consider this part of the cost of goods sold. However, for understanding the income statement and cash flow, it is helpful to have depreciation isolated.)

The *interest expense* is of course the interest charged for the project's use of debt-based financing.

The *taxes* are the taxes directly connected to the project and project profit.

Another consideration is that post-project costs usually decrease over time as workers become more experienced with the production or operating process. This decrease can be calculated with the business systems calculator by estimating the initial cost and the annual rate of decline. Cost and price often decline together. However, price declines as a result of market forces, whereas cost declines as a result of organizational experience. For instance, the business calculator and Newprod examples in Chapter Five assume an initial price of $300 per unit for a new product and an erosion rate of 5 percent per year. This erosion is assumed to begin when the market begins, not just when Newprod is ready. Costs are set at $240 per unit, declining at 8 percent per year, but this decline is based on experience, so it does not begin until the organization begins making the product. The graph in Figure 6.4 illustrates the relationship between price and cost if the organization makes the market. This graph is part of the calculator output. Here the price-cost difference is at its widest. If the project duration is longer and the outcome misses the market, the price will have started to decline before the organization develops any production experience. In that case the price-cost difference will be less.

FIGURE 6.4. PRICE AND COST WHEN THE PRODUCT MAKES THE MARKET.

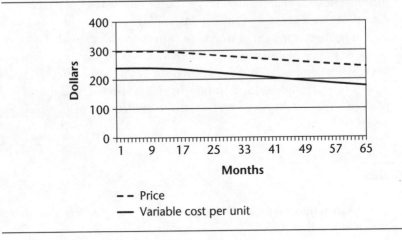

Break-Even Analysis

Given an understanding of the types of costs, project managers can calculate the operating income and cash flow for the project and the project outcome. Using the cash flow with capital charge as a measure of the results of the endeavor, the project manager can learn the time to the project's break-even point, as shown in Figure 6.5, another output graph from the business systems calculator.

This graph illustrates the results for both the project and the project outcome. It is similar to Figure 1.5, except that the operating income line has been eliminated to make it easier to read. Above the x-axis are two lines. The first line represents the project investment and the other represents the cumulative operating income for the project outcome. The break-even point is the point at which the cash flow without capital charge line crosses over the x-axis. It is at this point that the project outcome has generated enough operating income to pay back the investment in the project. In the example in Figure 6.5, this happens after about thirty-eight weeks. This net cash flow is the summation of all money spent and all money received as a result of the project. It goes negative in the beginning, representing the expenses incurred for the project. The turnup begins when project expenses stop and income begins. Crossing the x-axis represents the point at which the income covers all the expenses, the point at which the project breaks even.

The bottom line is labeled *cash flow with capital charge*. This line represents the net cash flow line minus the cost of the capital employed during the project. It is this line that indicates true economic value. At the break-even point the share-holders have not received any value as they have not yet received any return on their investment. Shareholders receive value only when the project outcome begins to pay back the cost of the capital employed to create it. The payback of all capital charges is indicated when the cash flow with capital charge crosses the *x*-axis. At this point the shareholders have received the value they expected. In Figure 6.5, this point is reached in the forty-third month. It is after this point that the project begins to add value beyond what was expected, and thus it is called the point of *economic value added*. We turn to a consideration of that topic in Chapter Seven.

Examples

The decision making for the Newprod and Newsys projects also needs to incorporate production costs.

FIGURE 6.5. PROJECT RETURN GRAPH.

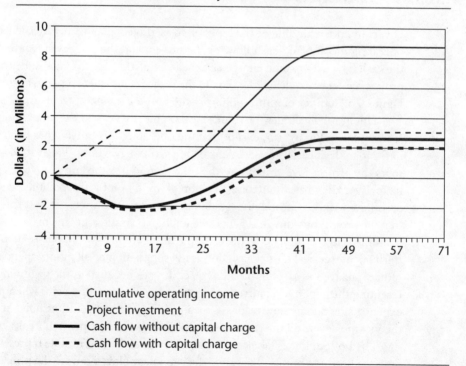

Newprod Project

To help make the decision on whether or not to add the suggested additional feature, you need to consider the effect on the product production costs of using an outside firm in order to add the feature and bring the project in on time. The production manager on the core team estimates that using the outside firm will add $5.00 per unit to the cost of goods sold. Figure 6.6 adds these production costs to the data given in Figure 5.7.

Once you and your team take product production costs into consideration, you see that using the outside firm is no longer the favored response. The increase in production costs more than offsets the revenue increase from being on time with the feature. You and your team decide to skip the feature and bring Newprod in on time.

This example has illustrated a lot of the power of the business systems approach. When we introduced this example in Chapter Four, the project manager and the team were going to incorporate the additional feature and delay project completion by one month. This tentative decision was based on cost considerations. When the effect of the delay on sales was considered, using an outside firm to add the extra feature was favored so as to avoid the delay and avoid losing market share. Finally, when the extra production costs associated with using an outside firm were considered, it became clear that it was best not to add the extra feature. The business systems approach takes all points of view into consideration by looking at the long-term consequences of project decisions.

Newsys Project

Your Newsys team determines, with the help of the finance department, that the new phone system is likely to reduce company operating expenses by 0.05 percent because the enhanced features on the phone are expected to increase productivity

FIGURE 6.6. CASH FLOW FOR THREE NEWPROD FEATURE OPTIONS WITH INCREASED PRODUCTION COSTS.

	Case 1: Use Outside Firm and Be On Time	Case 2: Use Team and Be One Month Late	Case 3: Have No New Feature and Be On Time
Project costs	$3,500,000	$3,250,000	$3,000,000
Duration	12 months	13 months	12 months
Product costs	$245	$240	$240
Market share	30%	20%	27%
Net cash flow with capital charge	$3,771,121	$1,559,395	$4,127,946

and lower phone rates. However, as illustrated in Figure 6.7, adjusted operating expense (expenses with the project) is still forecast to be more each year because of increases associated with the 0.10 percent increase in revenues from increased sales. You and your team members realize that you will not be able to analyze the whole picture until you have done a complete cash flow analysis (as shown in Chapter Seven).

FIGURE 6.7. PROJECTED OPERATING EXPENSE.

	Project Year 0	Production Year 1	Production Year 2	Production Year 3	Production Year 4	Production Year 5
Forecast operating expense (without project)	—	$(288,166,667)	$(376,133,333)	$(511,420,000)	$(579,227,133)	$(666,111,203)
Adjusted operating expense (with project)	—	(288,397,143)	(376,434,165)	(511,829,034)	(579,690,399)	(666,643,959)
Difference	—	230,476	300,832	409,034	463,266	532,756

FIGURE 7.1. BUSINESS SYSTEMS DIAGRAM.

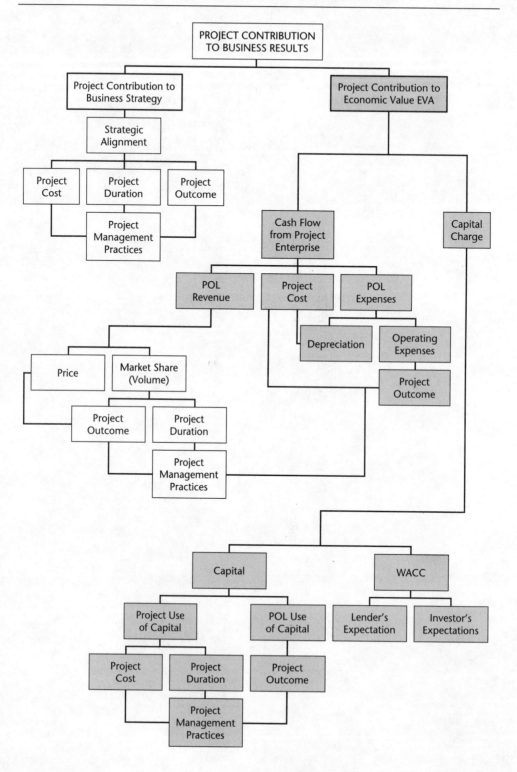

CHAPTER SEVEN

WHY FINANCE MATTERS
FOR PROJECT MANAGERS

They knew how to make a budget, but they didn't know how to make money.

C. MICHAEL ARMSTRONG, CEO OF AT&T (ABOUT HUGHES ELECTRONICS IN 1992), 1997

*The objects of a financier are, then, to secure an ample revenue; to impose it with judg-
ment and equality; to employ it economically; and, when necessity obliges him to make
use of credit, to secure its foundations in that instance, and for ever, by the clearness and
candour of his proceedings, the exactness of his calculations, and the solidity of his funds.*

EDMUND BURKE, *REFLECTIONS ON THE REVOLUTION IN FRANCE*, 1790

Finance matters for project managers because projects develop assets that produce a return to the company and its shareholders. This is what finance is all
about. Remember the cash cycle from Chapter Two? It begins with getting the
money to invest in and operate the business. It ends with returning money to those
who have supplied the cash. Unless a business demonstrates its ability to return
cash, it will not get the cash it needs to invest. No cash to invest means no projects
and probably no business. As the business systems diagram in Figure 7.1 shows,
finance adds new dimensions to costs. Financing results in a capital charge, which
combines with cash flow from the project enterprise. The *capital charge*, as we have
described, is the amount of capital used by the project and the project outcome
lifecycle (POL) multiplied by the *weighted average cost of capital* (WACC). WACC
is influenced by lenders' and investors' expectations. The project's use of capital is
influenced by project cost and duration. The POL's use of capital is influenced

---

This chapter draws extensively from the Strategic Management Group's *Why Finance Matters* (an
interactive CD-ROM), sections 8 through 10. ©1997 by Strategic Management Group. Used by permission.

by the project outcome. By the time you finish reading this chapter, you will have a fuller understanding of what these terms mean and how they interact to create shareholder value. (In this chapter we emphasize *shareholder value* rather than the more general term *economic value* because much of the analysis and the concept of Economic Value Added are from the world of private enterprise. However, project managers from not-for-profit and governmental organizations can effectively use their own equivalents of economic value and financial statements to build models to evaluate and plan their projects with financial consideration in mind.)

As stated in Chapter Two, *assets* are items of value that can be converted into cash. Projects produce all kinds of items of value with the potential to produce cash for the business. That potential is realized if the cash produced by the project outcome is greater than the cash used for developing and producing it. When this is the case, projects that produce items of value contribute a net positive cash flow to the finances of the company. Each of the three basic types of projects can contribute a net positive cash flow.

Research and development projects produce new products and services with the potential to generate net cash for the business. They do this by generating positive cash flow over the life of the project and of the project outcome that is greater than the use of cash to develop, produce, and support that outcome. These kinds of projects may produce

- Any new product, such as new computers, printers, drugs, cars, toys, cameras, global satellite phone systems, semiconductor chips, and so on
- Services, such as consulting processes, financial services, Internet sites, and so on
- Intellectual property, such as patents on technology or copyrights on software

Internal projects may create and fine-tune processes to potentially increase net cash. These processes may either increase the rate at which cash is coming in compared to the rate at which cash is going out or decrease the rate at which cash is going out compared to the rate at which cash is coming in. These kinds of projects make the company more efficient or more effective or both. Internal projects may also generate new cash flow by developing new facilities or by increasing the capacity of existing facilities. Thus internal projects may involve

- Reengineering
- Retooling
- Building various kinds of new production facilities
- Increasing the capacity of existing production facilities
- Developing new information and communication systems

Client engagement projects provide a direct service to the client. These projects generate net positive cash flow as well. They do this by generating a cash flow in from the client that is greater than the cash flow out to pay for the cost of production.

Financially, a company is a portfolio of assets produced through projects. The present operations of any company were developed by past projects. The present operations are improved and supported through current projects. And future projects will lead to the strategic implementation of future operations. This is why we say that from a financial perspective a company is no more than the sum of the projects in which it invests. If these projects do not meet the expectations of the company's investors, then it is unlikely that the company as a whole will be able to do so. This is why finance should matter very much to project managers.

If projects are investments, then project managers need to understand how they are financed. They also should understand how finance drives the business and should drive the project. Chevron executives refer to their project management process, Chevron Project Development and Execution Process (CPDEP, pronounced *chip dip*), as a strategy for remaining number one in stockholder return (Sullivan, 1998). What C. Michael Armstrong said of the managers of Hughes Corporation, quoted in the epigraph to this chapter, should not apply to a good project manager. A good project manager should be able to make a good budget and follow it, but ultimately that budget has to function in the service of making money.

Cost of Capital

Most managers focus on the operating costs of running their business. They often overlook or ignore the additional cost of acquiring the cash for purchasing the assets needed to support the operations. Project managers also tend to ignore the cost of acquiring the funds to finance their projects. This cost of acquiring the funds to finance a project is called the *cost of capital*. The cost of capital has important implications for project managers because their projects often require the use of cash for long periods of time before the outcome of the project can produce a return on that cash. When project managers ignore the cost of capital, they often make decisions that result in a return lower than the return the providers of the capital expect. Overall this is not good for the company.

The good news is that there are two sources for the cash to finance projects and operations. These sources are lenders and shareholders. The bad news is that these sources do not let a business use their money for free. Both lenders and shareholders expect to get their original investment back *plus* some additional cash called the *expected return*. This return is the payment that the company makes to its investors for the privilege of using their cash. For example, if you have a mortgage on your house with an annual percentage rate of 7 percent, this means that the bank has an expected return of 7 percent, or $7 per year for every $100 that you have borrowed and not yet paid back to the bank.

The cost of capital is the "amount of money that companies need to pay to their lenders and shareholders to satisfy their expected return" (Strategic Management Group, 1997, 8-A, p. 9). It is usually, as in the example of the mortgage, expressed as a percentage per year. What is the capital that businesses must pay the cost of? Capital is the total amount of cash that has been invested in the business. This cash is mostly in the form of assets. Capital may also be described as the sources of the cash the company used to purchase these assets. As the cash cycle in Chapter Two illustrated, a company gets the capital to invest during the first phase of the cycle (financing) and then buys assets during the second phase (investing).

Companies can determine the amount of capital they have in two different ways. One way is to look at the investment in the business, the total assets, then subtract current liabilities, the amount that must be paid back in the next year. The difference is net working capital plus net fixed assets, or the long-term cash that is tied up in the business. The second way is to look at the long-term financing: the primary source of cash the company used to purchase its assets. This financing is represented on the right-hand side of the balance sheet as the long-term liabilities and equity tied up in the business. Both the investment point of view and the financing point of view yield exactly the same amount. Conceptually, this description is a fundamental definition and measurement of capital. Many businesses, however, refine this basic point of view to fit the dynamics of their business. As a project manager, you will find it a good idea to know how your company defines capital for the purpose of calculating its cost of capital. It is also a good idea for you to know what part of that capital is represented by the investment in your project. Your friendly project accountant or core team member from finance should be able to help you learn this information.

If the cost of this capital is based on the expected return of lenders and shareholders, then it is important to understand the nature of their expectations. Lenders and shareholders have different expectations because they assume different levels of risk. Lenders bear less risk than shareholders when both are investing in the same company. When a lender loans money to a company, the company signs a commitment to repay that money. The company promises to repay the amount borrowed (the loan principal) by a specified date plus a certain percentage per year of that principal at specified intervals (the interest). The percentage, or interest rate, represents the lender's expected return. A shareholder who invests in the same company bears more risk than the lender because there are no specified guarantees for shareholders. When shareholders buy stock in a company, they expect to get back more cash than they originally paid. Sometimes the company will distribute cash to shareholders in the form of dividends (distributed profits not reinvested in the business). In addition, shareholders expect that the value of their shares will increase over time so that they will receive more money than they originally paid when they sell the stock to someone else. Shareholders are willing to accept more risk than lenders because they have the potential to make more money than lenders. The risk they face is that the price of the stock may go down instead of up and they might have to sell at a loss. There may be no dividends at all. In the worst-case scenario the company may declare bankruptcy, in which case the shareholders will never see their cash again. In the case of bankruptcy, lenders may get back their principal because, legally, lenders are first in line to be paid if a company goes bankrupt. However, if there is not enough money left, even lenders will not get paid.

Therefore, both lenders and shareholders bear risk when supplying capital to a company. The risk for lenders may be less than shareholders but so is the expected return. For both, the level of risk varies from company to company. With higher risk, lenders charge higher interest rates. Shareholders have higher expectations for dividends or for the appreciation of their stock and will shop around for better returns at the same level of risk. If they find it they will sell their stock to buy what they perceive as the better company. When this happens too many times, the value of the original company's stock goes down. Both lenders and shareholders assess risk based on similar factors. Lenders focus on the credit rating of the business. The higher the credit rating, the more likely it is that the company will be able to make its interest and principal payments. Stockholders and potential investors often rely on Wall Street analysts' reports to assess the financial health and long-term prospects of a business. Both lenders and shareholders assess the type of business. Is the company in a stable industry that tends to generate a steady cash flow (lower risk), or is it in a new field or in a cyclical industry with a more erratic cash flow (higher risk)?

Cost of Debt and Equity

The cost of capital is driven by these expectations of lenders and shareholders. Lenders issue debt and shareholders own equity. The cost of capital is a combination of the cost of debt and the cost of equity. The cost of debt is recorded on the income statement as interest. This is the payment owed to lenders during the period covered by the income statement. Determining the cost of debt is easy. The banks tell the company what their expectations are, and the company agrees to pay this amount.

The cost of equity is the return that shareholders expect on their investment. It includes dividends and the appreciation in the value of the stock. Because of these elements, determining the cost of equity is more difficult than finding the cost of debt. The payment of dividends is recorded in the cash flow statement and balance sheet; however, there is no line item on any financial report that shows the amount shareholders expect their stock to increase in value. This makes the true cost of equity difficult to assess, and therefore the cost of equity is easy to overlook or even forget. But even though shareholders are not guaranteed any return on their investment, they do expect one. These expectations play out every day on the stock market. Over the long run and on average, when shareholder expectations are met or exceeded, the price of the stock rises. When they are not met or exceeded, the price of the stock falls. For stocks in general, investors expect a return 6 percent higher than that available on long-term U.S. Treasury bonds, which are considered nearly risk free (Ibbotson and Sinquefield, 1989). However, your company may be more or less risky than the typical company, so the amount expected by shareholders needs to be adjusted accordingly.

Even though the cost of equity is more difficult to calculate than the cost of debt, the company will estimate it and then strive to meet or exceed it. If it does not and if the price of its stock falls as a result, the company will find fewer potential shareholders willing to invest the next time it tries to raise more capital by issuing more shares. Even if the company can find investors, in order to increase their expected return they will want to pay less money for their shares than they would have if the company had been more successful in meeting the cost of equity previously. This is more expensive for the company, which now gets less money for the same size piece of a share in the profits.

Weighted Average Cost of Capital

Companies determine the weighted average cost of capital by calculating the weighted average of the cost of debt and equity. The company first determines the total amount of debt and equity it has. Then it calculates the percentage of each in relation to that total and averages the expected return of each weighted by its percentage. This results in an overall rate of return that will satisfy the expectations of both the shareholders and the lenders.

For example, assume that a company needs to produce a 10 percent return to satisfy its lenders' expectations and a 20 percent return to satisfy its shareholders' expectations. As we discussed in Chapter Two, the proportions of debt and of equity appear on the right-hand side of the balance sheet (for example, Figure 2.11). The long-term liabilities section contains debt in the form of bank debt or other interest-bearing liabilities such as bonds. The equity section contains the sum of the original investment made in the company and the retained earnings, returns that shareholders have left in the company. A company with mostly debt financing will have a WACC closer to its cost of debt. A company with mostly equity financing will have a WACC closer to its cost of equity. WACC will always fall between the cost of debt and the cost of equity. More precisely, the calculation for WACC is (% of Debt Financing) $\times$ (Cost of Debt) $\times$ (1 $-$ Tax Rate) $+$ (% of Equity Financing) $\times$ (Cost of Equity).

For example, if a company's capital is 30 percent debt and 70 percent equity and if the interest rate on its loan is 10 percent and its cost of equity is 15 percent, then

$$WACC = (0.3) \times (0.1) \times (1 - 0.5) + (0.7) \times (0.15)$$
$$WACC = 0.015 + 0.105$$
$$WACC = .12$$

WACC is 12 percent. Notice that taxes lower the real cost of debt. When the tax rate is 50 percent, it lowers the cost of debt by half because the company deducts debt payments as an expense, thus reducing its taxes. This demonstrates just how important the cost of equity is and how dangerous it is for management to ignore it. Given that equity does not receive a tax deduction, its expected return is higher than the expected return on debt. In addition most companies hold less debt than equity; equity tends to push up the cost of capital. It is no wonder that shareholder value has become so significant in business today. It is both important and difficult to meet the investor expectations represented by WACC, usually heavily weighted by shareholder expectations over the long run. A net profit on the income statement shows that there is revenue left over after making debt payments and meeting tax obligations. However, it does not measure whether the amount of the profit meets shareholder expectations.

Project managers need to keep in mind that from a financial perspective, once again, their company is no more than the sum of the projects in which it invests. If these projects do not produce a return that meets or exceeds the WACC, then it is unlikely that the company as a whole will be able to do so. Admittedly, WACC depends on factors that project managers do not influence short term. These include the stock price and the cost of debt. However, good projects reduce the cost of capital over the long term. They raise the company's stock price and produce more internal capital, resulting in a higher credit rating that lowers the cost of debt. The direction for project managers should be clear: pay attention to rate of return during project selection and to the factors that might influence that rate of return as you manage the project. In addition focus on cash flow and on increasing the rate of cash flow when making project decisions in order to lower the company's WACC over the long run.

How Projects Contribute to Shareholder Value

It will be easier for you as the project manager to make better decisions while managing a project if you understand exactly how that project contributes to shareholder value. A concept that helps with this understanding is *economic profit,* also called *economic income* and *Economic Value Added* (EVA); the latter popular term for economic profit has been trademarked by the consulting firm Stern Stewart & Co. (Stewart, 1994). Economic profit measures the value created by a company after it has met the expectations of its investors. Any returns greater than needed to meet the WACC belong to the shareholders—hence the term shareholder value. Companies use EVA for a number of purposes, from evaluating the impact of strategic decisions to assessing the value of the company as a whole. Its most important use for project managers is in assessing the success of the project. Because the economic profit of a project and its outcome determines how much value the project and its outcome have contributed to the whole company, it is a very useful guide for project managers to use in decision making. Before you use this measurement as a decision-making tool for your project, however, you need to understand how it measures shareholder value. First, you should understand the measurement for your company as a whole, then for your project.

Determining EVA for the Company as a Whole

The Economic Value Added calculation first treats investors' expected return simply as a cost of doing business. This cost is the *capital charge.* As we described in the first two chapters, the capital charge expressed in dollars is equal to the amount of capital expressed in dollars times WACC expressed as a percentage: Capital Charge ($) = Capital ($) × Weighted Average Cost of Capital (%). So, if a project uses $1,000,000 in capital and the company's WACC is 12 percent, the capital charge is $120,000 per year. Next, the actual return generated by the project is calculated. This return is the *net operating profit after taxes* (NOPAT). On a traditional income statement, as you saw in Chapter Two, interest and taxes are subtracted from operating income to calculate net income. To calculate NOPAT from a traditional income statement, simply add back the interest expense to net income. Finally, to compute EVA, subtract the capital charge from NOPAT. The result is the economic profit or Economic Value Added. If EVA is negative, the company did not meet investor expectations. If EVA is positive, the company provided a return greater than expected by investors.

Companies with very high EVA, according to Stern Stewart & Co.'s 1999 rankings, include Microsoft ($3,776,000,000, with a WACC of 12.6 percent), General Electric ($4,370,000,000, with a WACC of 11.9 percent) and Intel ($4,280,000,000, with a WACC of 12.9 percent). Examples of companies with negative EVA include WorldCom (–$3,585,000,000, with a WACC of 12.6 percent), Motorola (–$2,830,000,000, with a WACC of 11.3 percent), and the lowest-ranked, General Motors (–$5,525,000,000, with a WACC of 9.4 percent) (Tully, 1999).

How can you apply this EVA calculation to projects? You can get the WACC for your company from the finance department. To calculate the capital charge for the company, you need to know the amount of capital employed by the company. As we described earlier, the amount of capital for the company as a whole can be calculated from the balance sheet. Capital invested in a project equals the amount of working capital that is tied up in the project plus the value of any long-term assets that the project is using, such as office space or equipment. It also includes the results of the same calculations made for the project outcome lifecycle, because capital will continue to be employed by the project outcome until the net cash flow generated by the outcome reaches the break-even point. Only by taking into account the full amount of capital used to generate the project return will the economic profit be a true measure of shareholder value.

The two project income statements for a million-dollar client engagement project illustrated in Figure 7.2 demonstrate the difference between calculating profit from the more traditional net profit perspective and calculating economic profit, EVA.

The more traditional income statement makes it look like the project made a profit. In accounting terms it did make a profit, but as the economic profit income statement shows, the project did not create value for the company's shareholders. It did not produce enough profit to pay the full capital charge for the project. Once

FIGURE 7.2. TWO WAYS TO CALCULATE PROJECT RETURN.

Traditional Income Statement		Economic Profit Income Statement	
Revenue	$1,000,000	Revenue	$1,000,000
Operating expense	933,916	Operating expense	933,516
Operating income	66,084	Operating income	66,084
Interest (partial capital charge)	15,054		
Tax	23,129	Tax	23,129
Net income	27,900	NOPAT	42,955
		Capital charge (complete capital charge)	53,530
		Economic Value Added	(10,575)

that return was calculated as part of the income statement, the project's short-comings became obvious.

A closer analysis of the calculation in Figure 7.2 shows that EVA is the actual dollar return of the project (NOPAT) minus the expected dollar return of the project. In Figure 7.2, NOPAT is the operating income ($66,084) minus taxes ($23,129), which equals $42,955. In the traditional income statement, management had charged the project only for interest on debt that was charged to the project. The project was not charged for the use of working capital supplied by the shareholders. For the economic profit income statement, management calculated the total of all the working capital and debt the project used as well as its use of long-term assets such as space and equipment. This was computed to be $446,083 over the yearlong project. Management felt that this was a more realistic estimate of the project's use of capital. Given a WACC of 12 percent, this raised the capital charge to $53,530 ($446,083 × 12% = $53,530). This is the dollar return of the project expected by investors (Expected $ Return = Capital Charge = Capital ($) × WACC (%)). Just as in calculating EVA for companies, if you subtract the capital charge from NOPAT in a project income statement, the difference is EVA ($42,955 − $53,530 = −$10,575).

In this case the investors required a greater return than the project generated. Now let's say that in this client engagement project, the project manager brought the project in on time, on budget, and to the original specifications. However, he neglected to work closely with the accounting department to invoice the customer on time. This greatly increased the amount of working capital tied up in the project and added greatly to the capital charge. So the project manager could have increased the project's EVA if he had managed the project differently. However, because he was not focusing on the invoicing process, the client was able to withhold payments until the project was almost completed. This resulted in the use of working capital of close to $350,000, including $100,000 for the use of long-term assets over the year. Had the project manager been able to accelerate the client's payments and to lower the working capital used by $200,000, the capital charge would have been reduced by $24,000 ($200,000 × 12%) and the capital charge would have been reduced to $29,530. Had this been the case, the project would have ended up with a positive EVA of $13,425 (NOPAT of $42,955 − Expected Return of $29,530).

This example is the least complicated for a project because it is based on a client engagement project. The cash flow and financing for this project is very much like the standard production process for a company. Product development and internal projects are quite different, and it is more difficult to calculate EVA for them. As we illustrate later in the chapter, the calculation of EVA requires the analysis of cash flows from both the project and its outcome lifecycle. In addition, as discussed in Chapter Six, companies will often capitalize their R&D costs for product development to reflect their status as an asset rather than an expense, even when they are classified as SG&A expenses for accounting purposes. Similarly, Digital Development Inc., the small company described in Chapter Two, capitalized the software code of its operating system and then depreciated that asset over time. How, then, can a project manager calculate the EVA for a product development project in a company that engages in this practice? He would treat the project as a long-term asset in calculating the amount of the capital used by any production process that manufactured a product developed by the project. This would then increase the capital charge for that product line.

The example in Figure 7.2 demonstrates the basics of calculating EVA. Actually, companies make all kinds of adjustments to their EVA calculations to reflect the realities of their business. They need to make sure that the amount of capital assigned to a project or product line reflects the true use of capital. Similarly, WACC needs to be a true indication of investors' expectations. The cost of debt is rather straightforward; figuring the cost of equity is more difficult. One interesting adjustment that some companies make is to increase the value of equity to reflect its market value (number of shares outstanding multiplied by the price per share) rather than its book value (the equity section of the balance sheet). They do this because shareholders base their expectations on what the stock is worth today rather than on what they paid for it and certainly rather than on what the person who bought that stock when it was first offered paid for it. Then there is the problem of determining current shareholder expectations. For example, "To derive each company's cost of equity capital, Stern Stewart determines what return investors expect from a basket of stocks in the same industry" (Tully, 1999, p. 280). Some other companies do the same for long-term assets, to reflect their market value as a kind of opportunity cost. If a project is using an office suite that was bought for $100,000 but is now valued at $1,000,000, the amount of capital in use is $1,000,000 not $100,000, even though the lower figure is what appears on the balance sheet.

It is important for project managers to understand company EVA and project EVA to be able to manage projects to optimize shareholder value. There are some principles companies can follow to improve EVA, and these principles apply to project managers and their projects as well. A company can increase EVA by managing its components: the actual dollar return and the expected dollar return. A company can improve the actual dollar return, or NOPAT, component of EVA by investing capital only where the return exceeds the capital charge. This requires careful evaluation of the return expected of all new capital investments, even if the investment seems like a logical or strategic use of capital. This is very important for project managers. It means that all projects should be justified by a business case demonstrating the expected cash flows and the projected actual dollar return. We have looked at some of this analysis in the previous two chapters on revenue and costs. In the next section we develop it further as investment analysis. The principal of investing capital only where the return exceeds the capital charge also means that the project manager needs to manage the project so that it actually produces the projected cash flow or at least attains the promised dollar return. In our experience it is becoming more common to justify a project with a business case, but it is not as common to actually manage the project with that business case in mind.

A company could also improve EVA by increasing its return on capital already invested. Increasing the use of existing equipment by running additional shifts rather than purchasing additional equipment could accomplish this. The company could also reduce unnecessary operating expenses associated with the capital already in place. These changes might include cost reductions for raw materials, labor, or the overhead associated with running the equipment. Finally, the company could increase output while maintaining the same level of operating expenses. Any of these initiatives could be pursued in the form of an internal project. For a product development project, all these strategies are opportunities to reduce the use of capital during the project outcome lifecycle.

To manage the expected dollar return, all managers need to remember that this expectation is a function of both capital and the cost of capital. So, reducing each of these elements can lead to improvements in EVA. A company could favorably influence the expected dollar return or capital charge by reducing the amount of capital employed at low returns. It should seriously consider getting rid of any capital that is not able to generate sufficient return to cover the cost of capital. For example, if a company owns a factory that consistently operates at a negative EVA, it should sell the factory. It can also lower the cost of capital. One way to accomplish this is to reduce the risk of the company's investments. Changing the way the company is financed can also lower the cost of capital. For example, the company could replace high-cost equity with lower-cost debt or exchange high-interest debt for lower-interest debt. These decisions are not in the domain of most project managers. Other managers make them outside the project. These decisions will, however, influence how the company evaluates your project. For this reason it is important to be aware of how and why these decisions are made.

Assessing Project Contribution to Shareholder Value

From management's point of view, projects are investments. So project selection requires investment analysis to determine the probable contribution to shareholder value of a proposed project. What follows is not meant to be a textbook treatise on project selection (see Meredith and Mantel, 1995, chap. 2). Rather it is meant to show in more detail than we have so far how management is most likely to assess a project's contribution to shareholder value for the purpose of project selection at the initiating stage and for project evaluation during the operating period or project outcome lifecycle. It is the responsibility of project managers to make sure that the expectations raised during project selection are met or exceeded during the project outcome lifecycle. Remember, if this is not your job yet, it will be soon!

Of course, in many companies, project selection is often a political process and the favored method of selection is a ritual that we call The Blessing of the Sacred Cow. In this ritual a person with great power in the organization makes it known that she favors a certain project, and all of a sudden it is chosen with great fanfare. Numbers appear magically that show that the project will return a great amount to shareholders. Inevitably, the failure of the project triggers a companion ritual, The Killing of the Scapegoat. Because the scapegoat is often the project manager, we will spare the reader the details. Needless to say, companies should avoid these rituals at all costs. They usually result in project failures that subtract rather than add value for shareholders. Companies should also be careful not to make financial analysis a mere ritual. Cooper, Edgett, and Kleinschmidt (2000) point out that financial analysis can be notoriously unreliable for project selection when the attitude of those who are developing the business case is exemplified in the phrase, "What number do you want to make this project a go?"

Any good selection process should include investment analysis of the project as one of the selection criteria. A project should return at least the amount of capital invested in the project plus the cost of that capital. If it does not, it will not add value for shareholders. There may be legitimate exceptions, projects that are necessary to meet regulatory requirements, to counter a competitor's move, or to implement a long-term strategy. Even when these types of projects show a negative EVA, management should be able to demonstrate that the value subtracted for shareholders would have been even greater if the projects had not been carried out.

We should also point out that EVA analysis should not be the sole criteria for project selection. Many experts in the project management field favor weighted scoring models over the exclusive use of financial analysis (Meredith and Mantel, 1995, p. 67). These models may include production factors such as length of work disruption during installation or safety of a process. They may include marketing factors such as the impact on the current product line or spin-off project possibilities, and they may include personnel factors such as the availability of required labor skills or requirements for training. They may also include other factors, such as patent and trade secret protection or the impact on computer or other corporate resource usage (Meredith and Mantel, 1995, pp. 44–46). We agree on the value of using multiple factors, but project managers should not lose sight of the larger picture that drives much of the behavior of competent senior managers, creating shareholder value. Many factors used in a weighted scoring model can be modeled according to their financial impact. A business case should be done carefully and should be more than a superficial numbers game. Projected cash flows, when done correctly with a careful consideration of assumptions and an attempt to model a realistic future, are similar to a weighted scoring model. Bordley (1999, p. 168) points out that a major function of *net present value* (NPV) analysis should be to promote effective communication between project leaders, management, and strategists to stimulate the creation of successful projects.

The quality of any investment analysis depends on the quality of the data and the assumptions that go into it. A business case should document the projected cash flows and the risks involved. It should include scenarios that incorporate a wide range of possible data. Each scenario should document the assumptions that drive the data and show how the data might change if an assumption proves incorrect.

To illustrate how a project proposal might be constructed as an investment analysis, we will use the example of an internal project to buy and install a new piece of equipment that will allow the company to add a new product to its product line. All the nonfinancial factors were considered first, and now management is relying on investment analysis to complete the selection process. As you read through the following steps, look at the figures provided that illustrate the analysis to make sure you understand each step. The goal of all this number crunching is simply to determine whether the estimated net cash flow from the project and the project outcome lifecycle will be enough to cover expenses, pay back lenders and investors who provided the capital used during the project and POL, and produce any additional value. If the project does this, it will have a positive NPV and should be a "go." If it does not, it should not be selected. Again, the primary purpose of this analysis is to stimulate thought and discussion among all the parties involved. It is not an exact, scientific process. Real-world dynamics often create distortions in this rational economic model (Thakor, 1993). However, we suggest that a process anchored with a rational model is better than one based on the distortions of real-world dynamics alone.

The cash flow statement in Figure 7.3 is different from the income statement in Figure 7.2. In a cash flow statement, only the actual dollars that flow into and out of the company are counted. Assume a project that will select, buy, and install and then test and start up a new machine to upgrade a factory. The useful life of the equipment is five years plus the product lifecycle of the new product that the company will now be able to manufacture and sell. The cost of the project is $600,000. The question for management is whether the return on the investment will create shareholder value. To answer this question, managers need to chart the projected cash flows that will be created during the project outcome lifecycle. When completed (Figure 7.3), the chart will show the additional or incremental cash flow, whether positive or negative, that the project will contribute

FIGURE 7.3. CASH FLOW ANALYSIS: NEW MACHINE FOR A NEW PRODUCT PROJECT.

	Project Year 0	Production Year 1	Production Year 2	Production Year 3	Production Year 4	Production Year 5
Investment required	($600)					
Revenue	—	$430	$510	$767	$706	$600
Operating expense	—	(273)	(308)	(442)	(395)	(335)
Depreciation expense	—	(120)	(120)	(120)	(120)	(120)
Operating income	—	37	82	205	191	145
Taxes	—	(14)	(31)	(78)	(72)	(55)
Incremental income	—	23	51	128	119	90
Depreciation adjustment	—	120	120	120	120	120
Incremental cash flow	(600)	143	171	248	239	210
Cumulative cash flow	($600)	($457)	($286)	($38)	$201	$411

Note: Dollars in thousands.

to the company each year if everything goes according to the plan. We have covered some of this analysis in the previous two chapters, but because the incremental cash flows are the foundation for analyzing the project as a time-based investment, we start with the cash flows here and then build the investment analysis from them.

In order to analyze the potential cash flow of the project for each year, the chart includes a column for each year of the estimated life span of the new machine being purchased. Year 0 represents the investment in the project. This amount includes the capital charge accumulated during the life of the project, to accurately reflect the total amount of the investment at the beginning of the project outcome lifecycle. Year 1 in this example represents one year in the future from the time of project completion. Each row of the chart represents a category for the investment analysis. These terms conform closely to the terms in an income statement. *Investment required* represents the cost of the project, which includes purchasing and installing the new machine and any other equipment or facilities required to support the new production process as well as any increases in net working capital the project required. *Revenue* is the anticipated cash flow coming in from sales of the new product. This is determined by multiplying the anticipated sales volume by the anticipated price of the new product. Additionally, if the sales and marketing research forecasts any lost sales due to cannibalization of existing sales, then the lost sales should be deducted from the revenue forecast.

Operating expense represents the manufacturing costs for the new product. These numbers are based on estimates of production costs and on the indirect costs associated with marketing, selling, distribution, and overhead. Representatives from production, sales, and marketing are among those who can help to determine these numbers. *Depreciation expense* allows the company to spread the cost of the machine and associated project expense over the machine's useful life. This expense reduces operating income and therefore the tax burden. The finance department most often determines these numbers. *Operating income* represents the amount of income generated by the operations associated with producing the new product. It is what is left over from the revenue after the operating expenses and depreciation expenses have been accounted for.

The *taxes* category indicates the amount of the additional taxes the company will have to pay on the operating income from the new product line. It also includes the impact of depreciation on reducing taxes, thereby increasing cash flows. The finance department usually determines this information. *Incremental income* is the amount of profit or loss generated by the project during the period. It represents what is left over after all the project's expenses have been deducted from its revenues. *Depreciation adjustment* is included because the end result of the analysis is cash flow, not income. The amount of depreciation deducted from revenue needs to be added back after taxes to show the correct cash flow for the year. *In-*

cremental cash flow represents the additional cash flow that will be generated in each period by investing in the new machine. These annual incremental cash flow numbers will be used in evaluating the long-term financial success of the project.

By the middle of Year 4 of operations the project outcome has paid back the investment in the project. The total *return on project investment* (ROPI), defined as the total of incremental cash flows over the project outcome lifecycle ($411,000), divided by project cost ($600,000) equals 68.5 percent. Does this mean that the project will be a success and that management should select it? Before anyone can really know if the project is an investment that will potentially add value for shareholders, he or she has to consider something called the *time value of money*.

Time Value of Money

To understand the concept of time value of money, consider the following question. If we offer you $9,700 right now or $10,000 one year from now, which choice would you take? If you say, "I will wait to get the greater amount," you are showing great patience and the ability to defer gratification (a measure of maturity); however, you are also showing that you do not understand the time value of money. We will put the $9,700 in the bank at 5 percent interest. At the end of the year, we will have $10,185. We then pay you $10,000 and have $185 left over. That $185 is how much more you would have received had you accepted the first alternative of taking the $9,700 right now. Projecting how much a certain dollar amount invested today will be worth in the future is referred to as *calculating the future value*. In this case that calculation is $9,700 × 1.05 = $10,185. Another way to look at the time value of money is to convert the $10,000 to be received a year from now into today's dollars to see how it compares with the offer of $9,700. This is referred to as *calculating the present value*. Ten thousand dollars in one year from now, adjusted for the 5 percent interest rate, is equal to $9,523.81 today ($10,000 / 1.05). As with the other method, the choice we offered is clear: $9,700 today is a better deal than $10,000 a year from now because the $10,000 is worth only $9,523.81 today, given the 5 percent interest rate.

The principle that underlies these examples is that in order to compare cash flows occurring over multiple years, the cash flows must be converted to a common time frame. Present value is most commonly used to do this comparison. Thus in investment analysis the incremental cash flows are converted to their present value. The process is called *discounting*. It gives managers the ability to effectively compare projects that have incremental cash flows expected to occur over different time frames.

In the investment analysis for the new product project involving a new machine, the project team has been asked to discount the incremental cash flows expected to come out of the project. In the previous discounting example, we used a bank interest rate of 5 percent as the *discount rate*. The team will use the company WACC as its discount rate. Remember that the weighted average cost of capital is the amount of return that the company must earn to satisfy its shareholders and lenders. If the money that the company invested in its business generates a return *less* than the company's weighted average cost of capital, the company will not be able to meet the expectations of its investors. For this company, the WACC is 15 percent. Applying the WACC as a 15 percent discount rate to the investment analysis produces additional sobering results.

The incremental cash flows that the team had estimated (Figure 7.3) represent the amount of cash paid out or received during each year of the project. Figure 7.4, on the line below those cash flow values, shows the cash flow for each year after it has been discounted to its present value. As we just described, discounting the cash flows lowers the present value of future year cash flows. This is because a dollar to be received in the future is worth less than a dollar to be received today.

The last row in Figure 7.4 shows the cumulative discounted cash flow for each year. The dollar amount in each column represents the total of the cash flow from that year plus all the years before it. For example, in Year 1, the cumulative discounted cash flow of negative $476,000 is the result of adding the $600,000 negative cash flow from Year 0 with the positive $124,000 cash flow from Year 1. The result of adding up the discounted cash flows for all the years of the project is the net present value of the project cash flow. For this project the NPV is $58,000. This number represents the amount of value created for the company over the life of the project. Whenever the net present value discounted at WACC is greater than zero, then the company has generated cash in excess of the amount required to cover the cost of capital. This means that the project has exceeded the investor's expectations and therefore created value for the company. If the net present value is less than zero, then the company used more cash than the project generated. This means that the project did not meet investor's expectations. If the net present value is zero, then cash from the investment would be exactly equal to the amount required to meet investor's expectations.

Risk is not included in NPV. Some companies consider risk by doing risk analysis of the cash flows, applying probability distributions to the cash flows for each year. The resulting cumulative discounted number is known as *expected present value* (EPV). A detailed description of this process is beyond the scope of this book, but project managers should understand this term. Again, EPV designates cash flows that have been adjusted based on risk factors and then discounted. Another, more sophisticated use of financial risk analysis for project selection involves using *options valuation* theory to identify the value of projects that have a negative NPV now but have a good chance of developing a positive NPV in the future (Luehrman, 1995, 1998). This model sets up categories based on the dimensions of value-to-cost (NPV) and volatility (risk). In the high value-to-cost space are the categories:

FIGURE 7.4. NPV OF CASH FLOWS: NEW MACHINE FOR A NEW PRODUCT PROJECT.

	Project Year 0	Production Year 1	Production Year 2	Production Year 3	Production Year 4	Production Year 5
Investment required	($600)					
Revenue	—	$430	$510	$767	$706	$600
Operating expense	—	(273)	(308)	(442)	(395)	(335)
Depreciation expense	—	(120)	(120)	(120)	(120)	(120)
Operating income	—	37	82	205	191	145
Taxes	—	(14)	(31)	(78)	(72)	(55)
Incremental income	—	23	51	128	119	90
Depreciation adjustment	—	120	120	120	120	120
Incremental cash flow	(600)	143	171	248	239	210
Discounted cash flow	(600)	124	129	163	136	105
Cumulative discounted cash flow	($600)	($476)	($346)	($184)	($47)	$58

Note: Dollars in thousands. Small discrepancies due to rounding.

do the project now, maybe do it now, and probably do it later, in order of increasing volatility. In the low value-to-cost space are the categories: maybe do the project later, probably never do it, and never do it, in order of decreasing volatility (Luehrman, 1998, p. 93). The more progressive companies that invest heavily in risky projects, such as firms in the petrochemical and pharmaceutical industries, are using this method.

The $58,000 net present value for the project in our example is exactly equal to EVA as long as the discount rate used to calculate NPV is equal to WACC. We illustrate this in Figure 7.5 by converting the NPV analysis of incremental cash flows into an NPV analysis of EVA. Converting a net present value analysis into an EVA analysis is not that difficult, and once you see this demonstration that they are the same, you can do either one to calculate how much your project is contributing to shareholder value. The EVA analysis starts with the *incremental income* line (Figure 7.5). This represents the net operating income after taxes (NOPAT). From this amount, rather than adding back the depreciation to get the cash flow, the EVA analysis instead subtracts the capital charge to get the economic income, or economic value added. Note that depreciation is not excluded, because it is assumed there is some deterioration in the economic value of the assets.

The capital charge represents the cost for the capital used each year by the project outcome lifecycle. The capital charge for the financing provided during the project is included in the project investment of $600,000. However, capital is still required until that investment is paid. In this case the firm has capitalized the investment, so it is paid through a depreciation charge of $120,000 per year for five years. Thus the required $600,000 investment in the first year is multiplied by the cost of capital, which is 15 percent in this example. The capital charge for this project, therefore, is $90,000 in Year 1. Note that the capital charge decreases over time to reflect depreciation.

The other difference between the calculations of NPV of incremental cash flows and NPV of EVA is that the latter does not subtract out the initial investment in Year 0 when computing the discounted EVAs. Just as in the cash flow analysis, in order to complete the EVA analysis you must translate the EVA for each year into present value by applying the same discounting process described previously. The results are shown in the line labeled *discounted EVA*. The result of adding up the discounted EVAs for all the years of the project is the *net present value of the EVA,* or the *cumulative NPV EVA.*

As with the original net present value analysis, the project team is looking for a cumulative NPV EVA that is positive, to show that the project will create value for the investors. In the example, both the NPV of incremental cash flows and the NPV of EVA are estimated to generate a cumulative NPV of $58,000. This means that even though the project costs $600,000, the cash flow from the project over five years will

FIGURE 7.5. NPV OF EVA: NEW MACHINE FOR A NEW PRODUCT PROJECT.

	Project Year 0	Production Year 1	Production Year 2	Production Year 3	Production Year 4	Production Year 5
Investment required	($600)					
Revenue	—	$430	$510	$767	$706	$600
Operating expense	—	(273)	(308)	(442)	(395)	(335)
Depreciation expense	—	(120)	(120)	(120)	(120)	(120)
Operating income	—	37	82	205	191	145
Taxes	—	(14)	(31)	(78)	(72)	(55)
Incremental income	—	23	51	128	119	90
Capital charge	—	(90)	(72)	(54)	(36)	(18)
Economic Value Added	—	(67)	(21)	74	83	72
Discounted EVA	—	(58)	(16)	48	47	36
Cumulative discounted EVA	—	($58)	($74)	($26)	$22	$58

Note: Dollars in thousands. Small discrepancies due to rounding.

- Generate sufficient cash to cover the cost of the project.
- Generate a return that exceeds the investment expectations of the company through an additional cash flow worth $58,000 in today's dollars.

As we have been emphasizing, project managers and their teams must remember that from the financial perspective a company is the sum of its projects. If, overall, the projects with their outcome lifecycles meet or exceed the expectations of investors then the company will be able to meet or exceed the expectations of its investors.

Creating Shareholder Value Through Projects

Positive EVA is a measurement of economic value that exceeds investor expectations. It is a contribution to shareholder value. To understand shareholder value better, project managers need to understand what shareholders want. This knowledge will lead to actions that project managers can take to better create shareholder value with their projects.

We talked earlier about investor expectations. What exactly are these expectations, and how do they play out day to day? Suppose you have $10,000 to invest. You go to your local bank and invest in a one-year certificate of deposit (CD). At the time you invest your money the bank is paying 4 percent—which means that at the end of the year, the bank will give you back your $10,000 plus $400 in interest. The day after you buy the CD, you decide you need the money back to make a purchase. You go to the bank and find out, first, that it won't give you your money back without penalties, and second, that interest rates have gone up overnight to 5 percent and so you feel that you got a bad deal.

At this same time, someone else comes into the bank with $10,000 to take advantage of the 5 percent CD rate. You really need your money back, so let's say you find a way to make a deal with the new investor to sell her your CD rather than having her invest in the CD from the bank. In order to make this deal you must think about what this investor expects. She expects to make 5 percent on $10,000 in one year, or $500. Your CD will get 4 percent on $10,000, or $400 in one year. In order to offer a deal that she will take, you need to make up that $100 difference in interest.

You can do this by selling her your CD for $9,900. That way, in a year the bank will give her the $10,000 plus $400, and you have already given her the extra $100 by cutting the price. For the investor, it's almost the same as if she had invested $10,000 in the bank at 5 percent. You, however, got a raw deal. You lost $100 because the bank CD rates went from 4 percent to 5 percent.

In a sense, this same process happens everyday when the stock market determines a company's share price. Shareholders have an expectation for the rate of return that they expect. Their expectations are established by looking at what returns are available. If you own shares of a company's stock that earns 8 percent and you want to sell the stock to someone who expects a 10 percent return—the market price will need to fall in order for the stock to meet the investor's expectation. This is generally how stock prices fall. Conversely, if the company's stock earns better than 10 percent, the market price could rise because the investor would be willing to pay more for that level of return. This is generally how stock prices rise. Essentially, the stock market trades every day and sets prices based on expectations of investors and how well the companies meet these expectations. Prices rise and fall based on investors' impressions of this balance. In some respects these dynamics seem to have been suspended as of the first quarter of 2000. A number of analysts are pointing out that the present valuation of some high-tech stocks is much too high for these stocks ever to meet the expectations expressed by the price investors are paying. Only time will tell if the nation is truly in a "new economy" or just an aberration of the old economy. However, one of the authors is constantly reminded of a statement made by the professor of his first finance class: "If you want to be considered a finance guru, just start any of your statements with the following two phrases: 'over the long run' and 'on average.' You will never go wrong." So once again, over the long run and on average, the stock market trades every day and sets prices based on expectations of investors and how well the companies meet these expectations. Prices rise and fall based on investors' impressions of this balance.

Given this understanding of shareholders' expectations, let's return to considering relationship between actual and expected return. The actual dollar return minus expected dollar return equals EVA. So far we have represented the actual dollar return by NOPAT and the expected dollar return by the capital charge. That version of the formula looks at economic value expressed in dollars. This is useful when evaluating projects or setting performance targets because it measures results in a tangible way. But you can also look at EVA as a percentage. This is useful because percentages allow you to compare the EVAs for different size projects or companies. Either way you calculate EVA, the results should be equivalent.

In order to look at EVA as a percentage you will use measures that are also expressed as percentages. To represent the actual return component of the formula, you use the *return on capital* percentage (ROC). This measure best evaluates the return generated from the capital invested in the company. To figure out the return on capital, look at the profit generated by the operations of the business after taxes have been deducted, NOPAT. As we illustrated in Figure 7.2, this value can be determined from the income statement. You then look at the total capital invested in the business (found on the balance sheet). ROC is the ratio, or percentage, that results from dividing NOPAT by the company's or project's total capital at the beginning of the year.

Investors' expected return is the WACC, as we explained earlier. Value added can be expressed as the difference between the actual percentage of return, as measured by ROC, and the expected percentage of return, as measured by WACC. This difference is known as the *spread*, between ROC and WACC. If the actual return is greater than the expected return, the spread is positive value that has been created. If the actual return is less than the expected return, the spread is negative. Value has been destroyed.

The relationship between actual return and expected return is what a company manages on a day-to-day basis. The expected return is not something the average employee can really influence over the short term, because it is largely a function of the company's debt and equity financing. However, managing the actual return is something that everyone can do. And of course, increasing the actual return can lower WACC over the long term. Project managers have a profound impact on ROC because they manage the asset development process that drives ROC over the long run. They should always look for opportunities to increase ROC. The process for doing this is more complicated than just controlling project budgets.

The analysis so far is represented in Figure 7.6. We are moving from left to right and have explained the first two nodes, EVA and WACC, and have started to explore ROC. Now we explore in more detail how to increase ROC, and we show how it relates to projects and project management.

There are four basic methods for improving return on capital:

- Increase profit without increasing the amount of capital employed.
- Generate the same amount of profit using less capital.
- Increase profit in excess of investor's expectations through new capital investments.
- Maintain or increase profits while reducing the amount of capital employed.

There are two components that affect ROC: profit and capital. Improvements to profit happen when employees make decisions that increase revenue or reduce operating expenses or do both. We explored this in the previous two chapters. Employees can effectively manage the capital resources by managing the investments made in long-term assets and working capital.

In order to maximize EVA a company must try to minimize WACC while maximizing ROC. Because investors' expectations are, to a degree, based on risk, managers can have some impact on WACC by their selection of projects and their attempts to minimize risk within the organization. Projects with higher risk should have a higher expected return relative to lower-risk projects.

In order to maximize the return on capital, a company should thoroughly evaluate all potential projects with an emphasis on accurately assessing their future cash

FIGURE 7.6. FACTORS THAT INFLUENCE EVA.

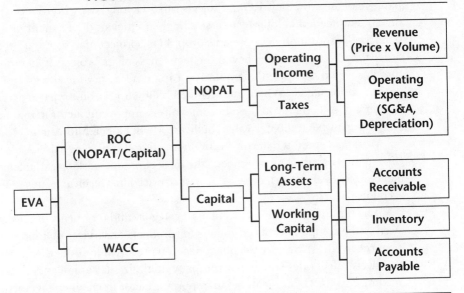

Source: Strategic Management Group, 1997, 32-D, p. 32. ©1997 by Strategic Management Group. Used by permission.

flows and all the relevant risk factors they involve. Capital should be supplied for these projects only when the expected return is sufficient. This means that all project managers should be able to manage the process of developing a business case for a potential project and that this case should include NPV analysis.

In this process of trying to maximize the amount of profit generated by its capital, a company must at the same time make judicious decisions about how much capital it should have. In calculating EVA, companies determine their net operating profit after taxes. Regardless of the specific way a company determines NOPAT, increasing the amount of operating income can maximize it. Because operating income is what remains when operating expenses are subtracted from revenue, to maximize operating income, a company must try to maximize revenue and minimize operating expenses. This was discussed in Chapters Five and Six.

Capital, the long-term cash tied up in the business, is the sum of the long-term assets and the working capital. Thus, to maximize EVA, companies try to minimize the amount of capital they have by managing both the long-term assets and the working capital. The most common long-term assets are property, manufacturing facilities, and equipment. These assets comprise a large portion of the capital invested in a company. By making decisions that either reduce the investment in long-term assets or increase the productivity of these assets, companies can improve their ROC. Projects can go a long way toward reducing the investment needed in long-term assets by their efficient deployment of capital. Chevron Corporation developed its proprietary project management process in order to increase the efficiency and effectiveness of its projects. Chevron knew that this would decrease the amount of capital necessary for any given level of project performance. When you spend $5 billion a year on projects, decreasing the amount of capital you need becomes a very important factor in maintaining and improving shareholder value (Sullivan, 1998; Cohen and Kuehn, 1996).

Working capital is determined by subtracting the current liabilities from the current assets on the balance sheet. The most common working capital accounts that employees affect on a day-to-day basis are accounts receivable, inventory, and accounts payable.

Accounts receivable is a current asset category and represents the cash that is owed to the company by its customers for products or services that have already been received. Any effort to collect accounts receivable sooner that does not negatively affect sales will help a company minimize its capital and, as a result, maximize its ROC. This can be an important factor in client engagement projects. Setting up a payment schedule in the original contract, invoicing on time, following up with the client when payments are late, and adjusting disputes quickly can have an important impact on project EVA. Yet a project manager often sees these issues as secondary to the technically oriented issues.

Inventory is a current asset and represents the value of the products that have been manufactured but have not yet been sold. As long as they remain in the warehouse, the cash used to produce these products remains uncollected. Only when a product is sold does the company receive cash from its customers. When project managers and their teams are designing a new product or production system, their choices can affect the level of inventory that has to be held at any given time. Initiatives such as employing JIT (just-in-time) inventory can certainly help in this regard. Project managers should strive to keep inventories at a minimum in the POLs that they design and develop (unless there is a compelling reason to do otherwise). Internal process improvement projects may have an impact on existing inventory as well. Installing an enterprise resource planning (ERP) system can have dramatic impacts on inventory control given increased coordinated information.

Accounts payable is a current liability category and represents the cash that a company owes to its suppliers. Because suppliers don't charge interest on the money owed them, accounts payable is often referred to as interest-free financing. Delaying payment to a supplier within the terms agreed on allows a company to use that cash owed to the supplier in other areas of the business. This is another factor over which a project manager has influence yet which he or she may not pay much attention to. Possible actions include making purchases of any kind as late as possible and paying as late as the vendor will allow without penalties. Given working capital considerations, renting or leasing equipment rather than buying it may prove to cost less in the longer run as well.

The most important point of all of this information for you, the project manager, is that you should always view your projects as vehicles for creating shareholder value. In order to produce a true return for shareholders, the project that you manage must return the capital used and pay the charge for its use, and then it can contribute profits toward producing more capital for the company. This leads to two important considerations. The first is that all other things being equal, the longer the project takes, the longer you use the capital invested and the more you pay for its use. This calculation needs to be part of the decision making when determining trade-offs. Delays without additional cost still incur charges for the use of capital for a longer period of time. They also increase the time to breakeven as well as the capital charge. This is why cycle time reduction and project time reduction can be so powerful in producing returns to shareholders, as long as all other factors remain the same or at least do not cancel out the gains (as discussed in the example of co-locating the team in Chapter Four). The possible actions suggested here should be the subject of the kind of ongoing analysis and dialogue about projects and project management that we have been illustrating throughout this book.

The second consideration is that the choice of marginal features for a project outcome should ultimately be based on financial arguments, not solely on whether the customer wants a particular feature and whether it is feasible. How much will the feature cost? How much will it delay the project and the break-even point? How much is the extra charge for the longer use of capital? Similarly, if you get a chance to buy time with money, you can use financial analysis to show the gains from reducing project time. Remember that in general, research has shown that a function set that meets customer needs has the greatest impact on the ability of a project outcome to generate sales and that this had the greatest impact on shareholder value (Turner, 1998, p. 5).

Finally, we have been concentrating on a new product example in our discussion, but internal projects should of course also be framed in terms of shareholder value. Any internal project should provide a net increase in cash flow by either increasing revenue, reducing costs, or doing both over the long term. Internal projects are subject to the kind of financial analysis we have been demonstrating. It is important to show how your solution is best by tracing the impact of the internal process improvement or other project outcome through the value chain of the company to show its ultimate impact in the market—the customer and competition. In this way you will be better able to demonstrate the project's impact on what most internal customers care about, shareholder value.

Managing Your Projects as If Shareholders Mattered

Finance matters throughout the project management process because shareholders matter. Remember that ultimately they own the company and that projects are instrumental in creating shareholder value. In addition, companies that create more shareholder value are also more productive, and grow employment faster than other companies (Bughin and Copeland, 1997, p. 157). At the national level, shareholder value has been linked to overall economic performance (Bughin and Copeland, 1997, p. 163). This means that sound entrepreneurial business management should be applied to the total project and project outcome lifecycle. Upper managers, project managers, and their teams should use sound financial and business analysis in selecting projects, thoughtful financial and business planning in the planning of all projects, and judicious financial and business management as an important element of controlling and executing all projects. As we have been illustrating, entrepreneurial business management goes beyond simply controlling the budget. It requires the kind of systems approach that we are advocating in this book. And it should be obvious by now that the job effectiveness of the project manager will soon be measured by the shareholder value produced. With the advent of new information systems and techniques like data warehousing, it is becoming much easier to measure projects according to their contribution to EVA and shareholder value. The chief information officer of Eli Lilly and Company for example, has declared that "with SAP [a total enterprise resource planning software system] and EVA, we've transformed how we've managed this company" (Zweig, 1996, p. 3).

The most important part of initiating a project is selection. Project selection too should be done using sound financial analysis, analysis that incorporates the principles discussed in this chapter. Break-even analysis, as exemplified in Figure 6.5, is a good beginning, but unless managers also incorporate the time value of money, WACC, and the true capital charge to measure project contribution to EVA, they are leaving out important factors that could influence the financial position of the company. Sound financial principles should also be incorporated into the project planning process. The various planning assumptions should be evaluated to assess their effect on the project time to breakeven, time to profitability, NPV, and EVA. A project plan should look like a business plan. The analysis that led to project selection should be refined and amplified as the project planning process uncovers more information. The project plan can then become a better guide for managing the project as a total enterprise, rather than as an isolated piece of work separated from its outcome. With a business-oriented project plan the project manager can better execute and control the project with the end in mind, the end being to optimize EVA and increase shareholder value. At the end of the project the most important principle should be that the project stays open until the outcome lifecycle is complete. Although this is difficult in the turbulence of today's business environment, it is essential to compare the results of the project outcome with the assumptions and plans generated during the project. The traditional lessons learned session that takes place at the end of a project but before the project outcome lifecycle fails to include this vital comparison. Did the projected financial return that justified the investment in the first place really happen? Could we have managed the project better to make the projected financial return happen or make even a better return? These are very important questions. Without answers to such questions, it is very difficult for a company to improve EVA at its source, the project portfolio. Process managers can incrementally improve EVA through intelligent day-to-day decisions, but they are limited by what project managers give them to work with.

Applying EVA Analysis to Project Decisions

Figure 7.5 is based on the conventions of investment analysis. It assumes that management is facing the future, trying to select the best project in which to invest. It treats the project as a lump sum of money to be invested in the POL. The POL then represents the return on that investment. But what about decisions once the project has been chosen and the project manager must try to use analysis of EVA as a basis for making decisions? Figure 7.7 shows how the project that was analyzed in Figure 7.5 might look from the point of view of the project manager rather than the financial analyst. It starts at the beginning of the project rather than with the POL. It assumes that the project manager is facing the projected cash flows as he or she is managing the project and that the project manager wants to use the model the figure represents as a decision-making tool during the project. It is this point of view that we have built into our business systems calculator. Both cumulative EVA and discounted cumulative EVA are measures of project success. Discounted EVA is useful when looking forward into the future, but cumulative EVA will look just fine as a historical number when looking back from the end of the POL.

The first column is no longer Year 0. It now represents the actual duration of the project. Numbers in this column will be discounted according to the duration of the project, which in this example is one year. The calculator will apply the WACC discount rate on a monthly basis for both the project duration and the POL. We have inserted the cost of the project on the *operating expense* line, because this is where the expenses for most projects will show up on corporate income statements. They are not usually depreciated. Product development, internal, and client engagement project costs are usually mostly salaries that are expensed. If the project

FIGURE 7.7. THE PROJECT AND THE POL: PROJECT MANAGER'S POINT OF VIEW.

	Project Duration	POL Year 1	POL Year 2	POL Year 3	POL Year 4	POL Year 5
Investment required						
Revenue	$0	$430	$510	$767	$706	$600
Operating expense	(560)	(273)	(308)	(442)	(395)	(335)
Depreciation expense	0	0	0	0	0	
Operating income	(560)	157	202	325	311	265
Taxes	212	(59)	(76)	(123)	(118)	(100)
NOPAT	(348)	98	126	202	193	165
Cumulative NOPAT	(348)	(250)	(124)	78	271	436
Capital charge	(40)	(44)	(25)	0	0	0
Economic Value Added	(388)	54	101	202	193	165
Cumulative EVA	(388)	(334)	(233)	(31)	162	327
Discounted EVA	(337)	41	66	116	96	71
Cumulative discounted EVA	($337)	($297)	($230)	($115)	($19)	$53

Note: Dollars in thousands. Small discrepancies due to rounding.

is depreciated, as a new facility would be, for example, then you should use the method for handling depreciation shown in Figure 7.5. In some cases, projects will have some elements that are expensed and other elements that are depreciated. These will need a combined approach of the two models. Operating income is negative because there is no revenue yet. We have inserted positive taxes to account for the savings on taxes that the project expense will provide for the company as a whole by reducing overall net profit. (This is probably the first time anyone has pointed out to you how your project adds value over the short term by spending money!) These positive taxes reduce the expense so that net operating profit after taxes is $348,000. The capital charge for the project is calculated by applying a monthly capital charge of 1.25 percent times the accumulated costs of the project each month. We assume that the project spent $46,655 per month, which spreads the total cost of $560,000 over the twelve months. (The capital charge will be greater when the project spends most of its total expenditure at the beginning of the project and smaller when the projects spends most of its total expenditure near the end of the project. This is yet another argument for paying attention to working capital management principles.) Using the compounding future value formula, the capital charge works out to a total of $40,000 for the year. The $560,000 cost of the project plus the $40,000 capital charge equals the $600,000 investment used to calculate EVA in Figure 7.5. The result is a negative EVA of $388,000 at the end of the project duration. This is the amount that must be paid back in order to break even on this investment. This happens during Year 3 of the project outcome lifecycle.

Revenue begins with the first year of the POL. The cash flow is quite similar that shown in Figure 7.5 except that there is no depreciation and the capital charge is based on the running outstanding balance of the negative EVA of the project. The capital charge of $44,000 in Year 1 of the POL is the result of the calculation $388,000 − $98,000 (NOPAT) × 15 percent WACC. In Year 2, it is $334,000 − $126,000 × 15 percent. It goes to zero during Year 3 when there is no longer an outstanding negative balance. Although the example of EVA in Figure 7.5 has a cumulative discounted EVA of $58,000, this example has a cumulative discounted EVA of only $53,000. Why? The primary difference is that the model in Figure 7.7 does not spread the project expenses over the five years of the project outcome lifecycle through depreciation. Cumulative EVA without discounting in the Figure 7.5 example is $141,000. In Figure 7.7, it is $327,000. So, on a year-by-year basis, this method based on a project manager's point of view actually produces a higher EVA, but because it incurs all of the capital charges early in the venture, the cumulative discounted EVA is less. If we were to do a similar calculation on the NPV of the cash flows in Figure 7.4 by starting the discounting in Year 0 instead of Year 1, there would be a similar reduction in NPV. In this case it would occur because even though discounting in the first year would reduce the negative $600,000 to a negative $522,000, the positive cash flows would be discounted even more because they are moved outward an extra year. Such viewing of a venture from the present to the future for investment analysis demonstrates the power and importance of cycle time reduction and revenue acceleration. However, each year the POL is producing Economic Value Added for shareholders. While managing the project, the project manager wants to make decisions to maximize the amount of that EVA each year and push as much of it as possible earlier rather than later in the project outcome lifecycle. In the end, either point of view, the financial manager's or the project manager's, produces essentially the same results and dynamics. Each should be able to support the other in adding to shareholder value.

Examples

The Newprod and Newsys project examples are a final demonstration of the importance of finance to the project manager.

Newprod Project

The Newprod project decision not to include an additional feature was made in Chapter Six. The team also found from the calculator output that the net present value of the choice was $2,900,751. The NPV was calculated using the company WACC of 15 percent. A positive NPV using the company WACC means that the cash flow is greater than investors' expectations. This positive NPV is equivalent to a positive EVA.

Newsys Project

Figure 7.8 shows the marginal cash flows for the Newsys project. The cost of the project including the capital charge is entered under Year 0. In this case the company is depreciating the phone system over five years, which is reflected in the *depreciation expense* and added back in in the *depreciation adjustment*. The overall savings from the project were forecast to be positive as shown in the *adjustment* line, which reflects the difference in operating expense with and without the project before depreciation. This line is the result of adding the change in revenue and the change in expense each year to calculate the net change in revenue. This amount then becomes the basis for a cash flow analysis to determine the value added by the project. This turns out to be a promising venture. It has an overall return on project investment of 197 percent, with an average of 39 percent per year over the five years. The marginal cash flows resulting from the project are used to analyze NPV. You can see that the contribution to shareholder value of this project, if it goes according to this forecast, will be $385,000. It will break even during the third year. When members of upper management reviewed the business case, they subjected it to a very conservative rule of thumb (ROT). Because cost overruns always seem to happen and revenues or cost savings are almost always overestimated, they reduced both savings and increased revenue by 50 percent. The NPV still came out to be $60,442. Then they assumed that the project would take ten months instead of seven and would cost $500,000. Given the original assumptions about revenue enhancement and cost saving, NPV was still a positive $266,358, but using the conservative ROT, NPV went to a negative $58,670. However, assuming that everything would not go wrong at once, they approved the project. The team now had some parameters to use in making decisions about time and cost overruns and about possible effects on the project outcome lifecycle.

FIGURE 7.8. NPV OF MARGINAL CASH FLOWS: NEWSYS PROJECT.

	Project Year 0	Production Year 1	Production Year 2	Production Year 3	Production Year 4	Production Year 5
Forecast revenue	—	$411,666,667	$537,333,333	$730,600,000	$827,467,333	$951,587,433
Forecast operating expense	—	(288,166,667)	(376,133,333)	(511,420,000)	(579,227,133)	(666,111,203)
Adjusted revenue	—	412,078,334	537,870,666	731,330,600	828,294,800	952,539,020
Adjusted operating expense	—	(288,397,143)	(376,434,165)	(511,829,034)	(579,690,399)	(666,643,959)
Adjustment	—	181,191	236,502	321,566	364,201	418,832
Depreciation expense	—	(72,857)	(72,857)	(72,857)	(72,857)	(72,857)
Operating income	—	108,334	163,645	248,710	291,345	345,975
Taxes	—	(41,167)	(62,185)	(94,510)	(110,711)	(131,470)
Incremental income	—	67,167	101,460	154,200	180,634	214,504
Depreciation adjustment	—	72,857	72,857	72,857	72,857	72,857
Cash flow	(364,284)	140,024	174,317	227,057	253,490	287,361
Discounted cash flow	(364,284)	125,021	138,964	161,614	161,098	163,056
Contribution to shareholder value	(364,284)	140,024	174,317	227,057	253,490	287,361
Cumulative contribution to shareholder value	($364,284)	($239,262)	($100,298)	$61,317	$222,414	$385,471
NPV	$385,471					
Break-even period	3					

FIGURE 8.1. BUSINESS SYSTEMS DIAGRAM.

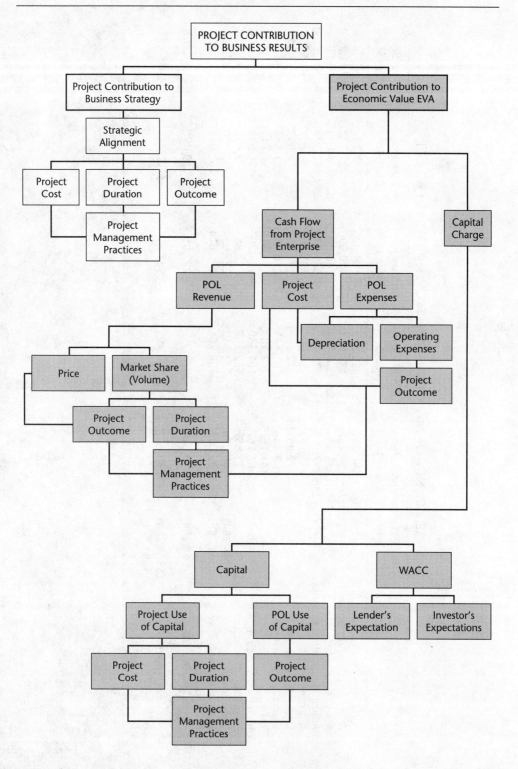

CHAPTER EIGHT

DECISION MAKING AND THE BUSINESS SYSTEMS APPROACH

Chance favors the prepared mind.

LOUIS PASTEUR, REPORTED IN 1927

In this chapter we illustrate how an understanding of business systems can help you in making project management decisions. We use our business systems calculator, which is based on our business systems diagram (Figure 8.1), and illustrate how various project management decisions can be evaluated based on their effect on economic value.

Uses for the Business Systems Calculator

There are three basic uses for the business systems calculator. First, project managers and other managers can use it to develop a better understanding of the interactions among the variables in business systems that work to produce economic value. It is one thing to talk about such an interaction and the effects of different variables, but a clearer understanding develops when you see the numerical effect of changes in the variables on the value created by the project outcome. We invite the reader to use the on-line calculator provided with this book to work through the examples in this chapter and solidify the knowledge gained from the last seven chapters.

Second, project managers and other managers can use the calculator to discover which project management variables, or factors, are most important for producing economic value and which factors cause the biggest change in that value. This tells the project manager which factors deserve the most attention. More specifically, the relative importance of the factors is determined by analyzing the sensitivity of cash flow to changes in these factors. This is called *sensitivity analysis,* and the process is shown in this chapter.

Third, project managers and other managers can use the calculator to evaluate the effects of various decisions normally made during the execution of a project. This chapter includes examples of such decisions as they affect different types of projects, and it shows the procedure for analysis.

In the previous chapters we have presented many of the steps in using the business systems calculator. With the information from the last chapter, we can complete the description of the calculator here. The final three input variables are the WACC, the tax rate, and the number of months to be considered in calculating net cash flow and net present value (NPV). Output variables include cash flow, both with and without considering the cost of capital, and NPV. The complete set of data and the results are illustrated in Figure 8.2. The net cash flow figures are the summation of all cash flows from the beginning of the project until the end of the time considered. That is, they are the difference between all cash in and all cash out. The net cash flow with the capital charge is thus the shareholder value that is created as a result of the project.

Sensitivity Analysis

The best way to perform a sensitivity analysis is to start with a base case that describes the most likely scenario for the project and then vary the assumed input values one by one to see which has the most effect on cash flow. The base case should come from the business case used to decide on doing the project. In the following examples, the base case assumptions are the ones used in Figure 8.2 for the Newprod project and shown in Figure 8.3. The various results from the calculator have been entered into tables so they can be easily compared.

To begin a sensitivity analysis, you might examine the effect of changing the total project investment and then the project duration, both by 100 percent. We show this change for two types of product development projects. The first is a radical new product, one that carries a penalty in market share if you miss the market (Figure 8.4). The second is an incremental product, one for which it is assumed there is no market share penalty for missing the start of the market. Incremental products are often new versions of current products and are not usually as sensitive to market timing (Figure 8.5).

For this project in which market share drops when you miss the market, it is better to be 100 percent late than to spend 100 percent more. This shows us that

FIGURE 8.2. BUSINESS SYSTEMS CALCULATOR COMPLETE CASE.

Project

Project duration	12
Total project salaries	$3,000,000
Total project investment (including other expenses)	$3,000,000
Project investment with capital charge	$3,171,037

Market demand

Length of time until the market for this product begins	(months)	12
Length of time after introduction to peak of market	(months)	24
Length of time after peak of market ends	(months)	20
Sales volume at market maturity	(units/month)	20,000

Revenues

Price	($/unit)	$300.00
Price deterioration	(%/year)	5%
Expected market share if first to market	(%)	30%
Expected market share otherwise	(%)	20%

Costs

Costs of goods sold	($/unit)	$240.00
Cost reduction	(%/year)	8%
Selling, general and administration (variable)	(% of revenues)	0%
Selling, general and administration (fixed)	($/month	
Depreciation	($/month)	—
Other expenses	($/month	—
Tax rate	(%)	33%
Company WACC	(%/year)	15%

Breakeven

Approximate time to breakeven	(months)	33

Net cash flow (NCF)

Period of time to be considered in NCF calculation	(months)	55
Net cash flow without capital charges		$2,622,504
Net cash flow with capital charges		$1,955,345
Net present value		$1,152,361

FIGURE 8.3. BASE CASE VALUES.

Investment	$3,000,000
Project duration	12 months
Market begins	12 months
Market peak	20,000 units, 24 months
Market share	30% if first, 20% otherwise
Sales price/unit	$300
SG&A	5% of sales revenue
Total unit costs	$240
Tax rate	33%
WACC	15%
Net present value	$1,152,361
Net cash flow (with capital charge)	$1,955,345

FIGURE 8.4. ANALYSIS OF INVESTMENT AND DURATION CHANGES FOR RADICAL PRODUCT.

	Base Case	Change Investment	Change Duration
Investment	$3,000,000	$6,000,000	
Project duration	12 months		24 months
Market begins	12 months		
Market peak	20,000 units, 24 months		
Market share	30% if first, 20% otherwise		
Sales price/unit	$300		
Total unit costs	$240		
Net cash flow (with capital charge)	$1,955,345	($1,410,388)	($1,039,217)
Time to breakeven	33 months	44 months	72 months
Difference from base		($3,365,733)	($2,058,562)

the typical argument in new product development is not always true. This disagrees with the results of the McKinsey & Company study mentioned in Chapter Four (Dumaine, 1989) that missing the market has a much greater effect on cash flow than does missing the budget. Here missing the budget had a greater effect than missing the market.

Assume now that the product involves not a radical development but rather a small change. In that case the penalty for a project of longer duration is likely to lie in lost sales during those extra months and not in lost market share. For this product for which market share remains the same, the effects of changes in investment and duration show that it seems better to spend less and have a longer

FIGURE 8.5. ANALYSIS OF INVESTMENT AND DURATION CHANGES FOR INCREMENTAL PRODUCT.

	Base Case	Change Investment	Change Duration
Investment	$3,000,000	$6,000,000	
Project duration	12 months		24 months
Market begins	12 months		
Market peak	20,000 units, 24 months		
Market share	30% if first, 30% otherwise		
Sales price/unit	$300		
Total unit costs	$240		
Net cash flow (with finance charge)	$1,955,345	($1,410,388)	$160,455
Time to breakeven	33 months	44 months	38 months
Difference from base case		($3,365,733)	($1,794,890)

duration on the project. In these cases the financial managers are finally vindicated. Doubling the project costs puts the endeavor in such a hole that it takes six months longer to start making a profit than it does when the original time is doubled. So although the cash flows without capital charges are fairly similar, the extra six months of paying capital charges makes the double investment case less attractive.

You might continue your sensitivity analysis by returning to the base case for the radical product and examining the effect of the market assumptions. Again, assume you overestimated by 100 percent in setting up the base case and that the market peak is not twenty thousand units but rather ten thousand units. Also look at the effect of overestimating by about 100 percent on market share.

Figure 8.6 illustrates that cutting market share in half is identical to halving the total market, as expected. Comparing the results to the results in Figure 8.4 shows that overestimating the market peak by 100 percent has a lesser effect than doubling the cost of the project, even when both outcomes make the market. In this case the model seems more sensitive to cost estimates than to sales volume estimates. Thus, in the radical product case when there is a decrease in market share when you miss the market, the developing priority for your attention as the project manager seems to be project cost estimates first, duration estimates second, and sales volume last.

In the case where the market volume is set at ten thousand and there is no decrease in market share when you miss the market, the net cash flows are the same

FIGURE 8.6. ANALYSIS OF MARKET FACTOR CHANGES
FOR RADICAL PRODUCT.

	Base Case	Change Market Peak	Change Market Share
Investment	$3,000,000		
Project duration	12 months		
Market begins	12 months		
Market peak	20,000 units, 24 months	10,000, 24 months	
Market share	30% if first, 20% otherwise		15% if first, 10% otherwise
Sales price/unit	$300		
Total unit costs	$240		
Net cash flow with capital charge	$1,956,345	($705,194)	($705,194)
Time to breakeven	33 months	43 months	55 months

as for the assumption that the project makes the market. In this case, comparing these results to those in Figure 8.5, the priority so far for incremental projects is project cost first, sales volume second, and duration last.

Your sensitivity analysis could move from here to examining the effects on the base case for the radical product of changes in price and in WACC (Figure 8.7). Doing the same analysis for the incremental product, you would find identical results. The model is not as sensitive to these variables. In particular, changing the WACC affects only the net present value of the cash flow, because the WACC is used as the discount rate.

The next step you would take in your analysis is to list the changes from the base case for all variables tested so you can determine which variables seem to have the most effect on cash flow. From the list in Figure 8.8, it seems that missing the project cost estimates had the most effect for both project types. For radical projects this variable was followed in importance by, then market peak, price-cost differences, and lastly, WACC. Of course this is not a totally valid comparison, as mixing the variables is like mixing apples and oranges—the duration variable is time based and the market peak variable is volume based. However, the comparison does indicate where the project manager's attention should be directed in this example. In addition, the market duration result is driven by loss of market share. The penalty for longer projects is found both in increased capital charges and in gaining a smaller market share. The drop in market share is by far the larger factor. Therefore, market peak and duration are measuring essentially the same thing, sales volume.

FIGURE 8.7. ANALYSIS OF PRICE AND CAPITAL CHARGE CHANGES FOR RADICAL PRODUCT.

	Base Case	Change Price	Change WACC
Investment	$3,000,000		
Project duration	12 months		
Market begins	12 months		
Market peak	20,000 units, 24 months		
Market share	30% if first, 20% otherwise		
Sales price/unit	$300	$270	
Total unit costs	$240		
Net cash flow with capital charge	$1,955,345	($703,383)	$830,841
Net present value	$1,442,000 (12%)	$700,000 (24%)	
Time to breakeven	33 months	44 months	33 months

FIGURE 8.8. RANKING THE CHANGES.

Variable	Change	Cash Flow with Capital Charge for Radical Product	Cash Flow with Capital Charge for Incremental Product
Base case		$1,955,345	$1,955,345
Project costs	Double	($1,410,388)	($1,410,388)
Duration	Double	($1,039,217)	$850,345
Market peak	Half	($705,194)	($705,194)
Price-cost difference	Half	($703,383)	($703,383)
WACC	Double	$830,841	$830,841

The picture is different for the incremental product project. It seems that changes in the costs had the most effect for this project, followed by the market peak, price-cost differential, project duration, then WACC. It seems the budget is more important in this instance than cutting duration, as there is no penalty for missing the market. So it seems that financial managers have been right all along for the example projects. Costs do matter when the capital charge is considered!

Now that you know the important factors, the next question you need to answer is how far would your assumptions about these factors have to be off to make the project unprofitable. By itself, a 50 percent decrease in market peak sales yields an unprofitable project. Likewise a 100 percent increase in WACC still yields positive cash flow. But you might ask what the results would be if you were only 50 percent off on both these factors, would cash flow be positive? Figure 8.9 offers two examples of changing several variables at one time for a radical product project. If you feel, as in this example, that your cost estimates could easily be off by $1,000,000 and your sales estimates off by five thousand units at peak demand, then your project needs further study. The two cases with the changes have positive cash flow, but the negative NPV indicates that this cash flow does not cover investor expectations, so neither of these potential changes in the project would add value to the organization.

Decision Making

The kind of analysis we have been discussing gives you important information for making individual decisions during your projects. Consider the Newprod project once more. In that case you, as the project manager, and your team members rejected an additional feature when you assumed that all your competitors would include that feature and that the customer would not pay a premium price for it in your product. Now suppose a suggestion for a new, unique feature is forwarded, a feature that competitors would not have time to include and that customers would pay a premium price for of $25 per unit. Sensitivity analysis can assess the practicality of delaying the product one month at the cost of an additional $250,000 so your team can produce the new feature compared to the practicality of using an outside firm to produce the new feature with no delay but at a cost of $500,000 more in project investment and $20 more per unit in production costs. Which of these is the better case? Again, as Figure 8.10 illustrates, even when the customer will pay a premium of $25 per unit, the new feature does not seem that appealing, although using the outside firm deserves further study. Now assume you add another factor to the analysis. You decide that you might realistically gain an additional 5 percent in market share if you are first to market with the new feature. Adding that to the calculator run yields a net cash flow of $3,509,000 and NPV of $1,636,880 when using the outside firm. Now that option is definitely worth considering.

We have been focusing on product development projects in our examples so far. However, much the same procedure applies for decision making for internal projects. Assume that you are trying to decide between two internal projects. The first would add production capability for an existing product, decreasing costs by an extra 5 percent per year. This project would cost $1,000,000 and would take six months. Because the product already exists, you can forecast the market and your share fairly accurately, and you know that there would be no market penalty

FIGURE 8.9. CHANGING A COMBINATION OF VARIABLES.

	Base Case	Market Peak = 10,000 and WACC = 30%	Investment = $4,000,000 and Market Peak = 15,000
Investment	$3,000,000		$4,000,000
Market peak	20,000	10,000	15,000
WACC	15%	30%	
Net cash flow with capital charge	$1,955,345	($2,897,211)	($437,639)
Net present value	$1,152,361	($726,844)	($218,290)

FIGURE 8.10. MAKING A PRODUCT FEATURE DECISION.

	Base Case	Add Feature with Team	Add Feature with Outside Firm
Investment	$3,000,000	$3,250,000	$3,500,000
Project duration	12 months	13 months	12 months
Market begins	12 months		
Market peak	20,000 units, 24 months		
Market share	30% if first, 20% otherwise		
Sales price/unit	$300	$325	$325
Total unit costs	$240		$260
Net cash flow	$2,662,000	$2,107,000	$2,673,000
Net present value	$1,442,000	$789,000	$1,094,000

for being late to market. The second project would be a Web site that would make it easier for people to order the product. The Web site project would cost $1,500,000 and take three months, but you think it would capture an additional 10 percent market share. To determine which project is the better deal, you develop a base case of a future without either project, then you compare the two proposed projects to that base case, as shown in Figure 8.11.

For the base case you expect $5,691,000. Doing the cost reduction project will reduce cash flow to $4,530,000, so this project should not be done. The Web site project, however, looks like a winner, increasing net cash flow to $5,707,000. This supports the results of the sensitivity analysis for the product development project discussed in the first part of this chapter: changes in the market tend to be more important than price-cost differentials.

FIGURE 8.11. COMPARISON OF TWO INTERNAL PROJECTS.

	Base Case	Cost Reduction Project	Web Site Project
Investment	$0	$1,000,000	$1,500,000
Project duration	1 month	6 months	3 months
Market begins	1 month		
Market peak	20,000 units, 1 month		
Market share	30% if first, 30% otherwise		40% if first, 40% otherwise
Sales price/unit	$300 (5% erosion per year)		
Total unit costs	$240 (8% reduction per year)	$240 (13% reduction per year)	
Net cash flow	$5,691,000	$4,530,000	$5,707,000

In working with any kind of project, any number of combinations of prices, competitor reactions, market conditions, and so forth can be considered. Of course it is important to remember that the data you get from these analyses are indications, not definitive answers. The beauty of making these analyses, with the calculator or on your own, is that you can collect multiple indications so that you are weighing more of the available evidence in making your decision and so that you can give these multiple indications to people whose perspectives may be limited by their corporate function. Suppose the marketing manager says you will lose 3 percent of market share without the new feature. That manager may be concerned only with the market share and not with the project and production costs of getting the feature into the product and still getting the product out on time. With the calculator output, you can show this manager the overall results of the situation. In this case the results are that a 3 percent loss in market share reduces net cash flow to $2,159,000 whereas adding the feature with the outside firm reduces net cash flow to $758,000. Results like these, which take many factors into consideration, can help the project manager broaden the perspectives of everyone involved in a project.

Conclusion

Will using the business systems calculator or doing similar calculations on your own solve all your project management problems? No, it will not really *solve* any of them. What it will help you do is broaden and clarify how you think about the problems in your projects. This will enable you and your team to develop better solutions than you would with less information and analysis. In this important respect the calculator contains the essence of what we are trying to communicate in this book. Project management must expand from a narrow approach driven by the traditional triple constraint thinking to a broader, more inclusive approach driven by business systems thinking. The calculator is a simple model of a company's overall business system. As you apply its functions to your present situation and possible future situations, you will get a better feel for how that system works and for how the parts of the system interact with each other to produce an outcome. Similarly, the outcome with which project management is directly concerned must also change from the outcome of the project itself to the total outcome of the project and project outcome lifecycle. This is the outcome that ultimately contributes to shareholder value.

Finally, here are six basic questions that you should ask about your project to begin thinking like a CEO and acting like an entrepreneur. These questions also serve as a review of the previous chapters.

1. Is the project aligned with the strategy of the larger organization (department, division, business unit, and business)?
2. Have you used all of the project management and leadership factors possible?
3. Are you focused on the customer, the end-user, and the competition in order to maximize the revenue of the project outcome?
4. Have you considered all the relevant cost factors—the cost of the project, the cost of the project outcome, and the capital charge against the project investment—in order to decide on appropriate costs?
5. Do you know why finance matters for your project and how the time value of money will affect the project outcome lifecycle, positive cash flow, and shareholder value?
6. Have you explored all these issues systemically, using the calculator to determine project sensitivities to variations in time, money, and outcome factors?

When you can answer yes to all these questions, you will be well on your way toward developing the business skills required for project managers to succeed in the future.

CHAPTER NINE

THE PROJECT VENTURE DEVELOPMENT PROCESS

Much of our American progress has been the product of the individual who had an idea; pursued it; fashioned it; tenaciously clung to it against all odds; and then produced it, sold it, and profited from it.

HUBERT H. HUMPHREY, ADDRESS TO THE JUNIOR CHAMBER OF COMMERCE, DETROIT, MICHIGAN, 1966

The fundamental question you may be asking now that you have read the first eight chapters is, So what do I do now? To help you answer this question, we offer you a *thought experiment* that will allow you to experience the practical implications of the principles we have been discussing for your job as project manager. Following this experiment, we outline a project venture development process intended to depict an ideal desired state for project management in the future. The process is also based on the principles discussed in this book, and it takes the concept of the project-based organization to its logical conclusion. We conclude by offering a list of things you should focus on and do at each stage of a project to act more like an entrepreneur and think like a CEO.

A Thought Experiment

Imagine, if you will, a company that has organized all of its work around ventures. A *venture* is a potential business that an individual or a company will invest in to realize a return on its investment. For our purposes, we define a venture further as consisting of a project and a project outcome lifecycle (POL) coupled together to constitute a viable business model. Ventures selected will have the potential of providing a better return on investment than any other competing for funding in the company venture funding system. For each of the company's ventures, the venture team consists of the project team and the implementation team; together these teams contain all the people necessary to develop, and operate the venture throughout its lifecycle. Bonus compensation for the project and implementation managers is heavily dependent on the success of the venture. This makes it very much in their financial interest for the venture to succeed. A venture failure will leave them with less compensation than they would normally expect, but a venture success will be very rewarding. The team members are compensated in a similar fashion, but in general they have a smaller percentage of their compensation at risk. Any manager or team member can choose to increase the amount of his or her compensation at risk, which increases the potential reward from success and also the potential loss from failure.

This model is very close to what is going on right now in e-commerce new venture start-ups (Platten and Weinberg, 2000). It is not much different from standard compensation plans that are based on economic value or other performance goals and that provide incentive payments or stock options when goals are met (Delves, 1999). This thought experiment simply creates a bonus directly tied not to the economic value of the company as a whole but to the long-term economic value of the venture.

How would you manage your venture given this kind of environment? We suggest that these principles would underlie your management behavior:

- The venture should be a viable business that combines all the elements of a value chain necessary to serve a customer base that will sustain the business over the long run.
- Like a project core team that consists of a person from every function necessary to produce the project outcome, the venture core team should consist of one person from each link in the value chain necessary to delight the customer. This may require including suppliers and intermediary customers on the core team.
- Those with the responsibility for implementation of the POL will want to be on the venture core team to give their input. Because your ultimate success will depend on how they operate the POL, you too should want them on the team. The right incentives can create strange bedfellows.
- Both project and POL team members should work toward a perfect handoff of the project outcome to the POL team so that implementation begins as soon as possible and revenue flows in as soon and as fast as possible. One team blaming the other for problems and delays won't help anyone. The incentive built into the system should encourage all team members to roll up their sleeves when it is necessary to fix something that has gone wrong.

- The project team should strive to keep costs down during the project, in the design of the POL, and during POL operations (without sacrificing the quality of the outcome and thus customer satisfaction), thus both optimizing revenue and maximizing EVA.
- The project team should be available as long as necessary to get the POL started successfully, as long as the cost to keep the team available does not outweigh the financial gain from its help.
- Throughout the course of the project you should make decisions with the end in mind. Whenever there is a trade-off between time, cost, and quality, you should choose the solution that maximizes EVA and shareholder value.
- In short, all members of the venture team should strive to maximize EVA. Why? Because they now have the same interests as shareholders. The more value they create with the venture as a whole, the more they will earn for themselves.

This thought experiment illustrates an ideal set of circumstances that would support managing projects in a way to maximize their economic value. If you, the project manager, can immerse yourself in these imagined circumstances it will help to drive home the impact on your motivation and behavior of managing a project as if shareholders mattered. It will also suggest some practical implications for your job as a project manager. It is likely that you will see you need to manage projects more like business ventures and less like technical or scientific undertakings. In the end, project management is not a technical process. It is a business process. To thrive it needs to be incubated in a business-oriented environment.

The Process

To support a venture-oriented project management system, we recommend a business-oriented process that is modeled to some extent on the venture capital system that has become so ubiquitous in the high-tech world of e-commerce and the dot-coms. Think of the company as a venture incubator, an environment structured specifically to promote the growth and well-being of new ventures. These ventures, as we have said, are the projects coupled with their project outcome lifecycles so as to constitute viable business models worthy of investment. The project selection process is run as a venture capital selection process and the project office becomes the venture development center. Venture team members own their ventures through a system of virtual stock options that convey rights to virtual stock in the venture, valued according to the venture's contribution to the EVA of the company (for examples of corporate venture compensation plans, see Block and MacMillan, 1995, pp. 125–143). How different would the project management process be in this environment? Different enough to promote and emphasize managing the project for business results. Consider the highlights of this changed process, which has five stages:

Initiating the Venture

- The business case is developed by the venture core team (one member from each link in the value chain from the initial process to the customer) led by the project manager and the POL manager.
- An internal venture capital board funds or rejects the venture, as part of developing and maintaining a portfolio of ventures. Critical selection criteria include strategic fit, competitive advantage, and potential return on investment of the venture (Block and MacMillan, 1995). Board members' incentives are based on how well the portfolio of ventures fares over the long run.
- The venture is staffed with the end in mind in order to support the total POL and to make sure that all links in the value chain are represented on the core team and will participate in the overall planning.

Planning the Venture

- The venture team refines the business case and converts it to action steps and major milestones in order to develop a plan that can guide the venture to the end of the POL.
- The team plans the phases of the project and POL, initially providing a higher level of detail by major milestones for the project than for the POL.
- As the project rolls out, the venture team adds detail to the POL part of the plan.
- All aspects of the venture become part of the budget, schedule, and specifications.
- The plan is constructed from the perspective of the venture as a whole rather than from the project perspective.

Executing and Controlling the Venture

- The venture team implements the business plan.
- The team treats all assumptions of the business plan as working hypotheses and the venture as an experiment.
- At each major milestone, the team checks the plan's assumptions against what has happened. If there is a gap, the team changes the assumptions accordingly and retests the plan for feasibility. Then the team decides whether to continue or stop at this point (Block and MacMillan, 1995).

Transitioning (Closing) the Venture

- The project team hands off the project outcome to the POL implementation team.
- Key members of the project team are linked to the implementation team to support the transition for as long as is necessary to facilitate a fast, cost-effective start up.

Operating and Evaluating the Venture

- The organization endeavors to broaden the traditional lessons learned discussion to include business execution and project implementation. The goal is to learn how to carry out better ventures for a greater return on the investment of capital.
- A process is set up to monitor the POL in order to compare the business results to the expectations stated in the business plan and to conduct lessons learned sessions at useful stages of the POL.
- Systems are put in place to measure contribution to EVA on a venture-by-venture basis. When ventures return a positive EVA, the venture team is compensated accordingly.

Things That You Can Do Now

We realize that not all companies will embrace the principles outlined in this chapter. Therefore, for most readers, the most immediate question will be, What can I do now given a standard corporate environment for projects? In the remainder of this chapter, we provide a list of suggestions. We are also providing a space on our Internet site (www.projectmanagersmba.com) for you, the reader, to add more suggestions based on your experience trying to apply the principles of this book to your own project management. We can all learn from both successes and problems. In addition, if your company does not have a standard process and template for creating a project business plan, the Appendix to this book contains a practical template that you can use as is or as a basis or creating your own template. You can also download an electronic version from the Internet site www.projectmanagersmba.com.

1. *Develop a business case for each project.* This is a step many companies use for project selection. One example is a financial services company that is a client of one of the authors. Even though most of this company's projects are IT-based internal projects, the company requires a business case for each one. The case

template requires that the project be based on specific client needs and on what the competition is likely to do to meet those same needs. This requires tracing the value chain through internal customers to the ultimate outcome for customers in the marketplace. A business case should perform these functions, at the very least (for further details see the Appendix):

- State where the numbers for the estimated price, sales volume, and production and operating costs come from.
- Specify the accuracy of these numbers.
- Identify the assumptions that drive the numbers. Go back to the business assumptions underlying the origination of the project. Do not only accept outcome, cost, and schedule. Go back to all of the business assumptions that went into the origination of the project.
- Most important of all, identify the business model that suggests this is a sound investment for the company.

2. *Think strategically.* Consider your project in its wider context. What are the links in the value chain that connect this project to the ultimate customer and end-user? How does the project fit into the wider strategy of the company to either support an existing, sustainable competitive advantage or create a new one? You should be able to do the following:

- Describe the big picture.
- Identify the type of business strategy the project is supporting.
- Identify the ways in which the project will promote this strategy of the company.
- Determine the ways in which the project will sustain the competitive advantage of the company.
- Know how the other projects in the company implement the company's strategy.
- Define how fulfilling the business case for this project will implement the strategy.
- Link the numbers of the business case to the strategy.

3. *Turn the business case into a true business plan to guide the project.* To do this, you will incorporate all the elements of the business case into a plan for action and integrate that plan with the rest of the project planning. All this needs to be done with the project team, not in isolation. You should pay particular attention to these steps:

- Remember that you are responsible not just for the project but also for the POL performance.
- If the project is internal, compare the net return on investment for doing the project and for not doing it.
- Refine the numbers and then refine them again. Assign risk probabilities if possible.

- Use the calculator for sensitivity analysis.
- Do more market research. Determine the market demand figures as best as you possibly can and research detailed competitor information.
- Think about your budget as an investment rather than an expense. Consider how to use it to get the best return possible.
- Assemble the core team and do all the business planning with that team.
- Make sure the core team includes important POL implementers such as people from manufacturing engineering, technical support, sales, the training staff, and the maintenance staff.
- Trace through the value chain to identify everything that must happen outside the boundaries of the project to make the POL a success. Trace the value chain even if the project is internal and seems remote from customers and competition.
- Identify the major milestones at which you will stop and check your assumptions.

4. *Execute and control the project through the business plan.* There was a reason why you spent all that time integrating the business plan into the project plan. It should be an integral part of project control. Do not make the mistake of doing all that business analysis on the front end but using only triple constraint thinking to control the project. Focus on these actions and understandings:
   - Use the language of the business plan to negotiate with upper management.
   - Focus on the POL rather than the end of the project.
   - Manage the risks for the POL as well as for the project itself.
   - Use rapid prototyping to stay close to the market and end-users.
   - Check in constantly with customers and end-users.
   - Keep competitive implications in focus (this applies to internal projects too).
   - At each major milestone, compare the results thus far with your assumptions. Ask what changes in assumptions you must make. Ask how these changes will affect the rest of the project.
   - Keep the ultimate business objectives in mind by making all decisions as trade-offs within the business equation. Always ask which alternative will ultimately provide the best competitive advantage and economic value.
   - Understand that the correct response to a request for a change is no longer, "In the next version," or more simply, "No, it is too late." The correct response is a question for analysis, "What is the effect on economic value if we incorporate this change at this late date?"
   - Act strategically by constantly checking that the project is still aligned with its strategic objectives.

5. *Transition smoothly to the project outcome lifecycle.* The end of the project is not the end of the venture but the beginning of its implementation. The project team needs to run alongside the new toddler to keep it from falling down.

- Track the POL, and make sure that project team members stay available to the implementation team as long as they are needed. Balance the cost of these team members against the cost of a slower start-up if the team members were not available to support the POL.
- Write a final project report with numbers, projections, and assumptions that everyone on the core team signs off on and that is checked against reality over the course of the POL in order to promote organizational learning.

6. *Operate and evaluate.*
   - Remember, it ain't over til the POL is over.
   - Check the POL assumptions at the major POL milestones. Take corrective action to improve performance if necessary and possible.
   - When the POL is complete, write a final venture report that compares the actual POL performance with the assumptions in the final project report. Disseminate the final venture report to promote organizational learning.
   - Compensate the venture team according to venture performance.
   - Celebrate success, learn from failure.

APPENDIX

AN OUTLINE FOR BUILDING
A PROJECT BUSINESS CASE AND PLAN

The following outline can be used to develop a business case for a project. The project team can then develop more detail for the business case during the planning process, when the business case becomes a business plan. The major difference between a business case and a business plan is the level of detail and the purpose.

The purpose of a business case is to examine the business dynamics of a proposed project as part of the evaluation and selection process. The business case demonstrates how the project coupled with its project outcome lifecycle (POL) is a complete business venture that will contribute to business results. Thus the case also demonstrates in concrete terms how the project will align with and support the strategy of the organization. Finally, it demonstrates how the project will contribute to the company's economic value.

The business plan adds analysis and data collected during the planning phase of the project. It also highlights the assumptions that went into the business case and now are going into the plan and the actions, tasks, and events that need to take place to make the plan a reality. These assumptions and these actions, tasks, and events should be integrated into the project planning documents. They should become a living part of the project's control process. The business plan should continue to be used as an active planning document during the project outcome lifecycle, serving those who have the responsibility of managing the POL. It is the most important baton that the project team hands over to the implementation team in support of the success of the venture.

The following outline includes cross-references to the chapters that contain concepts important to the outline point at hand. For more detailed explanations of how to work on some of the outline items and of how to go about business planning in general, we recommend that you begin with Tiffany and Peterson (1997). Ignore the title, *Business Plans for Dummies.* It is a good, solid introduction to business planning from an entrepreneur's point of view. Now that you have read *The Project Manager's MBA,* you are prepared to apply this business planning to projects and POLs. Henricks (1999) and Rich and Gumpert (1985) are two more resources worth looking at. Block and MacMillan (1995) and Pinchot and Pellman (1999) provide a perspective on venturing within the larger corporation.

I. Executive summary (three- to five-page summary of the following information).
   A. Description of the project.
   B. Market, customer, and competition.
   C. Cost-benefit analysis.
   D. Sensitivity, risks, and contingencies.
   E. Definitions of success and failure.
II. Description of the project.
   A. *Purpose of the investment.* Summarize what the company should expect to gain from its investment in this project (see Chapter One).
   B. *Key reasons for pursuing the project.* Answer the questions: What are the major reasons for pursuing this project and not other projects like it? What is the business model that drives this project, and how will it contribute to a sustainable, repeatable, scaleable process for positive cash flow? Why does this project make the most business sense? (see Chapter One).
   C. *Strategic alignment.* Answer these questions: How will the project support the company's strategy for sustaining competitive advantage? Is the POL part of a portfolio of outcomes that represent the implementation of a strategy, or is it an element in developing a new strategy? If it is simply a reaction to a development in the market, how will it support the strategy or at least not damage it? (see Chapter Three).
   D. *The value proposition.* Answer this question (make your comments concise): What are the core characteristics that make this venture uniquely valuable to its customers and that will allow continued success over time?
   E. *Project requirements.* Prepare an executive overview of the requirements document for the project. The overview should connect the require-

ments with specific contributions to the business success of the entire
venture (the project and the POL).

F. *Project goal, milestones, and major deliverables.* List these items and relate them
to the business success of the entire venture.

III. Market, customer, and competition (see Chapter Five).

A. *Market analysis.*

1. *Critical success factors.* Answer these questions: What critical success
factors that the company depends on to compete in the marketplace
will be supported, enhanced, or created by this venture? How will this
project sustain, protect, or advance competitive advantage?

2. *Weaknesses.* Answer this question: Are there any weaknesses along
the value chain of this venture that must be strengthened to ensure
success?

3. *Opportunities.* Answer this question: What opportunity in the market
is this venture going to capitalize on?

4. *Threats.* Answer this question: Are there problems or threats that this
venture must be aware of or problems that it has to solve? Address
marketing risk as well as technical risk.

5. *Structure and size of the target markets.* Describe these factors.

6. *Market trends.* Describe the market growth the company might expect
over the POL.

B. *Customer and end-user analysis* (see Chapter Five).

1. *Customer and end-user identification.* Be specific about exactly who is expected to buy and who is expected to use the outcome of the venture.
If it is an internal customer, trace your value chain out beyond that
internal customer to the external customer who actually pays the bills,
and if necessary to the end-user beyond that.

2. *Fulfillment of customer and end-user needs.* Answer these questions: Why
will the targeted customer and end-user want to use the outcome
of the venture? What would they do if it did not exist?

3. *Customer and end-user benefits.* Be specific about what the venture will
do along the value chain of the company to delight customers and
end-users.

C. *Competitive analysis* (see Chapter Five).

1. *Identification of competitors.* Answer these questions: If potential customers and end-users do not use the outcome of the project, what
other product or service are they likely to use in its place? Who would
provide this other product or service to them? (These are your competitors.) Supply this information about competitors for internal
projects too.

2. *Competitors' offerings.* List the reasons why your customers would buy a competitor's offering instead of yours.

3. *Competitive advantage.* Describe the ways in which the project investment will enable the company to provide a better product or service to its customers than competitors can provide.

4. *Countermoves competitors might make.* List the things competitors might do to block the desired advantage that your company intends to derive from the venture.

5. *New competitors.* List potential competitors, those who are not active now but who might come out of nowhere to blindside the project.

6. *Contingency plans.* Describe what you intend to do to meet countermoves by existing competitors and to prepare for new competitors.

IV. Cost-benefit analysis.

A. *Financial model.* Present a financial model. For internal projects, compare the projected financial statement that would result if the project were not done with the projected statement that would result from doing the project. The net difference reveals the NPV, or EVA, of doing the project (see Chapter Two).

1. *Cash flows in.* List the POL revenues and where they will come from (see Chapter Five).

2. *Cash flows out.* List expenses including the cost of goods sold and SG&A expenses (see Chapter Six).

3. *Financial analysis.* Prepare financial statements projected out for five years, including the following (see Chapter Seven):
    a. Income statement.
    b. Balance sheet
    c. NPV.
    d. Discounted EVA.

4. *Assumptions.* List all the important assumptions you have made about the financial model, market, competition, technology, and every other contingency you can think of that may influence the projected numbers of the financial analysis and consequently the success or failure of the venture.

5. *Assumption tests.* List all the milestones and other opportunities that will allow testing of the assumptions in your models.

B. *Nonquantitative factors.* These factors are especially relevant when a project is being taken on for strategic reasons and is difficult to justify financially.

1. *Opportunity costs.* Describe the opportunity costs of doing this project. What else could the company do if it did not do this project, and what would it gain by doing the other project?

       2. *Benefits.* Describe any benefits that are difficult to quantify, such as supporting general capabilities of the company or providing benefits for other ventures not directly connected to the project.

V. Sensitivity, risks, and contingencies.

  A. *Sensitivity analysis* (see Chapter Eight).

       1. *Critical assumptions.* From the complete list of assumptions you made earlier, identify those that are the most critical to the results of the venture by performing a sensitivity analysis on each one.

       2. *Assumption changes.* List the most critical factors identified by the sensitivity analysis, and show how they influence the results of the venture.

  B. *Risk analysis.*

       1. *Identification of risk.* Identify as many events as you can that might influence the critical factors.

       2. *Quantification of risk.* Assign a subjective probability of occurrence to each event, or simply rate each one high, medium, or low probability.

       3. *Management of risk.* Describe what you can do to prevent the high-probability events from happening.

       4. *Contingency plan.* Describe what you will do to minimize damage if a high-probability event occurs. Describe how you will monitor the medium-probability events.

  C. *Contingencies and dependencies.*

       1. *Value chain analysis.* List the things that must happen beyond the boundaries of the project to make the investment successful.

       2. *Responsibility charting.* List the roles of the people who will be responsible for making these things happen.

VI. Definitions of success and failure.

  A. *Metrics.*

       1. *Economic factors.* List the economic measures that will be used to define success.

       2. *Strategic factors.* List the strategic measures that will be used to define success.

  B. *Methods.*

       1. *Process.* Explain how data will be collected to report metrics.

       2. *Responsibility.* List the roles of the people who will be responsible for collecting the data.

GLOSSARY

Accelerated depreciation: A method of calculating depreciation in which the depreciation is higher in the early years of its useful life and lower in the later years.

Account balance: The dollar amount currently remaining in an account.

Accounts payable: The opposite of accounts receivable. Money owed to suppliers for purchases not yet been paid for.

Accounts receivable: Money owed by customers on sales already recognized for goods or services purchased on credit.

Accumulated depreciation: The total of the annual depreciation charges. It represents the total cumulative loss of book value on assets.

Acquisition: The purchase of another company with cash or stock.

Advertising expense: Money spent on advertising.

This Glossary draws extensively from the Strategic Management Group's *Why Finance Matters,* an interactive CD-ROM glossary. ©1997 by Strategic Management Group. Used by permission.

After-tax income: What is left of revenues after all expenses and income taxes are paid.

Amortization: The repayment of a loan by installments or the depreciation of an asset, tangible or intangible, over its expected useful life.

Assets: The total resources of a corporation, such as cash, fixtures, real estate, buildings, equipment, and so forth that can be converted into cash. On balance sheets, most assets are listed at book value or at their original purchase cost minus accumulated depreciation.

Asset turnover: A ratio that expresses how a company finances the capital invested in its business. It is long-term debt divided by capital. It answers the question, How much debt do we use to finance the business?

Balance sheet: A statement of financial position that shows total assets equal to total liabilities plus owners' equity. It answers these two questions: How much is invested in the business? How is the investment financed?

Bank loan: Money borrowed from the bank, usually short term.

Bond: A certificate that is evidence of debt where there is a trustee to represent the lenders. Bonds pay interest to the creditors. Bonds are liabilities and must be repaid.

Book value: The value of something on the books. Typically book value refers to investment in an asset minus depreciation. Also known as historical cost and acquisition cost.

Business case: A document that outlines the strategic, marketing, and financial justification for doing a project.

Business plan: A more detailed version of the business case that includes further research, confirmation of data, and the actions necessary to ensure that the project is a commercial success.

Cannibalization: The loss of sales from an existing product due to the introduction of a new product.

Capital: The total cash invested in a company that must generate a return. Capital is usually defined as assets minus current liabilities (or long-term liabilities) plus owners' equity.

Capital budgeting: A process of analyzing proposed investment projects at the plant and division level. It attempts to ensure that projects are worth pursuing by examining their overall rate of return measured against expectations.

Capital charge: The amount of economic profit that must be earned to satisfy shareholders and lenders. It is the weighted average cost of capital (%) multiplied by the capital ($) invested in the company.

Capitalizing expenses: Amortizing long-term expenses over a multiyear period. These expenses could represent spending on plant, buildings, advertising, and so forth.

Cash cycle: The process in a company or project of raising, investing, generating cash, and providing a return to lenders and investors.

Cash flow: The amount of cash that flows into or out from a project or company. Some companies refer to cash flow as *net income plus depreciation,* or *an approximation of the cash flow generated from income.*

Cash flow statement: A report that summarizes activities that generate and consume cash in order to reconcile the change in cash balance from period to period. It groups activities into one of three areas: operating activities, investing activities, and financing activities. Also referred to as the *statement of cash flows.*

Cash inflow: Cash coming into the company, also known as a *source of cash.* For example, during the financing stage of the cash cycle, a company's receipt of a bank loan is a source, or inflow, of cash.

Cash outflow: Cash flowing out of the company, also known as a *use of cash.* For example, during the investing stage of the cash cycle, a company's investment in new property and equipment is a use, or outflow, of cash.

Common size analysis: Analysis that expresses each expense on the income statement as a percentage of total revenues, and each asset, liability, or equity account on the balance sheet as a percentage of total assets. Expressing items by the same measure is useful for making an apples and apples comparison of items that are otherwise apples and oranges.

Common stock: Stock representing the class of owners that has residual claims on the assets and earnings of a corporation after all debt and preferred shareholders' claims have been met.

Concept lifecycle: The process over a given period of time through which an innovation is adopted by users from innovators and early adopters to laggards.

Cost: The amount of cash that a company has to pay to acquire the goods and services that it uses to conduct business.

Cost driver: Anything that influences the cost of a cost object.

Cost object: Something that analysts want to know the cost of.

Cost of capital: The rate of return required to meet investor expectations. The cost associated with acquiring cash from both lenders and shareholders. The cost of capital is expressed as a percentage (for example, 10 percent).

Cost of goods sold (COGS): The expenditure on the production of the goods and services sold (not just produced) in a given operating period. Cost of goods sold is often called *product costs*.

Current asset: An asset that is typically converted into cash within one year.

Current liability: An obligation owed to creditors that must be paid back within one year.

Current ratio: The ratio between a company's current assets and its current liabilities. This ratio is useful for measuring a company's liquidity. It is determined by dividing the current assets by the current liabilities. It answers the question, Does the business have more cash coming in from assets than it must pay out in liabilities in the next year?

Customer intimacy: A business strategy that emphasizes identifying the customers who are willing to pay for tailor-made service and then delivering that service to them.

Debt: Short, informal term for liabilities.

Deferred revenue: Money received from customers in advance of performance of revenue activities. This money will be spent on goods or services or will be repaid to the customer.

Depreciation: The loss of economic value of an asset. It represents the reduction in value of an asset over time. It is also the portion of an investment that can be deducted from taxable income. The word *amortization* describes the depreciation of an intangible asset (for example, patents) or an asset with a limited life. The word *depletion* describes the depreciation of a waiting asset (for example, oil, gas, or coal).

Depreciation adjustment: Adjustment made in a discounted cash flow analysis that adds back depreciation to show the correct cash flow for the year.

Depreciation expense: Expenses associated with the depreciation of an asset.

Direct cost: A cost that can be traced to a cost object in a practical, economically workable way.

Direct expense: An expense directly tied to the creation of the product. Also known as a *product expense.*

Directed strategy: What upper management does to develop and facilitate a vision and a strategic plan.

Discount rate: The rate used to calculate the present value of incremental cash flows. It represents the rate of return needed to satisfy investor expectations.

Discounted cash flow analysis: An analysis of whether a project will meet expectations. It converts incremental cash flows to their present value using a discount or hurdle rate. In calculating discounted cash flows for a project investment proposal, the weighted average cost of capital (WACC) is often used as the discount rate.

Diversification: An attempt to reduce business risk by offering multiple products or entering multiple businesses that are in some ways unrelated.

Dividend: A payment (distribution of earnings) by a company to its shareholders.

Dividends payable: Money owed to shareholders for dividends that have been declared but not yet paid.

Economic value: Returns generated by a company that are above the level needed to meet the WACC.

Economic Value Added: (See EVA.)

Efficiency: How well a company is using its assets.

Emergent strategy: What middle and project managers actually do as they implement directed, planned strategy

Equity: The ownership interest in a business. It is made up of the initial investments of the owners plus any income not paid out as a dividend. Equity is often called the *residual value,* because owners get what is left after all liabilities have been satisfied. Equity may also be called *net worth.*

Equity investors: Investors who are owners of the business.

EVA (Economic Value Added): A financial management system developed to quantify the value a company provides to its investors. EVA is calculated by subtracting the expected return, represented by the capital charge, from the actual return that a company generates, represented by net operating profit after taxes. EVA is a registered trademark of the consulting firm Stern Stewart & Co.

External report: A report that provides high-level financial information for investors, creditors, suppliers, and others outside the company.

Financial leverage: Use of debt to increase the expected return on equity, measured by the ratio of assets to equity.

Financial leverage ratio: A ratio that expresses how a company finances the capital invested in it. The ratio is calculated by dividing long-term debt by capital. It answers the question, How much debt is used to finance the business?

Financial report: An external report that includes the company's financial statements. These reports must conform to a set of rules called generally accepted accounting principles (GAAP).

Financial statements: Usually the income statement, balance sheet, and cash flow statement and the notes thereto. When published for external purposes, these statements must conform to GAAP.

Financing activities: The raising of funds from investors and the returning of funds to those investors.

Fixed asset: An asset that is not expected to be converted into cash until it has been held for a year or more, also known as a *long-term asset*. Examples include property, buildings, and equipment.

Fixed cost: A cost that tends to stay constant for a stated period, such as the administrative cost incurred by an organization during the year.

Fixed production cost: Production expense that does not vary with production volume.

Forecasting: Estimating or projecting costs or revenues or both, or estimating the trend of the economy or any other variable.

Free cash flow: The difference between cash from operations and cash used in investing. If positive, it shows managers that the operating and investing activities of the company generate sufficient amounts of cash to preclude the need for external financing.

Funds: Generally, working capital or current assets less current liabilities. Sometimes used to refer to cash or to cash and marketable securities.

Future value: How much a certain dollar amount invested today will be worth in the future.

GAAP statement of cash flow: An external financial statement that conforms to GAAP and summarizes activities that generate and consume cash. It groups activities into three areas: operating activities, investing activities, and financing activities.

Goals: Specific objectives that relate to specific time periods and are stated in terms of facts.

Gross margin: The amount remaining after cost of goods sold has been subtracted from revenue. It represents the markup on a product or the difference between the cost to sell it and the revenue generated by the sale.

Gross margin percentage: A ratio that expresses the relationship between the money a company receives from selling its products and the money it uses to manufacture those products. It is calculated by dividing the gross margin by revenue. It answers the question, What is the markup on the products? or, What is the difference between the price and the cost of the product?

Gross profit: The amount remaining after cost of goods sold has been subtracted from revenue. It represents the markup on a product, or the difference between the cost to sell it and the revenue generated by sales.

Ibbotson study: A study by Professors Ibbotson and Sinquefield that examined the average rates of return for multiple investments in corporate stocks over a fifty-one-year period compared to risk-free investments. It showed that shareholders in large companies received a return approximately 6 percent higher per year on average than the return they would have received from investing in U.S. government debt.

Income statement: The statement of revenues, expenses, gains, and losses for a given period, ending with the net income for that period. Also known as the *profit and loss statement,* or P&L.

Incremental income: The amount of profit or loss generated by a project over a specific period.

Indirect cost: A cost that cannot be traced to its cost object in a practical, economically workable way, sometimes called an *allocated cost.* Instead, analysts or managers must use a logical method, called a *cost allocation method,* to distribute indirect costs across cost objects.

Indirect expense: An expense not directly tied to the production of a product. Selling, general, and administrative (SG&A) expenses are categorized as indirect expenses.

Intangible assets: Assets that are not physical entities or whose value goes beyond their physical presence and that do not have set values. Examples are brand names, patents, and customer lists.

Intangibles: Patents, goodwill, and other nonphysical, hard-to-measure costs.

Interest: The charge or cost for using money, expressed as a rate per period, usually one year, called the *interest rate;* or the amount of interest paid (*interest expense*).

Interest bearing liabilities: Liabilities that require payment of interest in addition to payment of principal. Short- and long-term debt are examples of interest bearing liabilities.

Interest coverage: Earnings before interest and taxes divided by interest expense. Interest coverage shows the ability of a company to pay its interest expense with its operating income.

Interest rate: The rate of return that lenders expect on their investment to compensate them for their risk and lost opportunities to use the cash elsewhere.

Internal analysis: An evaluation of the strengths and weaknesses of the company in the areas of manufacturing, marketing, technology, finance, human resources, and so on.

Internal report: A report developed for use inside the company to provide employees with detailed financial information. Companies may use any format for their internal reports, unlike external reports, which must conform to GAAP.

Inventory: Assets held in stock for future use in production or sales. Inventory represents the amount of money already spent to purchase or manufacture goods that will later be sold to customers but are currently unsold. Inventory can be divided into as many as four subcategories: raw materials, work in process, finished goods, and supplies.

Inventory days: A measure of the number of days that elapse until the inventory is sold. It is calculated by dividing inventory by the cost of goods sold and multiplying by 365.

Inventory turnover: A ratio expressing how many times each year a company sells its inventory. Inventory turnover is cost of goods sold divided by inventory. It answers the question, How many times per year can we sell our current inventory, based on our current level of sales?

Invested capital: The money long-term investors have put into the business. It is equal to long-term liabilities plus owners' equity or assets minus current liabilities.

Investing activities: Purchasing the long-term assets a company needs in order to make and sell its products, and selling the long-term assets no longer needed by the company.

Investment analysis: A rigorous process of evaluating proposed projects for capital spending. The resulting project proposal should document the projected cash flows and the risks involved with achieving those projections.

Labor: Work for wages.

Liability: A company's obligation to pay what it owes.

Liquidity: The state of having sufficient cash or capacity to raise cash to meet short-term obligations.

Long-term assets: Assets that will be converted into cash over a period of time typically longer than one year. Examples include property, buildings, and equipment.

Long-term liabilities: Obligations owed to creditors that are paid back over many years.

Market: Potential or estimated consumer demand for a particular product or service.

Market discipline: One of three generic business strategies conceptualized by Treacy and Wiersema (1995): product leadership, operational excellence, and customer intimacy.

Market segment: A group of customers or potential customers whose members have common characteristics relating to how and why they might buy a product or service.

Market segmentation: Division of a market into groups of customers or potential customers (segments) by factors relating to how and why each group might buy a product or service.

Market share: Percentage of the consumer demand captured by one company in relation to all the other companies selling to that market.

Market value: The value of an item (such as an asset) in terms of the price it would command today. Often contrasted with *book value*, the price originally paid.

Matching principle: An accounting principle of matching the expenses for making and selling a product with the sales revenue from that product. This principle ensures that the income statement reports expenses related to the revenue being reported.

Net income: The money remaining after all expenses are subtracted from revenue. If this amount is positive, the company has made a profit. If it is negative, the company has taken a loss.

Net operating profit after taxes (NOPAT): The profit generated by the company after taxes have been deducted and before interest is paid.

Net present value (NPV): The result of adding up all the discounted cash flows for all the years of a proposed investment.

Non-interest bearing liabilities: Liabilities that do not require an interest payment in addition to the principal payment. Accounts payable are an example.

Notes payable: Money owed to lenders, both short and long term.

Objectives: Broad statements of direction that are externally focused.

Operating activities: Producing, selling, and delivering the company's products and collecting payment from customers.

Operating expense: An expense associated with the manufacturing of a product and the delivery of a service.

Operating income: The profit generated solely from operating activities.

Operating margin percentage: A ratio that compares the money the company receives from selling its products to the money it uses to manufacture the products and operate the business. It is calculated by dividing operating income by revenue. It answers the question, How profitable is the business, regardless of how it is financed?

Operational excellence: A business strategy that emphasizes efficiency and effectiveness of operations to deliver greatest value at lowest cost for the customer.

Opportunity cost: The benefits a company forgoes because it cannot do something; usually it cannot do this thing because it has chosen to do something else instead.

Payables: Money owed.

Percent change analysis: An analysis that focuses on the differences in year-to-year results It allows a company to track key changes in financial results from one reporting period to the next.

Present value: The amount a certain dollar amount invested in the future would be worth today.

Product leadership: A business strategy that emphasizes product innovation and being first to market.

Product lifecycle: The effective life of a product as it is adopted by users from innovators and early adopters through to laggards.

Profit: The amount (if positive) that remains after expenses have been subtracted from revenue.

Profitability: The generation of a positive income from operations.

Property, plant, and equipment (PP&E): Long-term assets in the form of investment in land, buildings, and equipment less accumulated depreciation.

Project outcome lifecycle: The life of a product or other outcome of a project from launch at the end of the project until the company stops using that outcome to produce value.

Quick ratio: A ratio that expresses how much capital a company has invested in assets that can be quickly converted into cash. It is calculated by subtracting inventory from current assets and dividing the result by the current liabilities. It answers the question, Will the business have sufficient cash coming in to pay short-term obligations?

Ratio analysis: An analysis of the relationships between numbers on the income statement and balance sheet, used to examine a company's profitability, efficiency, and management of capital.

Raw materials: Components that can be converted into inventory.

Realized strategy: The results of a strategy.

Receivables: Any money owed to the company, whether or not it is currently due, for sales already made.

Retained earnings: Profits not distributed to shareholders but reinvested in the company.

Return on capital (ROC): A ratio that expresses the return generated by a company on the capital invested in it. ROC is the net operating profit after taxes divided by the total capital invested in the company. It answers the question, What is the rate of return on this investment?

Return on project investment (ROPI): A ratio that expresses the return generated by a project and project outcome lifecycle on the capital invested in it. ROPI is the net operating profit after taxes (accrual) divided by the total capital invested in the project or the incremental income cash flows of the POL divided by that total capital. It answers the question, What is the rate of return on the investment in this project?

Return on sales: A ratio that expresses how much net income a company earns from each dollar of revenue. It is net income divided by revenue. It answers the question, How profitable is the business?

Revenue: The cash a company receives from the sales of its products or services. It is the total amount of products sold multiplied by the price of all the products sold.

Risk: The possibility of loss or of nonpayment of an obligation.

Sale: An event during the selling process that allows the company to recognize revenue. This event can be variously defined; a company (or industry) selects a single definition to use when reporting the revenue from sales on its income statement.

Salvage value: Value of an asset at the end of its useful life.

Selling, general & administrative expenses (SG&A): Operating expenses not directly associated with the manufacture of a product.

Selling, general & administrative expenses (SG&A) percentage: This ratio expresses how much of each dollar on sales the company spends on expenses not directly related to manufacturing the product or supplying the service. It is SG&A divided by revenue. It answers the question, How much does it cost to run the business day to day?

Sensitivity analysis: Often called *what if* analysis. The process of changing a variable in a model to see how the change will affect the results.

Shareholder value: Any returns generated by a company that meet or exceed the WACC.

Shareholders: Investors in a business with an ownership interest.

Solvency: The ability to satisfy long-term obligations.

Statement of cash flows: A report that summarizes activities that generate and consume cash in order to reconcile the change in cash balance from period to period. It groups activities into one of three areas: operating activities, investing activities, and financing activities. Also referred to as the *cash flow statement.*

Straight-line depreciation: A method of calculating depreciation that assumes the depreciation expense remains the same for each year that an asset is being depreciated. That is, it assumes that the asset loses value at an unchanging rate over time.

Tangible assets: Assets that are physical entities and have a set value. Examples are property, inventory, and equipment.

Tax reporting: Reporting that provides information for government officials in all the countries and localities in which a company does business so that the proper taxes can be assessed.

Time value of money: The value of money given that it has the ability to earn more money over time.

Treasury stock: Shares repurchased by the company. Also a line item on the balance sheet representing the value of these shares.

Useful life: The period of time for which an asset will be of value to a company.

Value: How much a commodity or service is worth or the utility of something.

Variable cost: A cost that changes over time in relation to changes in a cost driver, such as a cost for materials that increases with the number of widgets manufactured.

Wages payable: Money owed to employees.

Weighted average cost of capital (WACC): The rate of return that must be earned to satisfy all investor expectations. It combines the return necessary to satisfy lenders and the return necessary to satisfy shareholders. It is calculated by determining the proportion of debt and the proportion of equity a company has and then averaging the expected return for each one based on the investment in each.

Working capital: The cash tied up in running a business day to day. Often defined as current assets minus current liabilities.

Working capital management: The process of managing the short-term cash needs of a business.

REFERENCES

Allen, J. T. *Managing the Flow of Technology.* Cambridge, Mass.: MIT Press, 1977.

Block, Z., and MacMillan, I. C. *Corporate Venturing.* Boston: Harvard Business School Press, 1995.

Bordley, R. F. "Keeping It Sophisticatedly Simple in R&D Project Management." *Engineering Economist,* 1999, *44*(2), 168–183.

Bourton Group. "Still in Development: A Survey of the Management of Innovation in Manufacturing Businesses." Rugby, Warwickshire, U.K.: Bourton Group, 1999.

Brooks, F. P., Jr. *The Mythical Man-Month: Essays on Software Engineering.* Reading, Mass.: Addison-Wesley, 1975.

Browder, S. "For Nordstrom, Great Service Wasn't Enough." *Business Week,* Apr. 19, 1999, pp. 126–128.

Bughin, J., and Copeland, T. E. "The Virtuous Cycle of Shareholder Value Creation." *McKinsey Quarterly,* Mar. 22, 1997, (2), 156–167.

Cadillac Motor Company. *Information Book.* Detroit, Mich.: Cadillac Motor Co., 1991.

Cleland, D. I. *Project Management.* New York: McGraw-Hill, 1999.

Cohen, D. J., and Kuehn, J. "Navigating Between a Rock and a Hard Place: Reconciling the Initiating and Planning Phases to Promote Project Success." In Project Management Institute, *Proceedings of the 27th Annual Project Management Institute 1996 Seminars & Symposium.* Newtown Square, Pa.: Project Management Institute, 1996.

Cooper, R. G., Edgett, S. J., and Kleinschmidt, E. J. "New Problems, New Solutions: Making Portfolio Management More Effective." *Research Technology Management,* Mar.–Apr. 2000, *43*(2), 18–33.

Delves, D. "Practical Lessons for Designing an Economic Value Incentive Plan." *Compensation and Benefits Review,* Mar. 1, 1999, pp. 61–65.

Deschamps, J.-P. "Mastering the Dance of Change: Innovation as a Way of Life." *Prism,* Second Quarter 1999, pp. 61–67.

Dillon, P. "The Next Small Thing." *Fast Company,* June–July 1988, (15), pp. 97–102.

Dumaine, B. "How Managers Can Succeed Through Speed." *Fortune,* Feb. 13, 1989, pp. 54–59.

Eisenhardt, K. M. "Strategic Decision Making as Improvisation." In V. Papadakis and P. Barwise (eds.), *Strategic Decisions.* Norwell, Mass.: Kluwer, 1997.

Englund, R. L., and Graham, R. J. "From Experience: Linking Projects to Strategy." *Journal of Product Innovation Management,* 1999, *16,* 52–64.

Floyd, S. W., and Wooldridge, B. *The Strategic Middle Manager: How to Create and Sustain Competitive Advantage.* San Francisco: Jossey-Bass, 1996.

Gauss, D. C., and Weinberg, G. *Exploring Requirements: Quality Before Design.* New York: Dorset House, 1989.

Ghoshal, S., Bartlett, C. A., and Moran, P. "A New Manifesto for Management." *Sloan Management Review,* Spring 1999, pp. 9–20.

Graham, R. J. *Project Management as If People Mattered.* Bala Cynwyd, Pa.: Primavera Press, 1989.

Graham, R. J., and Englund, R. L. *Creating an Environment for Successful Projects: The Quest to Manage Project Management.* San Francisco: Jossey-Bass, 1997.

Graham, R. J., Englund, R., and Cohen, D. J. "Is Your Organization Ready to Support World-Class Project Management? Results from the Project Environment Assessment Tool: PEAT." In Project Management Institute, *Proceedings of the 31st Annual Project Management Institute 2000 Seminars & Symposium.* Newtown Square, Pa.: Project Management Institute, 2000.

Grove, A. S. *Only the Paranoid Survive.* New York: Currency Doubleday, 1996.

Hax, A. C., and Wilde, D. L., II. "The Delta Model: Adaptive Management for a Changing World." *Sloan Management Review,* Winter 1999, pp. 1–18.

Henricks, M. *Business Plans Made Easy.* Irvine, Calif.: Entrepreneur Media, 1999.

Horngren, C. T., Foster, G., and Datar, S. M. *Cost Accounting: A Managerial Emphasis.* (8th ed.) Upper Saddle River, N.J.: Prentice Hall, 1994.

Ibbotson, R. C., and Sinquefield, R. A. *Stocks, Bonds, Bills, and Inflation: Historical Returns (1926–1987).* Charlottesville, Va.: Research Foundation of the Institute of Chartered Financial Analysts, 1989.

Jaafari, A. "Life-Cycle Project Management: A Proposed Theoretical Model for Development and Implementation of Capital Projects." *Project Management Journal,* 2000, *31*(1), 44–52.

Johann, B., Macesich, M., and Massoudi, B. "How Can E&P Executives Fulfill the Business Promise?" *Oil & Gas Investor,* Second Quarter 1998, (supplement), pp. 7–11.

Kaplan, R. S., and Norton, D. P. *The Balanced Scorecard.* Boston: Harvard Business School Press, 1996.

Kessler, E., and Chakrabarti, A. "Speeding Up the Pace of New Product Development." *Journal of Product Innovation Management,* 1999, *16,* 231–247.

Kleinfeld, J. "Stryke Force: How Ingersoll-Rand Beat the Clock." *New York Times,* Mar. 25, 1990, pp. 3-1.

Kopelman, O., and Voegtli, C. *QRPD: Quality Rapid Product Development.* (8th ed.) Palo Alto, Calif.: Global Brain, 1998.

Kotter, J. P. *A Force for Change: How Leadership Differs from Management.* New York: Free Press, 1990.

Koyama, H., and Van Tassel, R. "How to Trim Capital Spending by 25%." *McKinsey Quarterly,* June 22, 1998, pp. 142–153.

Lambert, D., and Slater, S. F. "First, Fast and On Time: The Path to Success, or Is It?" *Journal of Product Innovation Management,* 1999, *16,* 427–438.

"Learn to Play the Earnings Game." *Fortune,* Mar. 31, 1997, pp. 76–82.

Lewis, P. "With 2 Chips, the Gigahertz Decade Begins." *New York Times,* Mar. 9, 2000, Section G, p. 1.

Lohr, S. "When You Are First and Still Don't Succeed." *Sunday New York Times,* Mar. 19, 2000, p. Bu-4.

Luehrman, T. A. *Capital Projects as Real Options: An Introduction.* Harvard Business School Publication 9-295-074. Boston: Harvard Business School, Mar. 22, 1995.

Luehrman, T. A. "Strategy as a Portfolio of Real Options." *Harvard Business Review,* Sept.–Oct. 1998, pp. 89–99.

Meredith, J. R., and Mantel, S. J., Jr. *Project Management: A Managerial Approach.* New York: Wiley, 1995.

Mintzberg, H. *Mintzberg on Management.* New York: Free Press, 1989.

Mitchell, D. *Control Without Bureaucracy.* Maidenhead, England: McGraw-Hill, 1979.

Moore, G. *Crossing the Chasm.* New York: Harperbiness, 1999.

Moore, J. F. "Predators and Prey: A New Ecology of Competition." *Harvard Business Review,* May–June 1993, pp. 75–87.

Pinchot, G., and Pellman, R. *Intrapreneuring in Action.* San Francisco: Berrett-Koehler, 1999.

Platten, P., and Weinberg, C. R. "Shattering the Myths About Dot.Com Employee Pay." *Compensation & Benefits Review,* Jan. 2000, pp. 21–27.

Porter, M. *Competitive Advantage: Creating and Sustaining Superior Performance.* New York: Free Press, 1998. (Originally published 1985.)

Prahalad, C. K., and Ramaswamy, V. "Co-Opting Customer Competence." *Harvard Business Review,* Jan.–Feb. 2000, pp. 79–91.

Project Management Institute. *Guide to the Project Management Body of Knowledge.* Upper Darby, Pa.: Project Management Institute, 1996.

Rae-Dupree, J. "In the Pilot's Seat Mobile Computing Changed in the Palm of His Hand." *San Jose Mercury,* Nov. 10, 1997, Section E, pp. 1–3.

Rich, S., and Gumpert, D. *Business Plans That Win $$$.* New York: HarperCollins, 1985.

Ryan, W. P. "The New Landscape for Nonprofits." *Harvard Business Review,* Jan.–Feb. 1999, pp. 127–135.

Schmidt, W. H., and Finnigan, J. P. *The Race Without a Finish Line: America's Quest for Total Quality.* San Francisco: Jossey-Bass, 1992.

Schrange, M. "Faster Innovation? Try Rapid Prototyping." *Harvard Management Update,* Dec. 1999, *4*(12), pp. 8–9.

Smith, P. "From Experience: Reaping Benefit from Speed to Market." *Journal of Product Innovation Management,* 1999, *16,* 222–230.

Smith, P., and Reinertsen, D. *Developing Products in Half the Time.* New York: Van Nostrand Reinhold, 1991.

Stepanek, M. "How Fast Is Net Fast?" *Business Week e.biz,* Nov. 1, 1999, p. EB52.

Stewart, G. B., III, "EVA[TM]: Fact and Fantasy." *Journal of Applied Corporate Finance,* 1994, *7*(2), 71–84.

Strategic Management Group. *Why Finance Matters: Understanding Finance and Shareholder Value.* Philadelphia: Strategic Management Group, 1997. CD-ROM interactive learning program.

Sullivan, J. N. "Capital Efficiency: Importance to a Major Petroleum Company." Paper presented at the annual meeting of the Construction Industry Institute, Minneapolis, Aug. 1998.

Thakor, A. V. "Corporate Investments and Finance." *Financial Management*, June 22, 1993, *22*(2, special issue), pp. 135–142.

Tiffany, P., and Peterson, S. *Business Plans for Dummies.* Foster City, Calif.: IDG Books, 1997.

Toney, F., and Powers, R. *Best Practices of Project Management Groups in Large Functional Organizations.* Upper Darby, Pa.: Project Management Institute, 1997.

Treacy, M., and Wiersema, F. *The Discipline of Market Leaders.* Reading, Mass.: Addison-Wesley, 1995.

Tuchman, B. W. *The March of Folly: From Troy to Vietnam.* New York: Knopf, 1984.

Tully, S. "America's Wealth Creators." *Fortune*, Nov. 22, 1999, pp. 275–284.

Turnbull, C. *The Forest People.* New York: Touchstone Books, 1987.

Turner, J. R. "Projects for Shareholder Value: The Influence of Projects at Different Financial Ratios." In Project Management Institute, *Proceedings of the 29th Annual Project Management Institute 1998 Seminars & Symposium.* Newtown Square, Pa.: Project Management Institute, 1998.

Wall, S. T., and Wall, S. R. "The Evolution (Not the Death) of Strategy." *Organizational Dynamics*, Autumn 1995, pp. 7–19.

Zweig, P. L. "Beyond Bean-Counting." *Business Week*, Oct. 28, 1996, pp. 130–133.

INDEX